Western China on Screen
An Urban Exploration

Hongyan Zou

EDINBURGH
University Press

Edinburgh University Press is one of the leading university presses in the UK. We publish academic books and journals in our selected subject areas across the humanities and social sciences, combining cutting-edge scholarship with high editorial and production values to produce academic works of lasting importance. For more information visit our website: edinburghuniversitypress.com

© Hongyan Zou, 2021, 2023

Edinburgh University Press Ltd
The Tun – Holyrood Road
12 (2f) Jackson's Entry
Edinburgh EH8 8PJ

First published in hardback by Edinburgh University Press 2021

Typeset in 11/13 Monotype Ehrhardt by
IDSUK (DataConnection) Ltd

A CIP record for this book is available from the British Library

ISBN 978 1 4744 7785 7 (hardback)
ISBN 978 1 4744 7786 4 (paperback)
ISBN 978 1 4744 7787 1 (webready PDF)
ISBN 978 1 4744 7788 8 (epub)

The right of Hongyan Zou to be identified as author of this work has been asserted in accordance with the Copyright, Designs and Patents Act 1988 and the Copyright and Related Rights Regulations 2003 (SI No. 2498).

Contents

List of Figures v

PART I INTRODUCTION
1. Cinematic Western China: The Under-represented
   Cinematic Cities 3
      Chinese Western Cinema 4
      Chinese Cities and Cinema: An Imbalanced Representation 10
      Organisation of the Book 30

PART II CINEMATIC CHONGQING
2. History, Cityscape and Spatial Stratification 37
      Chongqing in Films: A Brief Account 38
      The Stratification of High and Low Spaces 43
3. National Project and Disappearing Space 61
      Rainclouds over Wushan: Lived Space Matters 61
      Still Life: Expectation becomes Stillness from
      Wushan to Fengjie 76

PART III CINEMATIC CHENGDU
4. Spaces of Consumption Replace Spaces of Production 91
      Chengdu in Films 91
      24 City: Making Way for a Modern Space 96
5. Natural Disaster and Trauma 119
      Buddha Mountain: Nature, a Railway Station and
      Religious Redemption 122

PART IV CINEMATIC XI'AN
6. From an Enclosed Traditional Space to a Sprawling
   Urban Space 133
      Xi'an and Adjacent Area on Screen 133
      Back to Back, Face to Face: The *Flâneur* Walking in
      an Enclosed Space 137
7. Female Space and Bodies 155
      The Story of Ermei: Female Social Status in Rural and
      Urban Spaces 156
      Weaving Girl: State-owned Enterprise and the Female Worker 165

PART V CINEMATIC LANZHOU

8. Contrast between the Urban and the Rural Regarding
   Mental and Social Space   181
       The Cinematic City as an Absent Presence   181

PART VI CONCLUSION

9. Cinematic Western China: An Open Space for Spatial
   Imagination   207

Filmography   213
Bibliography   217
Index   226

Figures

1.1	The mountainous landscape: in *Yellow Earth*	6
2.1	The stair-street in the opening sequences: in *Evening Rain*	39
2.2	The Chongqing cityscape in the opening shot: in *Chongqing Blues*	42
2.3	The temple and its surroundings: in *Crazy Stone*	46
2.4	Heipi pretends to be a *bangbang*: in *Crazy Stone*	49
2.5	The vertical view of the city through Mike's view: in *Crazy Stone*	58
2.6	Spaces the crooks inhabit and utilise: in *Crazy Stone*	59
3.1	Mai Qiang's daily routines: in *Rainclouds over Wushan*	64
3.2	Mai Qiang catches, selects and kills fish: in *Rainclouds over Wushan*	66
3.3	Chen Qing catches, selects and kills fish: in *Rainclouds over Wushan*	67
3.4	Wu Gang watches and catches fish: in *Rainclouds over Wushan*	68
3.5	The white board: in *Rainclouds over Wushan*	73
3.6	Han Sanming and his wife: in *Still Life*	78
3.7	Ruins, workers and death: in *Still Life*	80
3.8	The tower *hua* (華) and its quiet launching: in *Still Life*	84
3.9	The funambulist and Han Sanming: in *Still Life*	86
4.1	Street view of Chengdu: in *24 City*	97
4.2	The stage backdrop of the auditorium of Factory 420: in *24 City*	99
4.3	Factory 420 becomes Huarun Twenty-four City: in *24 City*	102
4.4	Construction sites next to Factory 420: in *24 City*	103
4.5	Panoramic view of Chengdu: in *24 City*	112
4.6	Still photographs of anonymous people: in *24 City*	116
5.1	The earthquake-affected area: in *Buddha Mountain*	123
5.2	The wrecked car in the garage: in *Buddha Mountain*	125
6.1	The guild hall: in *Back to Back*	141
6.2	The guild hall (the locus of the Culture Centre): in *Back to Back*	143

6.3	The welcome meeting for Lao Ma: in *Back to Back*	147
6.4	Thick walls and forts that enclose the city: in *Back to Back*	150
7.1	Walls and window frames: in *Weaving Girl*	169
7.2	The Soviet style outdoor stage: in *Weaving Girl*	170
7.3	A peddler passing by and a motorised tricycle: in *Weaving Girl*	172
7.4	Abandoned socialist factories: in *Weaving Girl*	173
7.5	The cityscape of Beijing: in *Weaving Girl*	175
7.6	The character *chai* (拆) and the ruins: in *Weaving Girl*	177
8.1	Latiaozi's home town and surroundings: in *A Fool*	186
8.2	A street scene in the town and the tunnel: in *A Fool*	189
8.3	The space under the stage and Latiaozi encounters Shaozi: in *A Fool*	190
8.4	The rear-view mirror scenes: in *A Fool*	192
8.5	Latiaozi becomes Shaozi: in *A Fool*	200

PART I
INTRODUCTION

CHAPTER 1

Cinematic Western China: The Under-represented Cinematic Cities

With China's massive urbanisation, the dynamic relationship between cinema and the city has been recorded, reflected and reconfigured through fictional mainland Chinese feature films. However, the vast western areas of China have long been depicted as remote barren countryside in Chinese cinema, given their underdeveloped status and their position away from the centre of political discourse and economic privilege. In the 1980s, the image of the western areas was associated with a primitive pre-modern agrarian China. In particular, the north-west area became known for its yellow earth, barren land, poverty and exotic traditional rituals. Meanwhile, China came to the threshold of modernisation when the distinctive boundary between countryside and city started to be challenged and rearranged. In cinematic representation, the city–countryside boundary created by the timeless Loess Plateau was broken, with towns and cities sprouting in the reform era. Accordingly, Chinese cinema received two critical new concepts – Chinese Western and Chinese urban cinema – as new aesthetic and ideological discourses. For western China, with the central government's sustained effort of developing the region through a series of national projects including the 'Third Front project' (1950s to 1980s), the Three Gorges Dam (1990s to 2020), the 'Great Western Development' (1990s to the present) and the most recent 'Road and Belt Initiative', the area has achieved enormous economic and social progress. Consequently, it becomes increasingly exposed on TV and films, displaying an alternative 'urban image' of modern China. Importantly, cinematic western China was positioned as a space of resistance against the meta-narratives of modernisation and globalisation, taking a critical stance to question the rationality underpinning the miraculous transformations under the grand ideology of social progress and modernisation.

Chinese Western Cinema

China's Western films, represented by internationally acclaimed works such as *Yellow Earth* [*Huang tudi*] (Chen Kaige, 1984) and *Red Sorghum* [*Hong gaoliang*] (Zhang Yimou, 1987), are predominantly set in the countryside. The term Chinese Western was first proposed by Chinese film critic Zhong Dianfei at the Xi'an Film Studio Annual Conference in 1984 (Teo 2016: 90). Zhong made a speech entitled 'Face the Grand West, Develop New Western Film', in which he advocated for the studio's filmmakers to explore the spiritual world of the people of the vast north-western area through the big screen (Zhou 2012: 49). The conceptualisation of the Chinese Western has since exerted long-standing influences on filmmaking, genre blending and the cultural consciousness of Chinese cinema.

Zhong's proposition regarding Western film stirred up a fierce debate among domestic scholars concerning the term 'Western'. To clarify the concept, Zhong set out to explain the term 'Western' in a further two articles, pointing out that the purpose of making Chinese Westerns was to strive for originality in cinematic style and form, and promote the local agenda in cinematic themes (Zhong 1994: 599). In response to this, assenting voices argued that borrowing the American term to label the new trend of filmmaking based on north-western China was a means of initiating and exploring Western films with Chinese characteristics. As China was predominantly an agrarian country, there was a call for Chinese cinema to realistically show how people emancipate themselves from agrarian economic constraints, and how the harsh environment shapes the people's personalities (Zhong 1994: 606–7). Conversely, some critics perceived the concept and practice of the 'Western Film' in mainland China as imitating the capitalist USA's Western cowboy films (Xiao 2009: 81). One of the most powerful critiques, made by Yuan Wenshu, claimed that the genre was 'inappropriate' for China, because

> in our political system, we need to construct a Chinese-style socialist nation . . . [T]his allows of no doubt. Of course, in advancing and developing our nation's socialist cinema, we need to borrow from foreign nations, but this borrowing can only be of their advanced experience and of their techniques that would be useful in expressing our own cinematic content. (Cited in Fried 2007: 1488)

This perception may remind readers of the far-reaching modernisation strategy promoted since the late Qing dynasty known by the saying 'Chinese culture for essentials, Western culture for application', and the long-standing ideological and political concerns in cultural practice since

Chairman Mao's era from the late 1940s. However, although these critics disagreed on the name of this newly found subject matter and the aesthetics represented by *Yellow Earth* (emphasising the endless and timeless space of the Loess Plateau and its far-reaching influence on the traditional culture and conduct, way of production and history of the region), there was 'no disagreement that national culture must remain unvitiated' (Fried 2007: 1490). The Chinese Western during its initial period, therefore, can be seen as national cinema accommodating the culture of the particular terrain and contemporary ideological concerns, and targeting no commercial nor cinematic industrial purpose (Luo 2005; Zhang 2003). It is a concept proposed in the initial period of China's economic reformation, when filmmaking concerns related more to aesthetic and ideological values than commercial interests.

Yellow Earth and *Life* [*Ren sheng*] (Wu Tianming, 1984), both made in 1984, inspired Zhong to propose the concept and flag the new cinematic aesthetic style and subject matter (*ti cai*, a certain type of character or situation presented in artistic works, a Maoist practice). The following years saw a sprouting of Western films, such as the family drama *In the Wild Mountains* [*Ye Shan*] (Yan Xueshu, 1986), the countryside feature *Old Well* [*Lao Jing*] (Wu Tianming, 1986) and the melodrama *Red Sorghum* (Zhang Yimou, 1987), where landscape – specifically, sky, mountains, rivers and barren lands – takes on attentive importance (Figure 1.1). These films became illustrations of Zhong's configuration of the Chinese Western. Set in the rural north-west, they represent and contemplate the relationship between humans and nature, tradition and reformation, everyday practice and individuals' spiritual struggling in the context of China's economic reformation. The barren land, brutal mountainous landscape and 'timeless space' that the local people inhabit have fostered particular cultural conduct of the western rural area. These yellow earth-based cinematic representations have become significant sites for cultural and historical reflection on the national identity and local specificity in the 1980s and 1990s. The cinematic western frontier of China, with images of harsh environment and isolated villages, foregrounds not only an unchangeable circumstance where characters are unable to escape from, but also a 'timeless collective life that goes beyond the confines of communist history' (Chow 1995: 39). Such representations of 'timeless' life and space became the signature of the 'New Chinese Cinema' (Browne 1994: 3), paralleling the 'new waves' that emerged from Hong Kong and Taiwan at around the same time.

Figure 1.1 The mountainous landscape: in *Yellow Earth*

Chinese film scholar Wang Yichuan categorises Chinese films into four sections according to geographical distinction: the eastern section represented by Shanghai, the southern section by Hong Kong, the western section by Chengdu, Chongqing and Xi'an and the northern section by Beijing and Changchun (Wang 2009: 55). The provincial regions of Shaanxi, Ningxia, Gansu, Qinghai, Xingjiang, Tibet, Sichuan, Chongqing, Guizhou and Yunnan Provinces are regarded as the geographical base of China's Westerns. As the frontier western area has been inhabited by many minority ethnic groups, such as the Tibetan (*Zang zu*), the Uygur (*Weiwuer zu*), Mongolian (*Menggu zu*) and Hui people (*Hui zu*), as well as the majority ethnic group Han people (*Han zu*), the Chinese Western also includes minority films in the context of China's complicated ethnic situations. However, as the filmmakers and production units involved are predominantly Han people from the studios of Xi'an, Inner Mongolia, Tianshan (in Wulumuqi, Xinjiang Uygur Autonomous Region) and Yunnan, cinematic representations of the region, despite the existence of ethnic minorities, are essentially 'Han-centred in the 1980s and 1990s.' (Li 2012: 89).

Horse Thief [*Dao ma zei*] (Tian Zhuangzhuang, 1986) is one of the most critically-acclaimed Chinese Westerns set in Tibet, and displays the primitive landscape of the Qinghai-Tibet Plateau, the ethnic region and mysterious religious rituals – the sky burial and the sacrifice dedication ceremony of Tibetan culture. Thematically, the film examines moral issues and religious redemption. Despite the minority subject, the film is a 'Han centred' narrative, a curious gaze from the perspective of the majority Han at exotic rituals and dwelling places (Zhang 2002: 167). Such Han-centred cinematic depictions of western China become cultural and historical sites of 'national allegory' (Jameson 1986: 69), resembling the occidental foreign gaze at the mystifying oriental country presented in films of the representative directors of the Fifth Generation of Chinese filmmakers who established their reputations through rural ethnographic narration between the 1980s and 1990s at international film festivals. More domestic filmmakers, therefore, made similar films to cater to the foreign gaze. Hence, cinema became an instrument to discover, represent or 'reinvent' China, and 'in effect help to "other" China through images of the unfamiliar histories, identities and livelihoods that persist peripherally in space and time' (Chow 1995: 43). However, such ethnographical and allegorical representations of Chinese culture, history and society soon lost their status with the emerging market economy accompanied by mass consumerism. With the intrusion of the market driven modernisation, the 'timeless space' has been constantly interrupted and stirred up by commercialism and massive urbanisation. In spite of the stubborn tenacity of the traditional rural culture, people from the enclosed mountain areas began to be inspired and stunned by the outside world through TV, radio and all sorts of mass media devices. Western-based films that strove to show spectacles of traditional customs, cultural conduct and the uniqueness of the local life soon reached a standstill and were denounced as unrealistic by the Urban Generation directors.

The new trend of Chinese Westerns in the late 1980s and the beginning of the 1990s was increasing representations of small towns, the intermediate area of the countryside and the big cities that provide country people with traces of economic and social reform. As Pickowicz contends, it was a space that contained the vestiges of late imperial culture, the remnants of the modern or bourgeois culture of the Republican era, the residue of traditional socialist culture, and elements of both modernism and postmodernism (Pickowicz 2012: 274). Films such as *Ermo* (Zhou Xiaowen, 1994) and *Woman Sesame Oil Maker* [*Xiang hun nü*] (Xie Fei, 1993) capture the shifting rural–urban boundary, and have in varying degrees recorded, reflected and participated in the process of China's commercialisation and marketisation, and more significantly, in shaping and reshaping Chinese cultural nationalism (Zhang 2002: 203).

The American Western, with a much longer history of production and screening than its Chinese counterpart, has developed a sophisticated set of characterisations, narrations and aesthetics over half a century of popularity. In the words of André Bazin, 'it is the only genre whose origins are almost identical with those of the cinema itself and which is as alive as ever after almost half a century of uninterrupted success' (Bazin 2005b: 142). In representative Westerns such as *Stagecoach* (John Ford, 1939), *High Noon* (Fred Zinnemann, 1952) and *Shane* (George Stevens, 1953), the wild and awe-inspiring Western landscapes, galloping horses, fights and masculine men have become the defining elements of the genre. More significantly, the pioneer spirit of conquering unknown lands and 'the conflict between the transcendence of social justice and the individual character of moral justice, between the categorical imperative of the law which guarantees the order of the future city, and the no less unshakeable order of the individual conscience' are the core of the genre (Bazin 2005b: 148). In decline after the late 1950s, the American Western is nevertheless the 'ideal representation of American values, character, and exceptionalism, providing a modern mythology for a nation without an ancient past' (Creekmur 2011: 397). Therefore, the American Western constructed the narrative forms that modelled national identity during the twentieth century in the United States.

Similarly, the Chinese Western in the 1980s has substantially contained Chinese reality, local characteristics and cultural connotations. Moreover, it has kept accord with and represented China's contemporary circumstances and transformations. With representative works awarded at various international film festivals, Chinese Westerns, to a certain degree, participated in establishing cultural identity and nationalism. However, the Chinese Western is not confined to isolated desert rural spaces. In Huang Jianxin's two urban features, *The Black Cannon Incident* [*Heipao shijian*] (1985) and *Dislocation* [*Cuowei*] (1986), urban spaces of the region are depicted to show the collision of the capitalist economy with socialist political institutions. Accordingly, the idea of the Chinese Western is associated particularly with the geographical and topographical features of China's north-west. Whether rural or urban spaces, this was the development strategy chosen by the local Xi'an Film Studio in the face of the economic reform in the film industry in the latter years of the 1980s (Ni and Xu 2012). Since the reform era, a majority of national film studios across mainland China have been designated as enterprises under economic reform. The previous state-financed cultural production units have been transformed into financially self-reliant enterprises regarding production and distribution. Consequently, local film studios across mainland China often struggled for a living in the face of a sharp decline in cinema audiences in the 1980s subsequent to the emergence of the TV and DVD industry.

However, Hollywood's influence on Chinese cinema became more extensive due to further 'opening up' from the 1990s. The Chinese Western started to borrow narrative techniques and genre elements from American Westerns, including the desert town, over-emphasised hoofbeats and the hero who rides off into the sunset, as, for example, in *The Swordsman in Double Flag Town* (He Ping 1991). Yet the turn of the millennium saw Chinese Westerns becoming a highly commercialised film genre that combines Chinese martial arts with suspense and action, as illustrated in the black comedy *A Woman, a Gun and a Noodle Shop* [*Sanqiang pai'an jingqi*] (Zhang Yimou, 2009) (a remake of the Coen Brothers' *Blood Simple* (1984)), the action film *Wind Blast* [*Xifeng lie*] (Gao Qunshu, 2010) and the dystopian allegory *No Man's Land* [*Wu ren qu*] (Ning Hao, 2013). *No Man's Land* features a lawyer, a symbol of justice and modern civilisation, who experiences chaos, violence, criminality and even death in an isolated dystopia set in China's western region. In the context of globalisation, the previous scope of the themes and geographical backgrounds of Chinese Westerns has narrowed, but aesthetically, they are approaching the classic American Westerns. In films such as *Hero* [*Yingxiong*] (Zhang Yimou, 2002) and *Seven Swords* [*Qi jian*] (Tsui Hark, 2005), the western landscape, with its isolated border towns, mountain ranges and desert, becomes a blank background where national epic glory can be played out by infusing elements from their Hollywood Western counterparts (Fried 2007: 1493). In the new millennium, especially after China joined the World Trade Organization, Chinese cinema has been undergoing an enormous development in the global cinema market. Significantly, Chinese Western films that emerged under the influence of the planned economic system and bore no commercial interest have declined. However, Western elements, especially the geographical and topographical aspects, and the traditional Chinese martial art film have produced blended genres in the above films.

The landscape in north-western China has been prominently featured and sometimes framed into spectacles and ethnographical images of the national image of China in these Western films from the 1980s onwards. Meanwhile, with the launching of economic reforms, the skylines of China's new cities and their inhabitants have also gained more exposure, with the state promoting a socialist modernity with Chinese characteristics. The idea of urban cinema and new urban cinema first appeared in 1986, and was defined by the journal *New Film* in 1988 under the title 'Urban cinema has great prospects' (Tang et al. 1988). Urban cinema was introduced to counterbalance the Fifth Generation's rural ethnographic narrations (Braester 2012: 352), and has provided its counterpoint to rurally based films by realistically reflecting everyday city life commensurate with the latest social changes.

Chinese Cities and Cinema: An Imbalanced Representation

Before moving on to discuss Chinese cinematic cities, it is necessary to clarify the different connotations conveyed by the English word 'city' and its Chinese equivalent, *Chengshi* (城市). In English, city derives from the Latin *civitas*, meaning 'city-state' and 'citizens'. It suggests 'an ideal of rational order', the rights and privileges of the citizens, and refers 'thus by extension to the mass of social principles that serve to organize a society and lend a specific quality to its life' (cited in Zhang 1996: 6). The 'city' therefore suggests not only a physical construction but also a 'moral order, or an ideal of rational order', which is 'invariably inscribed in the physical city, as well as in societies and institutions within the city' (Zhang 1996: 6). However, the equivalent Chinese expression, *chengshi*, has quite different connotations to its English counterpart:

> The term chengshi consists of two characters, cheng (meaning both 'city' and 'wall') and shi (meaning both 'city' and 'market'). A cheng, which may be as large as the capital city or as small as a county administrative centre, is typically a walled city, highly

organised, managed, and planned in detail. [. . .] The city walls (chengqiang) might originally have been built for military defence, but over the centuries they have come to function primarily as 'symbols of the state-imperial authority, designed to emphasise and glorify the city's role as the seat of power and control, part of an overall imperial plan'. (Cited in Zhang 1996: 6–7)

Therefore, the concept of 'city' in Chinese, not only refers to a metropolis, such as New York, London, Beijing or Shanghai, but also includes medium-sized cities as well as small towns or counties. The form of China's traditional city has been influenced by prevailing political forces, hence Chinese cities have been 'distinctly regulated by the administrative philosophy behind it, so much so that . . . [they] are very uniform in plan and outlook' (Hsueh 1995: 6). Transforming from a traditional agricultural China to a modern industrialised China, small towns serve as the transitional link between major cities and the countryside. In Chinese, the equivalent of town is *zhen*, referring to 'control or administration', and it is usually situated outside of the city walls and designated as a small market place (Zhang 1996: 6). As a transitional zone on the fringes of major cities, the town represents an underdeveloped space in the process of modernisation. Meanwhile, it retains direct communication with 'the earth' and 'agricultural practice', because it serves as the front locus for country people to experience the modern city and urban life. The social practices in the town bear both urban and rural characteristics; specifically, traditional rural agricultural views and conduct can still be traced in the town.

In films, such transitional spaces – the small towns or counties adjacent to bigger cities – provide an intriguing space of social relation and spatial practices. For example, Fengjie and Wushan, the two small towns near Chongqing municipality (the most significant representative urban area economically, socially and culturally in the south-west), inherently share the culture, language and geographical characteristics of Chongqing. Moreover, they add a sense of locality and nostalgia to the metropolitan city, with their preserved cultural conduct and social customs. Therefore, the cinematic cities examined in this book do not just refer to the metropolitan centres such as the four provincial capitals, but also include the small towns adjacent to them.

Cinematic cities on various scales have been closely associated with the Chinese Documentary Movement, which was initiated by Wu Wenguang with his documentary film *Bumming in Beijing* [*Liulang Beijing*] (1990). This is recognised as China's 'first independent documentary' characterised by hand-held on-location shooting, unclear synch sound and absence of artificial light. The spontaneous style (Wu had no budget funding for the documentary and used borrowed equipment) came to be known as *jishi zhuyi*, or 'on-the-spot realism' that diverges from *xianshi zhuyi* (orchestrated realism) (Berry et al. 2010: 5), and greatly influenced the Sixth Generation directors' aesthetic style and themes. With the influence of the Documentary Movement and the film theories of André Bazin, Siegfried Kracauer and Italian neo-realism introduced to China, some directors became vanguard observers and interpreters of the bewilderment and anxiety caused by the sweeping modernisation of China in the 1990s. Directors such as Zhang Yuan, Jia Zhangke, Lou Ye and Wang Xiaoshuai, as the representatives of the Sixth Generation, have made signature realistic features based on their home towns: Jia Zhangke's Fenyang, Lou Ye's Shanghai, Ning Ying's Beijing and Wang Quan'an's Xi'an. Given the misleading and overgeneralising generational lineage in use in Chinese film studies (i.e. Fifth/Sixth Generation), the term 'Urban Generation', which includes filmmakers who straddle generations, has been created and become a well-accepted rubric in Chinese cinema discourse (Zhang 2007). The term appreciates the directors' sense of social urgency and their cinematic engagement with the radical economic and social transformations underway in contemporary China. I will therefore use Urban Generation rather than Sixth Generation in my urban exploration journey of western China.

Films that engage with urban themes and urban–rural relations have a long history in Chinese cinematic representation. From film screening to film production, Chinese cities and cinema have been developing alongside each other. The first screening of short films happened in Shanghai in 1896 when a French showman displayed a series of short films at the Xu Yuan (the Xu Garden, an entertainment and recreation place) located in Shanghai (Leyda 1972: 1). These short celluloid clips were referred to as *xiyang yingxi* (lit. western (occidental) shadow play) by Chinese viewers. In 1902, a tea house called Fu Shou Tang (lit. Bliss and Longevity Hall) in Beijing screened several short films (Cheng et al. 1978: 10). From then on, film-watching gradually spread nationwide. *Yan Ruisheng* (Ren Pengnian, 1921), a highly acclaimed short feature, and *Orphan Rescues Grandfather* [*Gu'er jiu zu ji*] (Zhang Shichuan, 1923), the first long feature made in mainland China, both were set in modern cities and laid the foundation for Chinese melodrama. From the 1930s to the 1940s, Shanghai was intensively depicted in films such as *Fate of Graduates* [*Tao li jie*] (Ying Yunwei, 1934), *Street Angel* [*Malu tianshi*] (Yuan Muzhi, 1937) and *Crossroads* [*Shizi jietou*] (Shen Xiling, 1937). Cinematic Shanghai was depicted as a site of extravagance, materialism and extreme inequality in wealth and social status. Even though it was the most advanced and modern city in mainland

China in the 1930s, the cinematic image of Shanghai was hardly that of a modern city in the western sense, due to its social and economic limitations. Before the establishment of the People's Republic of China (PRC) in 1949, Chinese cinema was often associated with Shanghai's theatre, studios and cityscape, as the city was the centre of the Chinese film industry in the 1930s (Braester 2012: 347). Along with China's launch of reform in the 1980s, more cities came to be represented through films.

From the 1950s to the end of the 1970s, countryside-related topics – rather than those of the city – dominated film representation, and only a few films were based on urban spaces as a result of a series of political campaigns in mainland China under the new Communist regime. The Shanghai-based feature *Sentinels under the Neon Light* [*Nihongdeng xia de shaobing*] (Wang Ping and Ge Xin, 1964) configured the city as a highly commercialised, class-stratified and morally corrupted space. The intriguing and dynamic urban spaces triggered innocent people to betray their previous humble agrarian values, as Shanghai had been a city 'plagued by the reactionary propaganda of imperialism, feudalism and capitalism and a place influenced by bourgeois and petit-bourgeois ideas' (Zhang 2004b: 199). Towards the end of the Cultural Revolution in the 1970s, films withdrew from patriotic battlefield and revolutionary themes and began to ponder the devastating social, cultural and economic consequences of the event. Moreover, as the central administration under Deng Xiaoping shifted the focus from political campaign to economic growth, filmmakers were allowed to 'denounce the brutality of the Gang of Four during the Cultural Revolution and tested their new-found freedom by exploring previously taboo or sensitive subjects and genres such as political persecution, female sexuality and martial arts' (Zhang 2004b: 226). A prime example during this period was the urban drama *Troubled Laughter* [*Ku nao ren de xiao*] (Yang Yanjin and Deng Yimin, 1979). In the film, a sentimental and ironic atmosphere engulfs the urban spaces, and its characters' appropriation of urban areas is strictly confined in accordance with their political positions, showing the explicit affinity between power and space.

The city and cinema affinity became complex and intriguing in the reform era. In the 1980s, city films became an effective and powerful instrument to record and reflect economic and social transformation and modernisation. Yomi Braester contends that urban cinema is the cinematic response to China's urbanisation in cities on various scales, as the term 'resonates with the long-standing ideological tension between city and countryside, as well as with China's recent urbanisation on an unprecedented scale' (Braester 2012: 347). Films such as Zhang Liang's *Yamaha Fish Stall* [*Yamaha yudang*] (1984) are set in emerging metropolitan Guangzhou and examine the thriving private businesses there. Tian Zhuangzhuang's *Rock 'n' Roll Kids* [*Yaogun qingnian*] (1988) and Mi Jiashan's *The Trouble Shooters* [*Wan zhu*] (1988) are set in Beijing and reflect ambivalent social values and emerging occupations undertaken by young people. Meanwhile, urban melodrama *My Memories of Old Beijing* [*Chengnan jiushi*] (Wu Yigong 1983) and *Rickshaw Boy* [*Luotuo xiangzi*] (Ling Zifeng, 1982), also based in Beijing, convey a strong sense of nostalgia for the traditional dwelling space – the courtyard house – and emphasise traditional social order. Shanghai, on the other hand, as a port city, became the most significant and pioneering industrial site, singled out for industrialisation and modernisation. Cinematic Shanghai during the 1980s appeared in an open and progressive proletarian posture. This was precisely reflected in films *A Corner in the City* [*Dushi li de cunzhuang*] (Teng Wenji, 1982) and *Backlight* [*Ni guang*] (Ding Yinnan, 1982).

The urban cinema of the 1990s tended more to target vernacular everyday life in the urban area. Modern traffic, huge factories and gigantic industrial machines, working classes (urbanites) and their housing conditions, and commercial sites such as extravagant shopping malls and stock exchanges were frequently presented in films. Ruins emerged as another significant cinematic trope for urban China. Rubble and debris from massive demolition and dislocation, and alienated young rebels roaming in the disoriented cities were represented extensively, owing to China's state-driven modernisation. Almost all cities in mainland China involved in this urbanisation were characterised by the coexistence of construction and demolition (Braester 2007: 167). Old walls, streets and buildings were erased from the map of the city, while subways and new landmarks were built to adjust to the speed and efficiency of a modern city. The Urban Generation rose to fame internationally and domestically through their cinematic 'trademark' features of 'the ubiquity of the bulldozer, the building crane, and the debris of urban ruins' (Zhang 2007: 3). Long takes, tracking shots, over-the-shoulder shots and alienated protagonists became the signature aesthetic style of the Urban Generation, which was known as on-the-site realism. Their films recorded and examined the raw reality, and challenged mainstream representations of social and moral issues resulting from such massive social and spatial transformation. The close bonds between people who used to live in *si he yuan* (courtyard houses, common residential housing in Beijing) and *nong tang* (narrow lanes lined with low storey apartment buildings that can be commonly seen in Shanghai) have been broken down by life in high-rises. Modern residents in the city have become isolated behind their apartment doors.

The massive scale of demolition and construction in cities (the material space) runs in parallel to the loss of a 'master ideological signifier' in mainland China in the post-socialist era (McGrath 2008: 24). The establishment of the PRC in 1949 ushered China into a socialist era, when communism and collectivism dominated the ideological terrain, and the whole nation was under the rigid control of planned economy. However, the reform era saw collective values of the socialist era fail to accommodate to the post-socialist modernisation characterised by pluralisation, individualisation and commercialisation. People from diverse social strata lament the loss of humanist spirit and try to find a new perspective or ground for cultural critique. However, the effort to establish a collective value to guide social values and ease cultural anxiety seems doomed to fail in a rapidly changing and market-driven economic context. Cultural products such as films under the circumstances capture and reflect the crumbling of traditional value systems and ideological reference through themes including infidelity and the fetishisation of money and commodities. The fetishisation of material possessions is explicitly shown in films such as *Woman Sesame Oil Maker* (1993), *Ermo* (1994) and *Cell Phone* [*Shouji*] (Feng Xiaogang, 2003). Having become accustomed to 'stasis and naiveté represented by the vestiges of communism in the rural village' (McGrath 2008: 120), people from rural areas are plagued and surrounded by vacuity and a sense of nihilism in pursuing modern commercial and industrial products.

Cinematic Beijing- and Shanghai-dominated urban representation

The cinematic representation of certain places often runs parallel to the level of economic and political significance. Cities with important social, economic and cultural status often catch more media attention and are imagined and re-imagined in contemporary Chinese cinema. It is difficult for the hinterland cities of China to compete with Beijing and Shanghai, the most favoured filmic cities in mainland China. Beijing has been the capital intermittently for over 700 years, and its cityscape has been carefully designed and planned as the political centre and a space of national power and identity. The urban arrangement has been power-oriented, with the Forbidden City at the central point and ring roads built one after another, pushing the urban boundary further and further into the rural area. Its long imperial history leaves behind it an abundant cultural heritage, including splendid architecture and a complete set of cosmological theories of the city, power and the people, all of which have become emblematic signs of the city. Its political, cultural and economic privilege has won the city numerous opportunities to be filmed by both domestic and foreign filmmakers, for instance, Bernardo Bertolucci's *The Last Emperor* [*Modai huangdi*] (1987) and Chen Kaige's *Farewell My Concubine* [*Bawang bie ji*] (1993). As previously noted, Shanghai was the centre of Chinese cinema during the 1930s. Predominantly Shanghai-based melodramas, such as *Street Angel* (Yuan Muzhi, 1937) and *Crossroads* (Shen Xiling, 1937), have been intensively researched for their depictions of the earliest modernised Chinese metropolis and their profound explorations of gender, class and social transformation. The city witnessed filmmakers, crews, producers and actors leaving for Chongqing, Hankou and Hong Kong and studios shut down during the tumultuous years of the 1930s (Clark 1987: 14). It was one of the first places where major reform policies were implemented and massive constructions launched in the 1980s. Being the most advanced industrial site and the birthplace of Chinese cinema, Shanghai remains the most filmed city in contemporary mainland China. The 1990s and 2000s witnessed an astonishing transformation of cityscape in both Beijing and Shanghai, and motion pictures and movie theatres have exerted a stronger influence on the urban culture of the two cities (Lu 2010a: 292). As social stratification and inequality became more acute, the discourse of modernisation and globalisation started to be questioned and challenged by directors such as Lou Ye, Jia Zhangke and Zhang Ming through their films.

Western urban cinema as the witness to radical spatial transformation

Quite a few cities in the fast-developing western part of China (such as Chengdu, Chongqing, Xi'an and Lanzhou) receive cinematic attention for their geographical (inland and poor traffic conditions) and economic (economic performance lags behind the eastern coastal cities) disadvantages. Despite their increasing populations (28 million in Chongqing, 14 million in Chengdu, 8.5 million in Xi'an and 3.6 million in Lanzhou) (National Bureau of Statistics 2011) and the expansion of urban areas in the four cities in recent years, there are far fewer films set in these cities than in Beijing and Shanghai.

In the new millennium, each provincial capital of the region has been undergoing industrialisation, and trying to keep up with south-eastern coastal counterpart cities like Shanghai and Guangzhou. The significance of the four western cities lies in the following aspects: they are each capital cities in their respective provinces now, while Chongqing was designated as the only municipality in the western area in 1997; with the exception of Lanzhou, they were established as capital cities during the dynastic period in ancient China, which gave them evident historical and cultural texture. These historical and cultural traditions have played a significant role in shaping the images of the cityscape and the character of each city in an increasingly assimilated globalised context. The four cities are now the most developed hinterland cities in the reform era. Chongqing and Chengdu are geographically close and their citizens share similar dialects, so that they are often studied as a whole. With a population of over 28 million people, surpassing even Shanghai or Beijing, Chongqing and has become the economic and cultural centre of the vast western terrain. As the only municipal city in western China, Chongqing enjoys direct economic and political support from the central government. Chengdu, Xi'an and Lanzhou, as the provincial cities of Sichuan Province, Shaanxi Province and Gansu Province respectively, also possess the political and economic vantage to realise rapid development. Thus, cinematic representations of these cities have been increasing steadily in recent years. This opens up alternative facets of China to the world, making known the peculiar landscape and hybridity of the current trend of localised culture in the context of globalisation.

Films about the four cities have become increasingly numerous, coinciding with the economic boom they have enjoyed since the 1980s. The four cinematic cities are distinctively different due to their unique local characteristics of urban spaces that have been greatly affected by national projects carried out since the 1960s. Cinematic representation of the region has recorded and reflected the consequences of these projects, which were undertaken at different stages of the national plan. The production of space in these films represents 'a field of differentiation or uniqueness. Indeed, it is a method of locating distinctiveness' (Teo 2013: 133). The earlier Third Front project (*Sanxian jianshe*), implemented between the 1960s and 1980s by the central government under Mao's regime, greatly impacted the urban designation of the four major western cities. A great number of socialist factories were moved from coastal region to these cities, along with accompanying compound residential spaces with Soviet-style buildings. Cities were planned as production spaces rather than commercial centres. The Three Gorges Dam project was launched in 1994 and mostly completed by 2006. Chongqing was the major area affected by the project. As the largest integrated hydropower station built in the history of the world, the project has exerted massive social, economic and ecological impact on the region. Cities and towns in the area, some of which had always been tourist destinations because of their scenic views of the three gorges (Xiling, Wu, Qutang) of the Yangtze River, were flooded, and an unprecedented number of local residents were relocated. During its construction, a myriad of news reports, films and documentaries were made to record and reflect the gigantic project of mainland China's modernisation. In the late 1990s, the Great Western Development project was launched by the central government, showing that the state's regional development strategy of realising an integrated progress in both the eastern coastal Economic Special Zone and the western area, where the Silk Road, the cradle of Chinese civilisation, is located. The project has promoted the construction of infrastructure of traffic, housing and industry of western China, and channelled various resources, in particular, education and technology, to the region. In most recent years, the Road and Belt Initiative, an international economic cooperation program proposed by Xi Jinping's administration in 2014, aims at an unprecedented scale of investment in infrastructure construction in China's western area and its neighbouring countries along the ancient overland corridor of Silk Road and the maritime route. China's western region, which has been an economically and culturally marginalised zone in the context of China's miraculous economic advancement in the reform era, now gains increased national and international attention due to the enormous project.

These huge national projects have fundamentally transformed the cityscape and created a set of everyday life spaces influencing social relationships and daily practice. From a macro perspective, the projects were implemented in the context that China has long been divided into two distinctive spaces – an open and dynamic south-eastern China and an enclosed and inertial western China since the reform era. National economic and resource distribution policies carried out at different historical, social and economic stages (socialist, post-socialist) have shaped the built spaces of western cities, in addition to their geographical features. In cinematic form, these cities provide alternative images of China that diverge from cinematic Beijing and Shanghai. Through these diversified images, western urban cinema conveys and offers a vivid and convincing explanation of why there is such a contrast between east and west in contemporary China.

Western urban cinema displays a more critical stance than that of the established eastern coastal area in terms of examining economic and social uneven development in the reform era. It represents an enclosed and backward west resulting from geographical isolation and a series of national policies implemented before and after the reform era. Consequently, the cinematic representations of western China are frequently associated with wasteland (either natural or industrial), ruins, migrants, poverty, social tenacity, dislocation and uneven economic and social conditions on various scales. The distinctiveness of China's western-based urban films configures a 'Thirdspace' (to use Edward Soja's term) that is dominated and subjected to the front stage of China's images of technocratic metropolises designed to stimulate tourism and national power found in cinematic Beijing and Shanghai. With increasing media exposure and a critical stance of examining China's modernisation and urbanisation, the urban cinema of western China breaks the rigid 'dialectics of centres and peripheries, the conceived and the lived, the material and the metaphorical', to 'open up a new domain, a space of collective resistance' (Soja 1996: 35).

Such a spatial thinking of the cinematic cities located in western China is necessary in terms of enriching and completing the landscape of Chinese cinematic cities hitherto dominated by Beijing and Shanghai. In this book, I ask, therefore, whether the western area is still represented in a similar way to the 1980s avant-garde rural narrative after four decades of implementing open and reform policies? How have the overwhelming economic and social transformations affected people living in the region? Finally, how does government-oriented modernisation impact the cityscape and urban culture and population in the context of globalisation? These are all questions that need to be addressed, as the region has witnessed substantial transformations economically, socially and culturally since the 1980s. Films set in or depicting the region represent and participate in these ongoing transformations through their superior capability to configure, reflect and influence people's understanding and imagining of modern cities and rural–urban relations. Specifically, they demonstrate the complicated dialectic relationship between 'continuity and divergence, the local Self and foreign Other, past history and present response' (Wang 2013: 2). Therefore, many of the films in question will contribute to configure and reconfigure the collective consciousness of specific locations. The location-specific concern of this book is aimed at discovering a sense of subjectivity and a space of resistance that develops on the ground of shared history and experiences tied to a specific place and its geopolitical relation to other regions. This tendency follows Zhang Yingjin's idea of the 'polylocality and translocality' that challenges the concept of 'national' and reconfigures the relations between local, provincial, regional, national and global (Zhang 2010a).

Cinematic western China claimed international and national attention in the 1980s with awe-inspiring landscape (the timeless Loess Plateau) and provocative cultural reflection on China's history, tradition and society. These Loess Plateau-based cinematic representations contributed to the coinage of 'Chinese Westerns' represented by *Yellow Earth* and characterised by distinguished local conduct, and evolved from a deliberate rejection of Hollywood Western genre elements at the initial stage to the embracement of the formulated American Western narration, characterisation and action. The development of Chinese Westerns shows the inevitable trend of transnational cultural communication in the context of globalisation. Urban cinema, meanwhile, corresponds to China's contemporary urbanisation that has radically shaped and reshaped China's cityscape and skylines. City films set in western China, therefore, bear witness to the radical transformation from an agrarian rural space to a hybrid of pre-modern, modern and post-modern space, which actively encourages 'spatial thinking' of the region. In addition, they enhance audiences' understandings of western China in the context of modernisation and promote a critical view on cinematic cities, while also inspiring the formation of multi-temporal and multi-faceted cinematic cities based in the area. Each of the cities explored in this book represents its provincial area, and each group of films (examined in detail) set in the particular city reflects defining moments of its local and even national identity. More importantly, the cinematic depiction of the cities extends to concepts including socialism, post-socialism, modernity, urbanisation, alienation, class stratification and human desire, which all make a significant impact beyond their local, regional or even national realm.

Urban exploration: cinema and space

The spatial turn initiated in the later twentieth century drew academic attention to theories contributed by Henri Lefebvre, Michel Foucault, Edward Soja and Michel de Certeau, all of whom associated urban spaces with history and society, and connected the seemingly inhumane space with subjectivity, psychology and identity in the context of a modern/post-modern world. Cinematic cities, either filmed on location or in established studios, crystallise the real and unreal, subjective and objective. Cities are sites to record, imagine and even transform the urban reality along with its own development. Apart from the cities of varied scales depicted in films, the film industry, from production to distribution and exhibition, has become an inevitable component of modern cities. Since its birth, film has participated in shaping urban space and people's everyday practice in terms of architecture, fashion, entertainment and even ideology. Cinema and the city have created the Thirdspace that Edward Soja perceived as 'the real-and-imagined' place, an inclusive and dynamic space aimed at presenting, analysing and eventually emancipating the marginalised, the peripheral and the Under-represented space (Soja 1996: 54). In this perspective, the urban cinema of western China, which represents the long-ignored western region, overshadowed by the economically booming east, represents a journey to assure its significance, and move from the periphery to the centre, from the unknown to the known.

Edward W. Soja (1996) introduced the concept of Thirdspace based on an epistemology that tends to unlock the rigid binary understanding of space as merely material and mental. His spatial theory is based on Henri Lefebvre's groundbreaking monograph *Production of Space* (1991), in which Lefebvre divided human spatial experience into the perceived, the conceived and the lived. Perceived space refers to the material space that is sensible and open, and can be accurately described and measured (Soja 1996: 66), while conceived space, according to Lefebvre, is 'the dominant space' and 'the space of scientists, planners, urbanists, technocratic subdividers . . . all of whom identify what is lived and what is perceived with what is conceived' (cited in Soja 1996: 67). Lived space, which is linked to 'social space' by Lefebvre, refers to 'the dominated space . . . [that] imagination (verbal but especially non-verbal) seeks to change and appropriate' (cited in Soja 1996: 67–8). Based on Lefebvre's spatial exposition, Soja perceives the Firstspace as a material and physical space that can be mapped and measured; the Secondspace is the mental space that derives from conception, imagination and ideology; the Thirdspace is an inclusive and constant 'othering' space where 'everything comes together . . . subjectivity and objectivity, the abstract and the concrete, the real and the imagined, the knowable and the unimaginable and the unconscious, the disciplined and the transdisciplinary, everyday life and unending history' (Soja 1996: 56). Soja notes that 'there is no unspatialised social reality' (Soja 1996: 46). That is to say, from human body to constructed social spaces at varying scales (village, town, city, region, nation . . .), the spatial dimension of human existence is as essential as humans' historical and social attributes.

Space in cinematic representations is often perceived as the Secondspace that is 'mediated, [and] . . . in contrast to an actual city or urban space' (Mennel 2008: 16). In other words, the cinematic city often appears as a 'transcendental illusion', and as Soja explains, it belongs to 'the visionary and creative arts' . . . [and is] condensed in communicable representations and re-presentations of the real world to the point that the representations substitute for the real world itself (1996: 63). Such imagined and represented cinematic space does not define the reality of social space. In other words, material spaces, no matter whether they are built or natural, are objective and measurable and cannot be narrowly perceived in a subjective and idealised way. As one the most important components of contemporary culture, film per se has its physical existence in forms of theatres, screens and all sorts of technological devices in its production, distribution and exhibition. Spaces in films, in specific villages, towns, cities and countries projected in films, carry their original physical features; meantime, these cinematic sites are also embedded with clear cultural, social and economic characteristics of a particular place. The three dimensions of such cinematic space, which include 'the physical, the mental, the social – [can] be seen as simultaneously real and imagined, concrete and abstract, material and metaphorical' (Soja 1996: 65). Films, with their capacity of truthfully capturing the material space of a place and reflecting the subjective space of human beings, resounds with the real-and-imagined world where 'the physical, mental and social spaces' come together. The artistic representations of space on various scales – from cities, regions to countries – as Lefebvre and Soja confirm, can be seen as a lived space or a Thirdspace that 'stretches across the images and symbols that accompany it, the space of "inhabitants" and "users", [and is also . . .] 'inhabited and used by artists, writers, and philosophers' (Soja 1996: 65). Specifically, in order to capture the multiple facets of the city, filmmakers often artistically display the dominant natural and built environments with local characteristics (Firstspace). In addition, the spirit of given cityscapes, and characters who interact with, escape from, or return to particular social spaces (the Secondspace) structure the film narration. Cinematic scenes about cityscapes and the ways that protagonists use particular spaces, such as walking, running, driving, or getting lost in the urban area show the hidden power relations that arrange the material space and manipulates the social spaces. Specifically, the power relations, which produce urban patterns and processes, are represented by social differences in 'class, gender, age, race, and ethnicity' (Mennel 2008: 15). Cinema as 'a peculiarly spatial form of culture' (Shiel 2001: 5) manifests such urban patterns and processes 'in how they code neighbourhoods as rich or poor or landscape as urban or rural. They reflect class in costume and setting, and in whether characters are positioned inside elaborate domestic space or outside in the urban public space' (Mennel 2008: 15). From this perspective, films can be seen as the Thirdspace that configures a space to reflect social class and cultural issues and involves producing and reproducing social relations by engaging with its audience concerning historical, social and spatial knowledge and power. As Soja contends, the 'Thirdspace' is:

> vitally filled with politics and ideology, with the real and the imagined intertwined, and with capitalism, racism, patriarchy, and other material spatial practices that concretise the social relations of production, reproduction, exploitation, domination, and subjection. (Soja 1996: 68)

The affinity between space, ideological and political power has been intensively illustrated in the spatial arrangement of urban space in China before the reform era. Urban development of most Chinese cities after the establishment of the People's Republic of China followed Chairman Mao's configuration to build 'a system of cities whose size was determined not by free market forces but by the ratio of the productive working population to the total population; an urban economy focused on production rather than consumption' (McGee et al. 2007: 34). Consequently, urban space in mainland China was arranged by 'the principles of uniformity, standardisation and classlessness' (McGee et al. 2007: 34). This was most clearly demonstrated where:

> housing was arranged and built in a standardised manner. There was no central business district, and the city centre was a ceremonial public space for political gatherings such as those found in Beijing's Tiananmen Square during the Cultural Revolution in the late 1960s. (McGee et al. 2007: 34)

The urban spaces, designed and built according to socialist ideals of uniformity and collectivism, are 'representations of power and ideology, of control and surveillance' (Soja 1996: 67). Such arrangements are fully exhibited in Jia Zhangke's Chengdu-based feature *24 City* (2008) and Wang Quan'an's Xi'an based *Weaving Girl* (2009), exemplifying that the concrete space is a result of 'political choice, the impetus of an explicit political project' (Soja 1996: 68).

The 'Thirdspace' of urban area is demonstrated through an array of politically oriented industrial production units spreading across the urban area. Administratively, a sophisticated bureaucratic system was developed to allocate jobs and residences for urbanites, and population mobility was monitored and controlled by the *hukou* system (McGee et al. 2007: 34). Spatially, working units for industrial and military production, usually with attached dwelling and entertainment spaces, were established across China in the pre-reform era. For instance, the Beijing-based military compound shown in *In the Heat of the Sun* [*Yangguang can lan de rizi*] (Jiang Wen, 1994) contains a teenage boy's fantasy of romance, heroism and his final disillusionment in the 1970s. In *Eleven Flowers* [*Wo shiyi*] (Wang Xiaoshuai, 2012), a community attached to a state-owned factory located in south-western China is depicted, showing a group of dislocated Shanghai workers' cautious conduct in a lingering revolutionary atmosphere in the 1970s. Similarly, Teng Wenji's Shanghai-based *A Corner in the City* (1982) features a well-organised industrial site juxtaposed with an urban village where the workers of the industrial unit dwell. Whether a compound community or an urban village, all the industrial units are built to ensure:

> neighbourhood familiarity, conformity and citizen involvement in public affairs, minimal differentiation in income, consumption patterns, religious customs and lifestyles, and rigid taboos on alternative forms of dress, expression, ritual life and communication that did not conform to the socialist convention. (Cited in McGee et al. 2007: 34)

This strategy of city planning transforms the urban space into a series of subordinate centripetal spaces where those who are able to settle down are regarded as having an 'iron bowl' that guarantees a position with high security and stability. Centripetal space in this case means that, in spatial terms, such kinds of state-owned enterprises with attached staff dormitory, school and even hospital confine people to a self-reliant and inclusive realm. Here, people undertake similar jobs, receive similar salaries, live in identical households and have the same group of people as colleagues, neighbours and friends. They all have one purpose – to play their trivial part in constructing an industrialised and powerful country. Temporally, insiders of this space are provided with a lifelong 'iron bowl', and usually the next generation are allowed to take over the 'bowl' from the retired parents. Given the adherent stability and decent social position, the socialist space is regarded as a desirable utopia for the insiders and outsiders in the socialist era, becoming a centripetal space that attracts people, resources and capital from outside. However, with the introduction of the reform policy in 1978, it became a space where inhabitants 'search for emancipatory change and freedom from domination' (Soja 1996: 70).

With the massive economic and social reformation that began in the early 1980s, such state-owned enterprises in many cities were demolished to make way for a consumer-oriented society. Entertainment and residential complexes sprang up across the urban space, and people, either from the city or the countryside, gained far more mobility than in the pre-reform era. Correspondingly, the uniform and collectivist arrangements and social relations rooted in socialist institutions began to be discarded and were replaced by commercialism and individualism. The 1980s becomes a watershed that breaks the centripetal space under the socialist economic system, and witnesses the formation of a centrifugal space created by a socialist market and facilitated by newly constructed inter-city and inter-provincial highways and railways. A similar phenomenon occurred in the 1950s in the USA, where the end of the Second World War and the growth of highways stimulated the transformation of urban representation and the role of space (Dimendberg 2004: 178).

The tremendous force of the socialist market with Chinese characteristics disperses capital, resources, technology and labour on various scales that ranged from the local, provincial, regional, national to transnational in the reform era. The commercial and consumer-dominated spaces constructed after the 1980s expanded the cityscape far beyond the original urban fringes and constantly redefined the skyline.

The radical transition from a centripetal space to a centrifugal space characterises cinematic western China, which can be seen in *Signal Left, Turn Right* (Huang Jianxin, 1996) and *24 City* (Jia Zhangke, 2008). The cinematic cities construct a space to record and reflect such transforming spatial practices and analyse the logic and ideals behind the spatial changes, namely, how the power (political, ideological, economic and cultural) controls and dominates the changing cityscape. Cinematic cities create an ideological and cultural space of 'epistemological power' that contains utopian thoughts and imagination of semioticians and artists (Soja 1996: 67). It is the 'conceived space' (in Lefebvre's definition) or alternatively, the 'Secondspace' (Soja's term) where filmmakers could make particular thematic and aesthetic choices to show how individuals appropriate and use urban spaces arranged by hegemonic political and economic power. What is more important is that this cinematic conceived space is also:

> tied to the relations of production and, especially, to the order or design that they impose. Such order is constituted via control over knowledge, signs, and codes: over the means of deciphering spatial practice and hence over the production of spatial knowledge. (Soja 1996: 67)

'The relations of production', in the background of mainland China before the reform era, followed a socialist institution under which the urban spatial design and city function were ascribed to a series of particular spatial practices and productions of space. Cinematic representation about the particular spatial arrangements and relationships between the space and people help us reflect and recognise the invisible power of space in the human body and mind and in interpersonal relations.

Moreover, the Thirdspace is also the 'terrain for the generation of "counterspaces", spaces of resistance to the dominant order arising precisely from their subordinate, peripheral or marginalised positioning' (Soja 1996: 68). Western China has long been regarded as the frontier, a marginalised counterspace characterised by agricultural and nomadic production and economically left behind in comparison with eastern and southern China in the reform era. To perceive western China represented in cinema as a Thirdspace will help illuminate how the uneven social and economic development has been spatially represented in films, how the oppressed and marginalised space represented in films shows the operation of power under socialist and post-socialist discourse, and how the cinematic western China becomes a space of resistance against the binary oppositions of the developing west versus the developed east, the rural west versus urban east, the culturally rooted west versus modern unrooted east.

Soja's view of imagining and appropriating the urban space resonates with the spatial exploration strategies and tactics elaborated by Michel de Certeau in his seminal essay 'Walking in the city' (Certeau 1984). Soja's Secondspace (representations of space) echoes Certeau's panoramic view of New York City from the World Trade Centre. This tremendous emblem of capital, power and modernity (before it was destroyed in the September 11th attacks in 2001) offers its viewer the concept of a modern city that can be found in the discourse of utopia. The God's view spectacle shows the architects, city planners and reformers' configuration of the city as a rational, readable and governable space. It is essentially an idealistic perspective aiming at rendering the city transparent. In contrast to the panoptic representation of space, Certeau offers a sympathetic account of a representational urban space which people inhabit. This lived space, in Soja's words, can be seen as the Thirdspace pervaded by personal memory and desire.

Two metropolitan experiences – looking down from the World Trade Centre to attain a panoramic view of the city and walking in streets to feel, to observe and to be reminded of the details and secret aspects of the city – are juxtaposed in 'Walking in the city'. Looking from the summit of the World Trade Centre, located towards the southern tip of Manhattan, Certeau is greeted by 'a wave of verticals' and the 'gigantic mass' that 'is immobilised before the eyes' (Certeau 1984: 91). New York City, specifically Manhattan, as the international financial and capital centre, is a concrete forest continuously exploding. The city,

> unlike Rome, has never learnt the art of growing old by playing on all its pasts. Its present invents itself, from hour to hour, in the act of throwing away its previous accomplishments and challenging the future. A city composed of paroxysmal places in monumental reliefs . . . in it are inscribed the architectural figures of the coincidatio oppositorum formerly drawn in miniatures and mystical textures. (Certeau 1984: 91)

The panorama of New York City can resemble that of any other metropolis across the world. In the battle between conserving the old and inventing the new, urbanisation is a compelling force that is capable of overthrowing the previous and the present, and forever looking toward the future.

When getting rid of the street and crowd and standing on the apex of the skyscraper, one is, according to Certeau:

> lifted out of the city's grasp. One's body is no longer clasped by the streets that turn and return it according to an anonymous law; nor is it possessed, whether as player or played, by the rumble of so many differences and by the nervousness of New York traffic . . . His elevation transfigures him into a voyeur. It puts him into distance. It transforms the bewitching world by which one was possessed into a text that lies before one's eyes. It allows one to read it, to be a solar Eye. (Certeau 1984: 92)

In other words, the panoramic perspective of the city turns the viewer into a reader, and at the same time, turns the city into a text, a concept that can be mapped, measured and analysed. In addition, the masses and their activities appear so small and remote that their mobility is almost invisible. Therefore, the 'voyeur' with a bird's eye view, can attain 'the concept of the city' (p. 93), which echoes the blueprint designed by city planners or institutional bodies that arrange the urban space according to rationalism and transparency. The other spatial experience, walking in the street, according to Certeau, contrasts with 'the collective mode of administration' as it represents 'an individual mode of reappropriation' (p. 96). Walking as a space of enunciation is inevitably full of infinite diversity. As an effective way of linking acts and footsteps, the names and symbols of a place provide meanings and directions to walkers. Besides, they would be changed or even vanish when spaces are emptied, or their original function is worn away.

Despite the consistent changing or vanishing of particular places, memories about places may linger on. Thus, it is through memory that people connect to certain places and spaces. Such connection remains personal, which in turn gives that place its character. It is a poetic journey to engage in walking through the same street time after time, pondering on the past and the present and moving forward to acquire a new self-knowledge and a new cognition of the city. Through the journey, one may be able to 'repeat the joyful and silent experience of childhood; it is, in a place, to be other and to move toward the other' (Certeau 1984: 110). Walking, as a pedestrian's speech act, is outside of the geometrical or geographical space of visual, panoptic or theoretical constructions. It is neither transparent nor rational enough to be concisely mapped or planned.

Certeau's dialectic view of urban exploration is what Soja tries to resist. But Certeau's observations of pedestrians' poetic and tactical way of appropriating or re-appropriating the complicated urban space affirm both the *flâneur* and urban drifters' urban exploration experience, oscillating between 'manipulating and enjoying, the fleeting and massive reality of a social activity at play with the order that contains it' (Certeau 1984: xxiv). *Flânerie* and drifting, as two archetypal modes of urban exploration, are often employed by cinematic characters to observe, interpret and interact with different urban spaces in their daily practices. With or without being conscious of their actions, individuals always deal with daily routine with some smart 'tactics' rather than being completely controlled or determined by 'strategies' imposed by institutional bodies. In the context of contemporary China, cinematic *flâneurs* and drifters can be found in a great number of urban films. They observe and experience the dramatic transformation in both material and psychological spaces, demystifying the enigmatic or Under-represented aspects of urban spaces, representing the experiences of modern populace attended by anxiety, insecurity and instability in the massive commercialisation and urbanisation being undergone in China.

Selection and analysis of films

Films selected for analysis in this volume vary in theme and characterisation, but most of them tend to employ a realistic style and represent an authentic local ambience and characteristics. Through editing and various filmic languages, the city and places that emerge or are created through city films form a virtual space based on actual urban spaces and offer proximity which enables viewers to see and feel the virtual presence of the city.

The films listed in Table 1.1 will be examined in detail. All of the films in question represent radical spatial transformations in the cities of western China. The previous dreary, highly politicised and enclaved spaces of cities have become, to varying degrees, commercialised and globalised. Rather than celebrating such a glamorous spatial reconfiguration, the urban films set in western China construct a Thirdspace that bears witness to and investigates ruined public spaces and marginalised private space, and the social groups who are living on the periphery.

In film, space is one of the critical media of visual communication. The way that characters are arranged in cinematic space (*mise-en-scène*) is illustrative of their social and psychological relationships (Giannetti 2008: 66). Scenes showing images of cityscapes and the way the protagonist uses the space (walking, running, driving, getting lost) will be closely examined; sounds (traffic noise, soundtrack, etc.) and shots that establish the ambience of particular places through lighting, framing, *mise-en-scène* and other techniques will be analysed to see how they engage with the state or process of China's urbanisation in the context of globalisation. As cinematic settings are not merely the background for the action, but also symbolic

Table 1.1 Basic information of films to be examined

City and its adjacent areas	Films	Director	Year
Wushan, Chongqing	*Rainclouds over Wushan*	Zhang Ming	1996
Chongqing	*Crazy Stone*	Ning Hao	2006
Chongqing	*Curiosity Kills the Cat*	Zhang Yibai	2006
Fengjie, Chongqing	*Still Life*	Jia Zhangke	2006
Chengdu	*24 City*	Jia Zhangke	2008
Chengdu	*Buddha Mountain*	Li Yu	2011
Xi'an	*Back to Back, Face to Face*	Huang Jianxin	1994
Xi'an	*Signal Left, Turn Right*	Huang Jianxin	1996
Near Xi'an	*The Story of Ermei*	Wang Quan'an	2004
Xi'an	*Weaving Girl*	Wang Quan'an	2009
Jingtai, Lanzhou	*A Fool*	Chen Jianbin	2014
Hexi Corridor	*River Road*	Li Ruijun	2015

extensions of characterisation and cinematic theme (Giannetti 2008: 266), characters from varied social strata will be examined in detail, especially when they physically or metaphorically cross social borders (boundaries between places, class, gender and ethnicity, etc.) or when their lived space is intruded upon and even demolished.

The *mise-en-scène*: the space between characters, the distance between character and camera and the depth planes within the frame will also be closely examined, as the spatial arrangement of 'virtually any kind of territory used by humans betrays a discernible concept of power and authority' (Giannetti 2008: 67). Accordingly, the power and authority demonstrated through the space structure represented both within and outside of the films will be included and closely examined, contributing to a spatial understanding of cities in western China. Shots of various length and shots that are tightly or loosely framed to demonstrate the mental space of characters, namely, their symbolic meanings in psychological and social dimensions, will be another focus of analysis. Chronologically investigating films made in and about each city will reveal the dynamic relationship between identity, gender, migration, class and place; it will create a collective 'memory map' of a city. Such analysis will reveal how a city creates, maintains and mutates its image on the road to modernisation. A spatial perspective looking at the physical and mental spaces represented by films made in and about cities of western China (in the context of modernisation) will draw a map of inequality in social and economic development, and show the nuanced cultural differences within this region.

Organisation of the Book

The first chapter starts with an introduction to China's Westerns and their territorial boundaries and cultural connotations by comparing them to Hollywood Westerns in terms of theme, genre, geographical setting and cultural significance. China's Westerns configured a rural and ethnographical image of the area from the 1980s to the 1990s, which therefore became stereotypes of the region, providing a stark contrast to the dynamic modern images of cinematic Beijing, Shanghai and Hong Kong. The chapter then briefly delineates China's eastern coastal-region dominated 'urban cinema' that resonates with the uneven urbanisation and modernisation in mainland China in the reform era. This historical account helps situate my chapters on Chinese Western urban film within a larger historical and social context. Finally, the discussion moves to national projects carried out in western China from the 1960s to the 1980s to explore the relationship between power, space, city and cinema. I will approach the cinematic spaces of four Han-dominated capital cities in western China by drawing on theories of scholars such as Henri Lefebvre, Edward Soja and Michel de Certeau.

The second chapter sets out to highlight the vertical cityscapes, local languages and old ways of living of Chongqing represented in films. The geographical isolation of the city makes it not only a historical and cultural 'interior other' in China, but a film centre during the revolutionary years (1937–46). The cinematic images of the city were associated with 'national rejuvenation' during the Anti-Japanese War, while it became a site of cultural and historical reflection of the Cultural Revolution in the 1980s. Contemporary history sees the city and its adjacent area as a site of a remarkable modernisation landmark, the Three Gorges Dam, which has been built to promote national industry and economy. I discuss the reasons why the city is favoured by filmmakers and how various modernisation projects attempting to tailor the city into a homogeneous urban centre become increasingly compromised, with filmmakers continuously capturing and representing Chongqing's mundane and vernacular facets. The next part explores, first, the black comedy *Crazy Stone* [*Fengkuang de shitou*] (Ning Hao, 2006), in which Chongqing appears as a melting pot characterised by immigrants, dialects and the lack of cultural originality and moral values. The film displays Chongqing's power to create disorientation, anxiety and social discontent owing to an increasingly complicated and unevenly developed technocratic society where great changes of identity, subjectivity and social class are underway. The second analysis is of the psychological horror *Curiosity Kills the Cat* [*Haoqi haisi mao*] (Zhang Yibai, 2006), which explores urban spaces pervaded by desire, infidelity and class stratification. Chongqing in the two films presents a literal stratification of its high and low spaces, with characters appropriating distinct urban spaces that correspond to their stratified social classes, and with tragic consequences ensuing when they transgress such stratified spaces.

Chapter 3 displays how material and cognitive spaces are shaped and demolished by a national project (the construction of the Three Gorges Dam) by examining Zhang Ming's 1996 *Rainclouds over Wushan* [*Wushan yunyu*] and Jia Zhangke's 2006 *Still Life* [*Sanxia haoren*]. The enormous national project represents the macro spatial view of rationalising and modernising the urban space, yet Zhang Ming chooses a micro perspective to examine the inertia and subjective dimension of the city. He creates a Thirdspace by showing the street view of the urban space and everyday life related to emerging commercialism and oppressed desire in a claustrophobic space, which opposes the grand discourse of building the Three Gorges Dam to national resurrection and modernisation. *Still Life* adopts the style of magical realism to convey the dramatic changes underway in the physical space and the consequent traumatic experiences in the mental space of characters. It works as a space of resistance by focusing on those marginalised people who make ruins, live in ruins, are exiled and even buried by ruins. Ruins, therefore, bear clear and indivisible class marks. The cinematic representations of the city resonate with the immensity and complexity of the trend toward urbanisation and modernisation.

Chapter 4 turns to cinematic Chengdu, the provincial centre of Sichuan province next to Chongqing municipality. The cinematic representations of Chengdu and its adjacent cities appear in two competing styles: either primitive or modern. The primitiveness of Chengdu results from its geographical isolation and underdeveloped economy, cinematically displayed through the distinctive natural beauty and primitive cultural landscapes of the area. Moreover, the remote geographical location of the city rendered it an industrial space designed in the service of national security under an enormous project – the Third Front (or Third Line) between the 1960s and the 1980s when mainland China was confronted with complex international circumstances (the Cold War). The cityscape of Chengdu, accordingly, was divided by an array of state-owned socialist 'units' involving in the production of military or heavy industry in China. These units functioned as centripetal spaces attracting talent, resources and capital with their promises of decent payment, city household registration and life-long career. Jia Zhangke's *24 City* [*Ershisi cheng ji*] (2008) represents such spatial arrangements and its disappearance in the reform era. The film demonstrates how and why such a socialist utopia was established and developed but has now disappeared. Moreover, it shows the transition of the urban space from a space of production into a space of consumption by exploring the generational gaps in characters' consuming and appropriating social spaces. I argue that the 1980s becomes a watershed that breaks the centripetal space under the socialist economic system and witnesses the formation of a centrifugal space created by a socialist market and facilitated by interprovincial highways and railways.

Chapter 5 begins with an overview of feature films and documentaries that proliferated after the 2018 Wenchuan earthquake, which has become the watershed in cinematic representations of the area. Ruins, heavy loss of life and local survivors' troubled situations wrought by the disaster have dominated cinematic modern Chengdu. Moreover, with the catastrophic disaster's ability of erasing physical spaces and producing traumatic experiences and memories, post-earthquake cinematic Chengdu becomes an optimal space for emotional remedy and contemplation on existence. In urban feature *Buddha Mountain* [*Guanyin shan*] (Li Yu, 2011), the ruins wrought by the Wenchuan earthquake symbolises the interior wasteland inhabited by film characters. The film juxtaposes the tragic disaster with the disintegration of traditional family units and the consequent psychological vacuum in modern families. Characters in the film are shown as drifters, driven from place to place because of the trend of demolition and construction, and impacted by accidents, mobility and imposed spatial oppression associated with urban spaces.

Chapter 6 starts with an overview of Xi'an represented in urban comedies and Huang Jianxin's two urban trilogies. Many urban comedies set in Xi'an employ local dialects and include landmarks of the city, fostering a strong sense of locale. Huang's first urban trilogy portrays Xi'an as an anonymous modern space, highlighting the conflicts between the intact socialist ideological/political order and the 'marching into the world' goal in modernisation at the initial stage of China's reform. His second urban trilogy diverges from acute political criticism, carrying more local characteristics of Xi'an through a *flâneur*'s street-level observation of ordinary citizens' daily practices. The following part explores Huang's *Back to Back, Face to Face* [*Beikaobei, Lianduilian*] (1994) and *Signal Left, Turn Right* [*Hongdengting, lüdengxing*] (1996). The two films capture the coexistence and hybridity of urban and rural values and conduct. In *Back to Back*, Xi'an is depicted within layers of walls and 'guild halls', creating an enclosed space overwhelmed by traditional power structures and rural values, and framing its characters in such spaces that overlook them, dwarf them and constrain their vision, perspective and behaviour. In *Signal Left, Turn Right*, the power of capital overwhelms traditional values and ways of conduct, and it also produces a sprawling urban space. Meanwhile, the phantom of obsolete political and ideological discourse persists in the daily practices of ordinary people.

Chapter 7 examines cinematic Xi'an as a capsule of rural inertia and socialist China by investigating the female appropriation of spaces in both rural and urban areas represented in Wang Quan'an's 2004 *The Story of Ermei* [*Jingzhe*] and 2009 *Weaving Girl* [*Fangzhi guniang*]. *The Story of Ermei* shows the protagonist's rural–urban experiences and the limited physical spaces she can access, and displays a complicated space–power relation which is not only limited to gender but also to social class and rural–urban disparities. *Weaving Girl* explores female bodies and human sufferings that resonate in grim anonymous industrial areas plagued with rundown factories, alienated streets and neighbourhoods. The cinematic image of Xi'an in this film is deprived of the thick historical and cultural sense, but is associated with fateful diseases suffered by female characters, which can be regarded as resonating with the collapse of the state-owned enterprise.

Chapter 8 examines cinematic Lanzhou, the capital city of Gansu province, which makes an 'absent presence' in films, as it often appears as the reference to modernity and a future destination in the eyes of film characters from the adjacent areas. Similar to cinematic Xi'an, Lanzhou and its neighbouring secondary cities in films are frequently associated with either Chinese Western genre, featuring vast expanses of desert, galloping horses and thrilling gun-fights, or minority films characterised by rural spaces, exotic costumes and mysterious religious rituals. In addition, the geographical conditions of the area nurture a nomadic way of production. Therefore, sheep, horse, camel or cattle herding becomes one of the overt images of the area, with protagonists in films often accompanied or symbolised by these animals. Chen Jianbin's directorial debut *A Fool* [*Yige shaozi*] (2014) is one example. The film is set in a small city adjacent to Lanzhou, and shows how the protagonist suffers from urban manipulative domination due to his low social status, inadequate knowledge about urban conduct and weak social connections. On a larger scale, the film demonstrates the sprawling urban spaces and the power of capital that transforms rural life and restricts the rural living space. Such a theme is further extended in *River Road* [*Jia zai shuicao fengmao de difang*] (Li Ruijun, 2015), a film featuring a disappearing ethnic minority in the Hexi Corridor. The film demonstrates that the transforming power of urbanisation appears even more dramatic in an ecologically fragile environment, with the inhabitants deprived of health, traditional ways of production and home.

This book concludes that city films set in urban centres of western China engage with, respond to and reimagine China's complex and heterogeneous urbanisation and modernisation in an increasingly globalised world. The four cinematic urban centres examined in this book configure a space of the subaltern, the marginalised and the dominated, defy the glamorised success stories of China's economic boost, question the dominance of political and capital power imposed on the designation and transformation of cityscape and urban life, assert the value of cultural and social pluralism and hybridity. However, limitations on the book's length mean it cannot fully cover all the urban centres in western China, such as Kunming, Lasa, Ürümchi, Xining and Hohhot, the capital city of Yunnan, Tibet, Xinjiang Uygur Autonomous Region, Qinghai and Inner Mongolia. These cities are inhabited by many minorities and often represented in minority films with their cultural uniqueness and religion foregrounded. With the implementation of the Belt and Road Initiative, and under the influence of expanding urbanisation and the ensuing social mobility and regional inequality, will their cultural and ethnic identities disappear? Will they be assimilated and transformed? Given the ambivalent and controversial relationship between minority groups and the dominant Han, the role of minority films in cultural intervention in central government's neoliberal policies, minority films set in western China are indicated as a new area for future studies.

PART II
CINEMATIC CHONGQING

CHAPTER 2

History, Cityscape and Spatial Stratification

Chongqing started its significant involvement in film production during the Anti-Japanese War of 1937–45, with the city designated as the temporary capital of the Nationalist government in retreat from Japanese-captured Nanjing and coastal territories. The short period of being the 'capital' of the Nationalist government brought the city to national and international attention and greatly accelerated the modernisation of the cityscape. Meanwhile, the city became the base of promoting national defence through propaganda films, which were thematically dominated by revolutionary stories and patriotic characters, although the city per se was not involved in these cinematic narratives. Before this film industry involvement in the 1930s and its status of being the temporary capital, the city has long been regarded as the 'interior other' in Chinese ancient history, owing to its remote geographical position and distinct cultural tradition.

Chongqing is the only inland municipality in contemporary China, and in addition to its metropolitan appearance, which shares homogeneous characteristics with other metropolises in China, has preserved many local traditions and characteristics. Filmmakers compliment the city on its unique spatial arrangements and the sense of magical realism engendered by enormously contrasted cityscape and social stratification. Consequently, recent films such as *Crazy Stone* [*Fengkuang de shitou*] (Ning Hao, 2006) and *Curiosity Kills the Cat* [*Haoqi haisi mao*] (Zhang Yibai, 2006) capture local features and dynamic development of the city, and focus on pressing social issues such as degraded mass culture, fake products, social stratification and infidelity.

The launch of the construction of Three Gorges Dam in the middle of the 1990s made the city a media focus. Wushan and Fengjie, the two towns adjacent to Chongqing involved in the national project, were partially demolished, which brought large-scale forced migration. *Rainclouds over Wushan* (Zhang Ming, 1996) (set in Wushan) and *Still Life* (Jia Zhangke, 2006) (set in Fengjie) feature enormous social and environmental transformation that bewilders and traumatises both local people and outsiders who break into the disappearing space. In these films, the ruined space brought by the monumental project, the huge gap between the lower and higher social classes, the natural beauty of the local space and the exiled population become critiques of the national dream of modernisation. Constructing the Three Gorges Dam was the central government's economic and political choice that was meant to be an impetus to give 'special attention and particular contemporary relevance to the spaces of representation, to lived space as a strategic location from which to encompass, understand, and potentially transform all spaces simultaneously' (Soja 1996: 68). The cinematic city, accordingly, not only is associated with the national modernisation dream, but becomes the Thirdspace that challenges the discourse of modernisation and creates a space of silent resistance that common people inhabit, work and try to survive.

Chongqing in Films: A Brief Account

During the Anti-Japanese War (1937–1945), the Nationalist government moved its capital from Nanjing up the Yangtze River to Chongqing. The state-owned Central Film Studio [Zhongdian] and the China Motion Picture Studio [Zhongzhi] also moved to the city in 1938 (Zhang 2004b: 92). A great number of filmmakers, scriptwriters and actors migrated to the city and continued to make films. The Nationalist government sponsored the making of patriotic films, and Chongqing arguably became the film centre from 1937 to 1946. For instance, director Shi Dongshan's anti-Japanese tetralogy *Defend Our Land* [*Baowei wo men de tudi*] (1938), *Good Husband* [*Hao zhangfu*] (1939), *March of Victory* [*Shengli jinxingqu*] (1940) and *My Homeland* [*Huan wo guxiang*] (1945) stimulated numerous young people to join the war for the sake of national defence and solidarity. *Storm on the Border* [*Saishang fengyun*] (Ying Yunwei, 1940) featured a love triangle story and advocated solidarity between the Meng minority and the Han majority in joint struggle against the Japanese invasion. After the establishment of the People's Republic of China in 1949, the Chongqing-based studios made a number of films to reflect the class conflicts of the Civil War, including the war drama *Living Forever in Burning Flames* [*Liehuo zhong yongsheng*] (Shui Hua, 1965) and the musical *Sister Jiang* [*Jiang jie*] (Huang Zumo and Fan Lai, 1978). These two representative cinematic works were based on true revolutionary stories of Communist soldiers. Places such as Bai Mansion (residence of a warlord named Bai Jü, transformed by the Kuomintang (KMT) into a prison to jail Communists during the Civil War), Refuse Pit (Zhazidong) and the Red Crag (Hongyancun) not only served as the settings of the above revolutionary stories, but also as symbols of the Red Spirit (the bravery and perseverance of the Communist warriors). All these places have been transformed into popular tourist destinations dedicated to the memory of the soldiers and their sacrifices.

In the 1980s, urban films set in Guangzhou, Beijing and Shanghai began to display the progress and processes of industrialisation and commercialisation, the thriving market and people involved in private businesses. In contrast, Chongqing and its adjacent area were represented as natural beauty resorts and a place for exiled victims of the Cultural Revolution in films such as *Evening Rain* [*Bashan yeyu*] (Wu Yonggang and Wu Yigong, 1980) and *Time until the Mountain Leaves* [*Dengdao manshan hongye shi*] (Tang Huada and Yu Benzheng, 1980). In the opening sequences of *Evening Rain*, a little girl runs via numerous stairs to the dock where a ferry is leaving for Shanghai. A long tracking shot follows her hurried steps from the city all the way to the dock, showing an old and scarcely populated stair street that runs up and down the hilly topology (Figure 2.1).

Figure 2.1 The stair-street in the opening sequences: in *Evening Rain*

In *Time until the Mountain Leaves*, the picturesque landscapes along the Yangtze River, especially the natural spectacle of the Three Gorges, and some local legends become the essential contextualisation that inspires its characters' passion for dreams and the pursuit of true love. The Three Gorges area began to draw national and international attention after the National People's Congress approved the immense national project to construct the world's largest hydroelectric dam, the Three Gorges Dam, in 1992. From this period onward, the hinterland area has been a constant focus of domestic and overseas media coverage. In the years 2000 to 2002, the processes of demolition, migration and transformation in the region attracted extensive media attention, engendering voluminous news coverage across the whole country (Lu 2010b: 101). Filmic representation of the area also increased, keeping spectators updated about the great changes occurring in the area. More importantly, films provided an alternative perspective from which to perceive the radical spatial changes underway in the area. The traumatic individual experiences and agitated collective memory of the local immigrants represented in some features contrasted with the upbeat tone conveyed by mainstream coverage. Films such as *Rainclouds over Wushan*, *Balzac and the Little Chinese Seamstress* [*Ba'erzhake yu xiaocaifeng*] (Dai Sijie, 2002), a Franco-Chinese romance feature, and *Still Life* contained a strong sense of agitation and sentimentality and became an acute critique of the discourse of modernisation.

The Three Gorges Dam project was launched in 1994 and the designation of Chongqing as the fourth municipality took place in 1997, after which time Chongqing began to attain increasing exposure in cinema. In 2000, the 'Great Western Development' [*Xibu dakaifa*] project was launched, targeted at solving the problems of regional inequality (the enormous economic gap between the coastal area, middle area and western area) and rural poverty. Overall, the plan aimed to improve the nation's economic strength by including relatively underdeveloped western and central China in the march towards an integrated modernisation (Lai 2002: 436). The other major cities in the west, such as Chengdu, Xi'an and Lanzhou, also benefited from the project economically, gaining more opportunities for filmic representation. From the year 2000 until the present, at least ten major films have been shot on location in Chongqing (including the urban area and the nearby countryside). Urban dramas *Chongqing Blues* [*Rizhao Chongqing*] (Wang Xiaoshuai, 2010) and *Chongqing Hot Pot* [*Huoguo yingxiong*] (Yang Qing, 2016) were named directly after the city and featured the city's distinctive aura and representative cuisine. In *Life Show* [*Shenghuo xiu*] (Huo Jianqi, 2002), *Curiosity Kills the*

Cat [*Haoqi haisi mao*] (Zhang Yibai, 2006) and *Deadly Delicious* [*Shuang shi ji*] (Zhao Tianyu, 2008) the city appears as an anonymous urban space entrapping the characters. The box office hit comedy *Crazy Stone* stands out for its employment of local dialect and black humour. Long features such as *Lost, Indulgence* [*Mi'an*] (Zhang Yibai, 2008), *Distant Thunder* [*Mi cheng*] (Zhang Jiarui, 2010) and *Forgetting to Know You* [*Wangle qu dongni*] (Quan Ling, 2014) alternate between urban spaces and adjacent industrial or town areas, showing the increasing mobility and instability of the city, and the danger and predicament induced by urbanisation. The diversified representations of this city not only show alternative cityscapes but also manifest the local colour of this transforming place. Filmmakers such as Huo Jianqi, Wang Xiaoshuai and Jia Zhangke made it clear that Chongqing distinguishes itself from Beijing, Shanghai and the coastal developed cities in terms of its unique urban space and preservation of vernacular culture. Huo Jianqi chose Chongqing as the setting for his film *Life Show*. He explained the reasons as follows:

> It is located on rocky mountain ranges within which flows the great Yangtze River. The geographical condition provides many angles and perspectives for cinematography. The cityscape offers an interesting amalgam of the newly built urban space and the long existing old space. Such a cityscape reflects the interdependence between the people and the environment (whether it is natural or built), and also shows the stress brought by constant changes in the city and in people's lives. (Huo 2002: 40)

He frames his story on Houci Street, an old street lined with numerous stalls and restaurants, engulfed by blocks of high-rise apartment buildings and shiny commercial complexes on the downtown peninsula of Chongqing. Revolving around the old street, which is designated to be demolished, *Life Show* showcases a disappearing living space, and represents common people's stress and agony brought by urbanisation. In the film, the mountain city is closely associated with dark private spaces, a jail and a bustling night market, creating an unstable and beguiling cinematic city. Similarly, Wang Xiaoshuai's *Chongqing Blues* captures a spatially fractured Chongqing where the modern high-rises engulf the dilapidated low-rise structures (Figure 2.2). Specifically, the film shows a multi-faceted cityscape. On the one hand, the city is characterised by night clubs, fancy shops and streets patronised by adolescents; on the other hand, it is the parental generation's socialist working unit characterised by old dilapidated factories and residences. The distinctive spaces used by the young and the old generations symbolise their grim relationships and misunderstandings.

Figure 2.2 The Chongqing cityscape in the opening shot: in *Chongqing Blues*

In an interview, Wang explained why he selected Chongqing as the filmic setting:

> In the process of urbanisation, Beijing turns from an interesting, humanist and passionate city into a concrete forest metropolis . . . what used to be intriguing about the city has been utterly destroyed, and the situation in Shanghai is even worse. However, Chongqing is quite unique. It is identical to any other metropolis concerning the same cold and hard urban spaces, while in terms of the fabric of the daily life and its inhabitants, the city holds onto its local tradition and a vulgarity that survives the sweeping force of modernisation. (Liu 2010: 96)

While the massive urbanisation and modernisation tend to tailor cities in a homogeneous manner across China, it has been a practice that becomes increasingly compromised in Chongqing. As filmmakers have been keeping discovering and representing alternative facets of the city by juxtaposing the newly accomplished modern cityscape with the traditional run-down urban villages, which becomes testimonies of a transitional era characterised by heterogeneity and hybridity. In *Crazy Stone* (Ning Hao, 2006) and *Curiosity Kills the Cat* (Zhang Yibai, 2006), such transitional characteristics of Chongqing are fully represented.

Crazy Stone, a low-budget box office hit comedy, was made with an estimated investment of CNY 3 million and eventually grossed CNY 23 million in China, and obtained great critical success as well. It sheds light on people from all walks of life in Chongqing and celebrates everyday life and common people's triumph over the power of authority and modern technology. *Curiosity Kills the Cat*, a thriller disclosing rigid social stratification through a shifting point of view of four characters, shows ordinary people's uncompromised desire for wealth and decent social status in a bustling urban space. Both films were regarded as successful genre films in mainland Chinese market after release, with their mimic of Hollywood style thrillers and gangster films. Chongqing in the two films stands out with its distinguished cityscapes, special traffic devices, enormous economic gap and spatial dichotomy. In addition, the cinematic city also impresses viewers by its tenacious hold on tradition, dynamism and dramatic modernisation in an increasingly globalised context.

The Stratification of High and Low Spaces

Crazy Stone, set in Chongqing, revolves around a precious jade stone that attracts the attention of three groups of people: the manager and workers from a near bankrupt state-owned handcraft factory who intend to sell the jade to resurrect the factory's fortunes; three crooks seeking wealth; and a shrewd real estate developer who wants the inner-city land owned by the factory and his hired international hustler, who aims to snatch the jade and deprive the factory of its last possibility of survival. In the film, Chongqing municipality is presented both through a panoramic view and a street view from below. It depicts a city pervaded with sensual stimuli, confronting viewers with a cluster of sounds (both diegetic and non-diegetic sounds, including the Peking Opera in chase sequences) and images of the intricate urban spaces experienced by people from all walks of life. Human bodies, especially half-naked male bodies, are frequently represented and associated with violence, desire and conspiracy, configuring the dynamic and vulgar ambience of the city. As a result, the characters' explorations of the urban space are no longer those of an intellectual's leisurely *flânerie* into the city or a response to modernisation. Rather, they are accelerated and violent individual experiences that lead to a sense of nihilism and absurdity.

With a panoramic view of the city in the early sequences of *Crazy Stone*, the camera spans over rows of black and grey low buildings engulfed by a circle of skyscrapers. Xie Xiaomeng (Peng Bo), the son of factory manager Xie (Chen Zhenghua), is trying to pick up a pretty woman as they travel in a cable car. A self-styled artist who is concerned with the beauty of the city and the people, he likens the city to a mother, whose womb is a habitat for humanity. Although Xie Xiaomeng continues pressing the girl, flirting and praising her with pretentious high-brow expressions, his suggestive words and behaviours fail to draw any interest from her. Instead, they only stir up annoyance in two middle-aged women who roll their eyes and curse him as a 'hooligan'. The girl then stamps her high heels on his feet, making Xie scream with pain and drop his Coca Cola can down from the cable car. The can tumbles down, turning into the name of the film in Chinese characters. The can, falling from a space high above, smashes the windshield of the minivan driven by Bao Shihong (Guo Tao) and becomes the first domino that triggers a series of misunderstandings and highly comedic incidents that turn the rest of the characters' lives upside down. The space displayed in this sequence is more than 'a medium, a milieu, an intermediary', as its role can hardly be perceived as 'neutral', but is rather 'active, both as instrument and as goal, as means and as end' (Lefebvre 1991: 410–11). That means, the spatial arrangement in the sequence exhibits the attribute of the material space of the city per se, and actively creates the encounters of strangers and generates ensuing incidents. Chongqing is one of the few cities in contemporary China that still utilises the cable car as a traffic shuttle in everyday life. The culture and history behind such a transport device is the result of the geographical conditions of the city, and now it has become the trademark of the city, carrying the cultural memory and collective identity of the city. The cinematic spaces inside and outside of the cable car become 'culturally positive' (Teo 2013: 134); that is, they realistically illustrate a city, with a long history and complicated geographical features, embrace the anxiety, desire, conflicts, possibilities and vulgarity wrought by temporal and spatial transformations.

In *Crazy Stone*, the desire for sex or affluence drives characters into extreme situations, but there are people who stay out of the 'wealth race', remaining upright and loyal to the socialist unit. Belonging to the same state-owned handcraft factory, Bao Shihong and manager Xie show a disparity in dealing with individual desire and public benefits when facing material temptation. Such personal disparity and social differences are ubiquitous in contemporary Chinese society where:

> an exuberant commercial and mass culture, enhanced by the popularisation of personal computers and the World Wide Web, has yielded an avalanche of images – big and small, still or moving. They literally engulf the city inside out: from building facades to the interiors, from the subway to the highways, from KTV rooms to Internet cafes. Meanwhile, this startling new and fast image culture is surreally contrasted with the uneven, often scarred, urban geography dotted with architectural and life ruins or traces from different epochs including the pre-communist and the socialist times. (Zhang 2010b: 97)

Such kinds of multiple temporalities unfold with the varied appropriation of urban spaces by different social groups. The first group is represented by Bao, the head of the security department in the factory, who holds onto socialist production and social practices. When central governmental policy shifted to the market economy in the 1980s, a great number of state-owned enterprises across mainland China lost financial and administrative support from the central state. They were thrown into the market to await their destiny – to either thrive or die in highly competitive commercial circumstances. In the film, the handcraft factory is one of those marginalised by this sudden advent of the market economy. Workers have nothing to do but go routinely to the factory, receiving no payment for months, in the hope that some property tycoons will purchase the land (the only property left) to attain financial compensation.

The discovery of the valuable gemstone provides a good opportunity to resurrect the factory; however, a number of people hatch plots to use the jade for their own benefit. From Bao's perspective, the stone represents the last hope of saving the factory, or at least bringing economic benefits for its 200 employees who have not been paid for eight months.

For Xie Xiaomeng, the value of the stone is as a means to pursue a girl. Manager Xie calmly holds onto his land and the gemstone, bargaining with the property developer for the best compensation for his old employees and himself. Echoing his son's comment, 'my father is an old bureaucrat', manager Xie eventually ends up using the stone to acquire a large sum in compensation and a decent retirement. The liberal market not only encourages a commercial and mass culture, but also emancipates people from the previous socialist oppression of any desire for wealth, sex and power.

Manager Xie puts up an exhibition in *Luohansi* (lit. Arhat Buddhism Temple) to auction the stone (Figure 2.3), as a means to force the greedy property developer Feng Hai (Xu Zheng) to offer a higher price for the land. However, it is outrageously dangerous to exhibit the precious jade in such a poorly equipped temple that doesn't even have a safe door.

Why is it not on display in an exhibition centre? Why isn't it kept in an insurance company for safekeeping? The following exchange takes place when Bao, as the head of security, complains about the poor security conditions of the temple:

Figure 2.3 The temple and its surroundings: in *Crazy Stone*

Bao: The high mobility of the crowd engenders potential danger in such a tourist attraction area.
Female worker: We are asking you to keep an eye on a piece of stone. Don't tell me your detective nonsense. We are aiming at a tourist attraction so that we can even save money from promotion. If we could have it exhibited in the Great Hall of the People [located in Beijing, the space of the highest political power in China], what are you doing here?

In manager Xie's words, the exhibition centre and insurance company charge too much, and the saved amount will make more compensation for the would-be laid-off workers. The modern practices of using insurance companies and exhibition centres for storage and display are perceived as worthless and unpractical. Rather, a temporary security team led by Bao and some handmade easy protection facilities are good enough. This rather anti-modern and anti-technology conduct reflects not only the embarrassing financial situation of this old state-owned factory, but also the old-fashioned way of management, which conflicts with the rational division of labour, profession and social spaces under the discourse of modernity. The state-owned unit and the temple stand for an outdated ideology and conduct. As material spaces, they used to be maintained for production and spiritual support. They are shared urban spaces that 'can provide the means of developing and living – in concrete, material, mundane, routinised ways – shared collective memories' (cited in Pratt and Juan 2014: 105). The state-owned unit once served as an enclosed realm that provided jobs, houses and all sorts of allocated welfare to its workers; at the same time, it also served as a spiritual harbour that promised a socialist utopia characterised by uniformity, equality and collectivity. However, under the shifting focus of political and economic concerns, the function of particular material spaces also undergoes change accordingly, leaving the people struggling between the old and the new systems.

When the factory in the film is facing disrepair and demolition and the temple functions as a temporary exhibition centre for commercial purposes, conflicts arise between the old users of the space and the new consumers of the space: consumed and possessed by property developers represented by Feng. The real estate developer, who has gained tremendous benefits under the market economy, represents another group that is fuelled by capital and is able to manipulate resources and even the lives of people in the emerging market. It is a transitional period when the old system is not yet dead and the new is not yet fully established. In this film, it is the poorly decorated temple and dilapidated factory that contrasts with the high-rise building that is designed to be erected on the land formerly occupied by the factory.

Urban village and its inhabitants

In *Crazy Stone*, the other typical space related to Bao and his co-worker Sanbao (Liu Gang) is the urban village. Among the skyscrapers and glassy complexes, there are dark, crowded and narrow 'villages' scattered at the bottom of the concrete forest. These urban villages provide dwelling spaces for people like Bao and his co-worker Sanbao. In one sequence, when Bao misunderstands that Sanbao intends to take the jade in exchange for money, he walks through a dark zigzagging lane lined with rooms. The shaking shots over the shoulder track Bao's furious steps into Sanbao's home where Sanbao's grandmother takes care of his bedridden mother.

The street scene and the unpleasant living spaces displayed in the sequences explain Sanbao's obsession with buying lottery tickets and his gullibility in falling for scams. Meanwhile, the grandmother asks Bao to keep Sanbao at work, as the factory exhibition needs him. The old temple, disintegrating factory, labyrinthine lanes and crowded small domestic spaces configure a city inhabited by the threatened state factory workers and their families. Such situations may remind viewers of the socialist space and its far-reaching impact on urban space and social relations in Jia Zhangke's 2008 docufiction *24 City*, set in one of the largest state-owned factories in Chengdu.

Another social group that inhabits such noir-like spaces is the '*bangbang*', itinerant porters for hire who use a length of bamboo with rope tied to each end to carry goods for customers for little pay. As a traditional port city along the Yangtze River for centuries, Chongqing needs large numbers of workers for the labour force undertaking the loading work around its harbour. During the era when loading relied on manual labour, *bangbang* became an essential part of the economic and traffic flux. In *Crazy Stone*, Heipi dresses like a *bangbang* (Figure 2.4) to scam passengers, but fails.

Bangbang appear in two more sequences: one occurs when Bao shouts at a group of *bangbang* standing near the temple, demanding that they keep away from the temple. Although they have not done anything wrong, they get yelled at with little respect, indicating their low social status and the harsh situation they face trying to make a living in the city. Then, after the theft incidents, Bao assumes they are accomplices to the abortive jade robbery. On both occasions, *bangbang* are perceived as potential criminals. Ironically, the group of *bangbang* is not aware that they are suspected of

HISTORY, CITYSCAPE AND SPATIAL STRATIFICATION 49

Figure 2.4 Heipi (the middle one) pretends to be a *bangbang*: in *Crazy Stone*

being accomplices. Therefore, when Bao offers them cheap alcohol and cigarettes, requesting them to stay away from the jade, they look confusedly at each other, whispering:

Bangbang 1: Must have something to do with the urban management!
Bangbang 2: Must be undercover cops conducting civil law enforcement!

How could such a seemingly 'friendly' treat be regarded as civil law enforcement? The *bangbang* are represented as a group of people who are able neither to figure out their roles in the unfolding situation, nor to understand the concept of 'civil law enforcement'. They are despised by urbanites and often the first to be suspected when crimes are committed. They are everywhere in the city, but belong nowhere.

To a certain degree, *bangbang* are a group of people who benefit from the country's grand blueprint of reformation in terms of attaining access to the big city. However, their social status, even though gradually freed from the household registration constraint, still remains at the lowest level. In the present day, they are inefficient compared to fast-developing modern traffic devices. Their working conditions and gathering places are characterised by darkness and chaos. By juxtaposing their circumstances with Feng Hai, the real estate tycoon, and Mike, an international thief, *Crazy Stone* reveals the huge material and cultural gap between different social groups in the city under the force of market stratification. The urban space they can appropriate, identifying with their low social status, is usually dark, secret, low and invisible. The theme of spatial segregation is extended in *Curiosity Kills the Cat*, with the underprivileged attempting to climb up the social ladder and eventually slipping into disastrous consequences.

Class stratification and infidelity

In *Curiosity Kills the Cat*, the stark material contrast between characters is explicitly shown in the spatial *mise-en-scène*, where the privileged couple, Zheng Zhong (Hu Jun) and Feng Qianyu (Carina Lau), possesses a luxurious apartment on the top of a premium apartment complex named Haike Yingzhou, while immigrants such as Liang Xiaoxia (Song Jia) and Liu Fendou (Liao Fan) occupy low, even underground basement spaces. People's social status directly corresponds to their access to difference places. Meanwhile, sexual desire, pursuit of wealth and decent social status, and curiosity about others' lives bring the privileged and the underprivileged together.

A young woman, Liang Xiaoxia, migrates to Chongqing and rents a room located at a dark corner of an alley that connects to the outside world via hundreds of steps zigzagging down to the Yangtze River. The old and dilapidated neighbourhood resembles Sanbao's dwelling space in *Crazy Stone*. Liang's small room looks like an attic attached to an old house, and outside it expands in a platform where Liang and Zheng Zhong, who are having an extramarital affair, can enjoy leisure time. Construction cranes and skyscrapers located blocks away overlook the small yard and the two lovers, which generates a sense of their being watched, as if they are under the control of invisible power. Zheng Zhong used to be a white-collar worker before getting married to Feng Qianyu, the daughter of a rich and powerful businessman. The marriage plucks him from obscurity and places him in a glamorous world of wealth and respectable social status. However, Zheng Zhong and Qianyu seldom appear in the same shot, and he constantly appears anxious (bites his nails) in Qianyu's presence. In their delicately decorated house, equipped with sophisticated facilities and stylish design (such as the glass arch on the top of the building and the ornaments attached to it), Zheng Zhong hardly feels at home. His conversations with Qianyu have to be cautious, as whatever disagreements or arguments happen at home will eventually find their way into the workplace. His only child, Xiaobai (Ma Qianli), is 'not only my son, but the only heir of your Feng family' (Zheng Zhong's words). Even though he has successfully stepped into the upper-class world through marriage, he is stressed, constrained and deprived of self-esteem and value.

Liu Fendou, the security guard at the apartment complex Zheng Zhong and his wife live in, Hanke Yingzhou, is situated even lower than Liang Xiaoxia's urban village. He lives in a small, dungeon-like basement room in the underground parking lot of the complex. After finding out about Qianyu's acts of sabotage on her husband to take her revenge for his infidelity, Liu becomes involved in them in exchange for material compensation. He then gets an opportunity to enter the living space of the privileged, and even requires Qianyu to make coffee for him. The way he drinks coffee (using a spoon) exposes his lowly origins and his desire to ascend to the rosier world above. Both Liang Xiaoxia and Liu Fendou attempt to climb up the social ladder through extramarital intimacy or participation in the conspiracies led by the privileged. However, they find themselves excluded and manipulated ruthlessly by the privileged class. Zheng Zhong and Liang Xiaoxia's intimate relations often take place in Liang's small dark room, while Qianyu and Liu Fendou's prompt intercourse happens at the underground parking lot. This spatial arrangement explicitly indicates a fact that the upper/privileged class's living space is highly exclusive.

In the film, the material gap between the rich and the poor illustrated by strictly divided spaces appropriated or used by characters demonstrates the power of capital that dominates social mobility and confines a particular social group to a fixed position. Director Zhang Yibai emphasises the dynamics and the growing economic gap between different social classes in one of his interviews:

> What has been displayed in the film – old neighbourhoods are demolished, and new buildings are constructed – exemplifies the happening urban life in contemporary mainland China . . . I capture the lives of various kinds of people, reflecting their fleeting desire and intimate relationships generated and manipulated by social classes and status. (Zhang 2008b: 102)

In *Curiosity Kills the Cat*, social classes empowered by capital can manipulate those from the lower social classes, both economically and sexually. This can be seen in the constant negotiation between Zheng Zhong and Liang Xiaoxia, and Qianyu and Liu Fendou. Realising that his extramarital affair has been discovered by Qianyu, Zheng Zhong terminates his relationship with Liang Xiaoxia by giving her a bank card containing 200,000 RMB. However, Liang uses the money to set up her own nail salon on the ground floor of Haike Yingzhou, an event that becomes the turning point in her tangled affair with Zheng Zhong. Their relationship is manipulated by Qianyu, who is aware of her husband's infidelity. Qianyu pays Liu Fendou to help her carry out a series of dreadful 'accidents' and plays the role of an innocent victim, making people believe that Liang Xiaoxia is not only breaking up her marriage, but also carrying out these malicious acts against her.

Qianyu ruins her luxury car by scratching and splashing red paint on it, and then pretends that someone has deliberately vandalised it, screaming for attention and finally making Zheng Zhong suspect that Liang Xiaoxia is responsible for the incident. She then asks Liu Fendou to pour red paint from the top of the glass room, and makes the gullible girl Momo, who owns a photo studio on the ground floor of Haike Yingzhou, a witness to the terrifying scene, which again draws public attention to her as a fragile victim of Liang Xiaoxia's brutal conspiracy. She even uses her son to stage a fake kidnapping, which finally convinces Zheng Zhong that Liang Xiaoxia has unscrupulously carried out all the wicked acts against her. This faulty assumption drives Zheng Zhong to murder Liang Xiaoxia and he himself is consequently arrested. That Zheng Zhong finally kills Liang suggests his insecurity about his identity and the social status that he has acquired as the husband of Qianyu and the son-in-law of a wealthy businessman. Liu Fendou, who has assisted Qianyu to frame Liang Xiaoxia, also finds himself tricked by Qianyu and commits suicide.

The film is told from four characters' perspectives but only Qianyu is aware of the whole picture of the sequence of events. As the one standing at the top of the capital pyramid, Qianyu possesses an omniscient perspective in her relationship with each of the three characters who come from the lower social class. The tragic endings of Zheng Zhong, Liang Xiaoxia and Liu Fendou show the dark side of the urban life, which can lead to uncontrollable situations and even death.

Since the 1990s, extramarital affairs have become a frequently discussed social issue in mainland China. Films such as *Woman Sesame Oil Maker* [*Xiang hun nü*] (Xie Fei, 1993), *Ermo* [*Ermo*] (Zhou Xiaowen, 1994), *Mr. Zhao* [*Zhao Xianshan*] (Lü Yue, 1998) and *Cellphone* [*Shouji*] (Feng Xiaogang, 2003) provide the rural (the former two) and urban (the latter two) landscapes of the changing views and behaviours around marriage, gender and infidelity in the reform era. Female protagonists from *Woman Sesame Oil Maker* and *Ermo* have extramarital relationships that introduce them to bigger cities and help them expand their family business. In *Mr. Zhao* and *Cellphone* we see how male intellectuals in metropolitan cities – Shanghai and Beijing respectively – oscillate between different females and deceive their spouses with various excuses and lies. The reasons for having extramarital affairs in the four films vary widely, but one of the shared social elements that increase the chance of extramarital affairs is the higher level of geographical mobility in the reform era. In *Woman Sesame Oil Maker* and *Ermo*, the female protagonists benefit economically and romantically from such mobility by travelling outside their home town and extending their family business to a larger market. Similarly, *Mr. Zhao* and *Cellphone* display the myriad of opportunities for male intellectuals, who possess high social status, to encounter extramarital sexual relationships in a highly mobile urban space. Moreover, the filmic infidelities in rural and urban areas indicate different layers of modernisation according to Jason McGrath: 'If the rural setting invokes the anxieties of incomplete modernisation, the urban milieu presents both the attraction and the dangers of a modernity that may be out of control' (2008: 124). The 'incomplete modernisation' in the rural setting eventually shows in the commodification of both labour and sex of the female protagonists, while the modernity appears quite hazardous in the urban setting where the modernisation is unfolded on a more massive and intensive scale.

Since the 1980s, globalisation, access to Internet, development of infrastructure of traffic, housing and commercial activities and large-scale rural–urban migration have impacted many areas of everyday practice, including people's sexual attitudes and behaviour. Personal choice, the individual's interests and rights, have been given great prominence in relationships and marriage as the result of the state's redefinition of marriage 'as a voluntary contractual relationship grounded in individual emotional satisfaction' (Davis 2014: 554). In this context, previous social norms that restricted premarital and extramarital affairs have relaxed and intimate relationships outside marriage have rapidly increased. In *Curiosity Kills the Cat* there are four main characters involved in extramarital relationships. However, the moral condemnation of the outside marriage sexual relationship remains strong under contemporary social and sexual norms in mainland China, which can be seen from the disastrous consequences for the protagonists.

The urban space, for immigrants represented by Liu Fendou and Liang Xiaoxia, is stratified physically as well as mentally in accordance with their economic and social status. Although the city provides them with opportunities and probabilities to reach an affluent life, they usually find themselves being excluded from desired positions and spaces. When they try to transgress the spatial and social class boundary, conspiracy and even death will ensue. Modernisation and globalisation emancipate sexual behaviours that were previously restricted by institutionally sanctioned rules or traditional values, and liberal beliefs endorse marriages or relationships as a way of self-development and emotional satisfaction. These rapidly changing attitudes and behaviours around intimate relationships, marriage and family, in addition to the frequent navigation between places, give different social classes more opportunities to have extramarital affairs, triggering a series of social problems concerning morality, marital and familial relationships.

City and the human body

Similar to Hong Kong, the Chongqing cityscape is also characterised by a vertical view rather than a horizontal one, as it sits high above the rivers and mountains below. Bridges, high-rise buildings and especially the crisscrossed rail transit system built high above the ground push the whole city upwards. In *Crazy Stone*, this vertical point of view overlooking the cityscape can be seen from the sequences showing a monorail leaping through a tunnel, racing alongside the river and breaking into the concrete forest, producing a strong sense of speed and instability. In such diverse circumstances, characters are plagued with physical pain, anxiety and craziness.

In the opening sequences, Bao's twisted face appears in close-up, screaming with pain when the doctor checks his prostatitis. Bao's physical suffering echoes his anxiety, produced by the bankruptcy of the factory, so that the body becomes more than just a biological existence. It is perhaps the most critical site to 'watch the production and reproduction of power' (Soja 1996: 114). The physical pain can be read not only as an emblem of individual anxiety, but as a metaphor of the agitated social transformation experienced by all walks of life. The body, disease and city become intertwined and reflect on each other in the film. As Hooper observes:

> body and city are the persistent subjects of a social/civic discourse, of an imaginary obsessed with the fear of unruly and dangerous elements and the equally obsessive desire to bring them under control: fears of pollution, contagions, disease, things out of place [for the ancient Greeks, the definition of 'pollution']; desires for controlling and mastering that [become] the spatial practice of enclosing unruly elements within carefully guarded spaces. (Cited in Soja 1996: 114–15)

In the film, Bao's disease-ridden body symbolises the dilapidated state factory. Correspondingly, his prolonged recovery from the disease runs in parallel to the long and difficult journey of resurrecting the factory by protecting the priceless jade stone. His desire to retain the state-owned factory and his position in it is projected through his determination and hard work to guard the temple that is designated as the temporary exhibition space for the jade stone. In contrast, the other two groups, the group of three crooks and Mike, the international thief from Hong Kong, become the 'unruly and dangerous' elements that threaten Bao's job as a guard and the city's stability. They intrude into Bao's carefully guarded space three times attempting to steal the jade, triggering massive chaos each time. Finally, the repeated theft irritates Bao, who furiously curses in a hoarse voice: [What is this?] 'Public toilet? Come and go as you wish?'

This comparison of the temple (exhibition space) with a public toilet emphasises the easy accessibility of the jade due to the poor facilities of the exhibition hall. The next sequences cut to a toilet, and zoom in for a close-up of Bao's profile. He is sweating and hitting his head against the wall. Zooming out, he appears in a sequence of fast cuts, losing his temper and randomly kicking and smashing toilet facilities. The grim face and violent actions show both his extreme physical pain caused by prostatitis and his unbearable mental torment triggered by the repeated thefts.

The space of the 'public toilet' appears many times in the film. As the space related to human defecation, it is often associated with filth and disgust, and metaphorically, indicates the morbid father–son relationship in the case of Xie Xiaomeng, who constantly swindles money from his father. For Bao, the dilapidated and filthy interior of the toilet resonates with his physical pain, mental uneasiness and stressful guard job. Such mutual projection between space and human body intensifies the characterisation, and shows the physical features of buildings in such a way as to have a psychological and emotional influence that may have nothing to do their practical use (Jorn 1996: 51). In the case of Brother Dao (Liu Ye) and his two fellow crooks Heipi (Huang Bo) and Xiaojun (Yue Xiaojun), their bodies and spaces they appropriate not only represent one another, but also demonstrate the flux of transnational capital, cultural products and talents, and the blurred boundary between the real and the imagined.

The three crooks in *Crazy Stone* are represented by a lack of refinement and physical filth and violence, which directly indicate their low-born tastes and inferior status. They are frequently framed in public bathrooms and toilets, with partially naked bodies and shampoo foam all over their faces or in defecation. When Brother Dao discovers that Xie Xiaomeng is sleeping with his girlfriend, the crooks beat Xie Xiaomeng ruthlessly and lock him in a suitcase. The physical torture becomes even more violent after the crooks find that Xie presents the jade as a gift to the girl, as they assume that Xie must have used a fake jade to seduce her. Under their torment, Xie gives random answers to appease Dao and stop the torment. To a certain degree, 'the randomly induced bodily destruction and interpersonal violence bespeak the ultimate absurdity and irrationality of contemporary urban life' (Liu 2018: 166). Afterwards, their focus shifts to stealing the real jade. A shabby motel, a public bathroom and even a toilet become their venues for making plans. They often wear serious faces when discussing their grand plan of stealing and how to conduct their 'business' professionally and in a proper manner. In particular, they attempt to conduct their robberies without using violence. Theft is perceived as a craft that should be conducted with calm and elegance. The group's attempt to verbally beautify their illicit conduct is humorous while at the same time manifesting 'cultural degradation' and 'subversively express[ing] the experience of the subaltern' (Liu 2018: 163). The amateur thieves and the well-trained professional hustler employ their respective methods to conduct thefts which contribute the most humorous episodes in the film.

In the scene where the three slip into the Temple where the jade is on display, Heipi assumes that the glass showcase containing the jade must be protected by infrared rays that would automatically activate the alarm system as soon as any accident occurs. Brother Dao refutes Heipi's assumption: 'How could high-tech possibly be installed here? You must have watched too many films.' Heipi may have watched similar foreign films imported in the early 1990s, like Hong Kong's *Once a Thief* [*Zongheng sihai*] (John Woo, 1991) or Hollywood blockbusters *Mission Impossible* (Brian De Palma, 1996) and *Ocean's Eleven* (Steven Soderbergh, 2001), in which hustlers possess practical skills and handy high-tech tools to facilitate theft. Nevertheless, neither of them truly believes that they need any high-tech tools to 'do their business' in this developing city. This coincides with the opinion of the owner of the jade, as manager Xie and some of his colleagues believe that money spent on promotion and insurance fees would be a waste.

While the crooks' desire to be 'professional' remains in words, the international hustler from Hong Kong demonstrates 'professionality' in action. In a sequence in *Crazy Stone*, Mike (Lian Jin) is suspended from the ceiling to steal the jade, recalling the scenes from *Mission Impossible* (1996) when Tom Cruise adopts the same strategy and accomplishes his mission. However, Mike's 'mission' is jeopardised as the rope is not long enough to reach his target. He then realises that he must have been short-changed by the dishonest rope seller. Cursing helplessly, he can only watch Xiaojun taking the jade away and is ruthlessly ridiculed. Mike's suffering reveals the chaos and loss of integrity and honesty in the market economy era. Mike's professional skills, outfits and instruments are identical with those employed by the internationally famed actors in Hollywood blockbusters. For him, the scenes from the fictional Hollywood story are his real life, and all the advanced and handy tools and techniques make him efficient and win him the reputation of 'Master Hand'. Meanwhile, when Xiaojun, the clumsy small-time thief, witnesses the high-end, tech-savvy method of stealing, he is reminded of *Spider Man* movies The above scenes relate to Hollywood franchises that are usually 're-exported' and flow into the mainland Chinese market through Hong Kong, showing Hong Kong as a 'transhipment point' in cultural exchange between China and the outside international world (Marchetti 2007: 165). Mike, as a 'Master Hand' in the field, is one of the characterisations essential in gangster genre films. In contrast to the 'unprofessional' crooks and the cunning rope sellers, Mike reiterates his established reputation as 'honest' and 'professional' – the qualities the crooks lack. The comparison emerges as a metaphor of the 'amateur' level of China's market economy, and also the chaotic and dishonest conduct that pervades the market.

In *Crazy Stone*, the hinterland city imagines metropolises like Hong Kong and Hong Kong people through Mike, as the representative of a highly developed capitalist city. Similar to Hong Kong, 'a profoundly vertical city', Chongqing is also built 'layer upon layer' in order to 'defy the limits of space' (Chow and Kloet 2013: 140). The horizontal space of Hong Kong is characterised by claustrophobia due to the dense population and narrow urban spaces. The vertical space, specifically the rooftops of high-rises, provides a temporary space of relief and sanctuary for people who have been regulated and supervised by the carefully planned and strictly divided street spaces. In Marchetti's words, the rooftops provide spaces that are 'separate from the quotidian workings of the city, above the business being conducted on the floors below, as well as privileged vantage points for surveying the Hong Kong cityscape' (Marchetti 2007: 44). In *Crazy Stone*, Mike often appears from a high position moving toward a lower place to conduct his 'business'. In the temple, he hangs down from the ceiling to reach the jade, which resembles a high-tech technocratic movement. After the first attempt fails, he quickly comes up with another plan and tries to accomplish the 'mission'. In his second attempt, he slides down from the top of the high-rise where Feng Hai, the shrewd real estate developer, runs his business. Mike locates Feng's office, and sneaks into the office swiftly. He quickly opens the steel safe, calmly turns around when Feng suddenly shows up, and flings a dagger towards Feng with considerable agility. The vertical spaces and high positions he occupies in the film show the city in a panoramic view (Figure 2.5). The inaccessible height of the high-rise is like a playground for Mike to present his individual show of magic and skills. As a well-trained thief, Mike is a confident decipherer of the city, taking the vantage position to look and walk in the city. This resembles the image of the *flâneur*, where he 'puts the city on hold . . . [and] pauses as if to interrupt the global city-as-machine' when he locates himself high up in the street (Chow and Kloet 2013: 144).

Figure 2.5 The vertical view of the city through Mike's view: in *Crazy Stone*

In contrast, the crooks are frequently seen in the street and occasionally go deep down into the drainage system to carry out their plan. Without professional tools, they deploy stockings as bandit caps; Heipi keeps a hammer at hand at all times, and Xiaojun hides in a dustbin to achieve good timing. The down-to-earth position of the crooks indicates their

HISTORY, CITYSCAPE AND SPATIAL STRATIFICATION 59

Figure 2.6 Spaces the crooks inhabit and utilise: in *Crazy Stone*

lack of skills and low social level (Figure 2.6). Such an image is further enhanced by their unrefined clothes, behaviour and abuse of human bodies. As immigrants in the city, the three live on the periphery, both physically and metaphorically. Identical with the other subaltern social groups, represented by *bangbang*, they occupy the dark corners of the city, mainly the streets and the urban village. In summary, the majority of characters in *Crazy Stone* are down in the street, even lower in the drain system, while the hustler from Hong Kong and the real estate developer Feng Hai occupy the higher space of the city, physically and metaphorically. Human bodies and the urban space are represented 'as a politics of difference, as segregation and separation' (Soja 1996: 115).

Although *Crazy Stone* has been perceived by many Chinese film critics as a black comedy for its satire on the morbidity, weakness and suffering of the subaltern group in a comic way, it is a realistic representation of the city and its residents more than a fictional one in terms of the mutual projection between urban spaces and their users. *Crazy Stone* exposes social issues such as fake products, dishonest conduct and degradation of mass culture that pervade the post-socialist market. More ironically, the film itself is self-consciously learning from the gangster genre epitomised by British director Guy Ritchie and Hollywood auteur Quentin Tarantino. As Liu Hui notes: 'Ning's films' self-reflexive vision of their own status as imitation commodities raises the question of artistic originality and innovation' (2018: 169). The film per se, the replicated jade and the imitation of the Thousand-hand Bodhisattva dance in the film demonstrate the 'fake plastic feature' of contemporary Chinese commercialisation. The lack of cultural originality and moral values, together with the thieves, professional or unprofessional, are emblematic of the city's ability of creating disorientation, anxiety, social discontent owing to an increasingly complicated technocratic society where great changes of identity, subjectivity and social class are underway.

CHAPTER 3

National Project and Disappearing Space

Throughout the 1990s and 2000s, the construction and completion of the world largest hydropower station, the Three Gorges Dam project, attracted sustained media attention. This enormous national endeavour has been regarded as the milestone of China's modernisation, and the state government generously provided financial and political support to accomplish the venture, which was anticipated to boost the development of the whole region. The cityscapes of cities and towns involved in this programme have been radically transformed and films based in the area have truthfully recorded, reflected and questioned the consequent relentless changes and dislocation. Features *Rainclouds over Wushan* and *Still Life* reflect the enormous social and environmental transformation that bewilders and traumatises the local people and outsiders who break into the disappearing space. The oppressed desire, the impending inundation, the ruined space brought by the monumental project, the huge gap between the lower and higher social classes and the exiled population become critiques of the national dream of modernisation. Cinematic Chongqing in the two films, associated with the national ambition of modernisation and prosperity, however, projects the Thirdspace that is lived by common people who only concern themselves with immediate daily routines and practices.

Rainclouds over Wushan: Lived Space Matters

Zhang Ming's 1996 debut *Rainclouds over Wushan* was highly acclaimed at various international film festivals. However, just like those works that are critically acclaimed overseas but either banned or a failure in the box office at home, *Rainclouds over Wushan* was banned in China without an explicit reason until it was eventually released in 2003. The film expresses 'individual subjectivity' realistically (Zhang 2010a: 104) through characters' subjective experiences. Also, the slowness of the characters' actions illustrates Zhang's resistance to the mainstream conceptualisation of the national project – the Three Gorges Dam. The idiom 'rainclouds over Wushan' refers to an ancient legend that the Goddess of Wu Mountain used to descend from the celestial palace to the area and assist the Great Yu (one of the three most ancient Emperors in Chinese legend) to dredge the watercourse and overcome floods. After the flood was tamed, the goddess and her sisters chose to stay on the mist-shrouded peaks of Mount Wu on earth to direct passing ferries and ships so as to protect people from danger (Mi 2009: 29). She remained on the mountain so long that she finally turned herself into a breathtaking peak, becoming the famed Goddess Peak (Shennü feng). Thus, 'rainclouds over Wushan' first connotes the mysterious beauty of the landscape shrouded in mist and praises the Goddess's beauty and sacrifice. Later during ancient times, legend said that a king had a fleeting sexual encounter with the alluring Goddess from Mount Wu. As a result, the expression carries another layer of meaning – sexual desire and encounter (Mi 2009: 29). The film projects a story about a lonely man and a distressed woman who lead dull and hopeless lives. They are finally brought together by a rape case investigated by Wu Gang, a local police officer. The mundane and trivial daily practices of the protagonists are in stark contrast to the great historical legend of the Goddess and the king.

The film slowly unfolds via a tripartite structure. It begins with Mai Qiang (Zhang Xianming), a signalman working at a river station called Qiu Shizi, whose life is punctuated by phone calls informing him of the navigation of ships on the Yangtze River and by changing signals on the station tower. The second section shows Chen Qing (Zhong Ping), a hotel receptionist anticipating her second marriage while stuck in an affair with Lao Mo (Xiu Zongdi), the hotel manager. The third part focuses on Wu Gang (Wang Wenqiang); preoccupied by his coming wedding, he is constantly distracted by Lao Mo, who reports a rape case that links Mai Qiang and Chen Qing together. The characters' complicated relations surface in the process of the interrogation of the case, and the film ends with Mai and Chen getting together. In the film, Wushan town is about to be flooded due to the construction of the Three Gorges Dam. The town used to be an enchanting place that inspired poets and painters to create beautiful works of art. The film, which is set in this disappearing space, displays the mundane daily practices of ordinary people and their silence or inertia in the shadow of the impending flood.

Commercialisation and desire

The two protagonists, Mai Qiang and Chen Qing, represent those who have been left behind by the nation's rising commercialisation. The film begins with a sequence showing Mai's routines – he pulls the rope attached to an arrow shaped navigation signal, fastens it to a wooden pillar and then walks back into the room (Figure 3.1). From a medium long shot, spectators can see part of the two-story building with a red balcony and a platform where the signal facilities are located. Following this, a black screen appears, on which emerge lines of white Chinese characters listing protagonist Mai Qiang's personal information: 'Mai Qiang, aged thirty, a signal operator at Qiu Shizi station. Ma Bing comes to visit with Lili in the afternoon.' The signal tower is situated on a hill cliff overlooking a muddy river. It is alienated from the surrounding houses and buildings. Mai's personality, in contrast to his friend Ma Bing's (Li Bing), is very conservative, introverted and indifferent to commercial allure. He works and dwells in the signal station, which is affiliated to the local river bureau. Mai is a member of the working class who has been doing this job as long ago as the planned economy era, as testified by Ma Bing when he introduces Mai Qiang to Lili (Yang Liu, a sex worker), stating that Mai was 'my master'.

'Master and apprentice' relationships used to be common among the working class in the planned economy system, but they have gradually dissolved in the reform era with increasing numbers of people dropping out of the working unit. Ma Bing is one such example. Among the social changes stirred up by the omnipresent market of 1990s China, one of the most outstanding changes was 'the wrenching psychological disruption caused when the working class rapidly fell from being Chinese society's leading class to being at the very bottom of all social, economic, cultural strata' (Dai 2002: 228). Apparently, Mai Qiang has become accustomed or insensitive to social changes. Despite having fallen from being a privileged and proud member of the working class to an alienated and lonely worker living at the bottom of society, he does not show dissatisfaction about his low social status, nor does he have ambitions to obtain a respectable social position by joining in the world of self-employed private businesses that is embraced wholeheartedly by some flexible minds, represented by Ma Bing.

Compared to his master Mai, Ma Bing is too worldly and practical to work at this place of solitude. He actively joins in the trend of commercialisation, putting a price on everything, including Mai's calligraphy paintings. Even when he is under interrogation concerning the alleged sexual harassment committed by Mai, he grasps the opportunity to promote a refrigerator to Wu Gang, the police officer who is investigating the case. He has actively joined the commercial world, seizing every opportunity to chase after profit. In the previous planned economy system, Mai was Ma Bing's master, but their roles become switched when Ma Bing brings a sex worker, Lili, to Mai's place in an attempt to show Mai how to enjoy life. Ma Bing becomes the master in this case, while Mai Qiang is an unqualified apprentice who

Figure 3.1 Mai Qiang's daily routines: in *Rainclouds over Wushan*

is passive and slow. Being teased and locked in the room with Lili, Mai sits nervously on a broken chair as they face each other in an awkward silence. Later they leave the room, coming to the river bank under the moon. Mai Qiang watches Lili calling out to moving ships and tries to prevent her from swimming in the chilly river. The night that should have been a night of 'rainclouds over Wushan' ends with the two sitting by the river until sunrise. Nothing has happened or changed. Mai resumes his mundane daily routine in the quotidian residential and working space the next day. Mai's residence, which is also his workplace, exterior and interior, can be seen as a personification of his personality. The isolated location resonates with Mai's solitude, as he lives out of the town totally alone. The simple interior decoration indicates a simple formulated way of living. His job, navigating the passing ships, has to be done manually. His presence is frequently associated with nature – the river, wind, moon, sunrise, etc. His TV set often loses its signal and he is virtually disconnected from any commercial exchange, except in the alleged rape case, which turns out instead to be a consensual act.

Mai is arguably a socialist son accustomed to the planned economy system, mirroring Chairman Mao's famous phrase that the individual is a 'screw' (*luosiding*) that should work for the operation of the gigantic machine: metaphorically, the nation. He stays content with his current condition and refuses to change in spite of being confronted with commercial and sexual allure. He never questions, refutes or explains anything, nor does he show any emotion. He appears as an emotionless man, but not the only one in this film. As seen by Lai:

> the protagonists of *In Expectation* [*Rainclouds over Wushan*] are permanently trapped in inertia ... They are taciturn, indecisive, their minds constantly drifting. Not much happens. Nothing moves forward, but rather everything goes around in circles forever 'in expectation' – of change, breakthrough, or even the stirring of a simple verbal utterance or minor emotional outburst. (Lai 2007: 221)

They are like the fish in a red bucket, waiting passively in expectation of something. The image of fish in a red bucket appears in each of the three character's narration. Stuck in the small space, these fish are caught, observed, selected and killed. Fish in Chinese conveys rich meaning. It is the most common food served on the average person's dinner tables, as it is for the protagonists. It can also be a small gift for friends, as in Wu Gang's case. When Mai Qiang overhears Ma Bing and Lili flirting, two fish on a cooking board are shown in close-up, which indicates an ongoing intercourse. Fish, thus, means sexual desire. What is intriguing is that the way Mai Qiang chooses and kills the fish is repeated by Chen Qing and Wu Gang (Figures 3.2, 3.3 and 3.4). Therefore, fish can also be regarded

Figure 3.2 Mai Qiang catches, selects and kills fish: in *Rainclouds over Wushan*

NATIONAL PROJECT AND DISAPPEARING SPACE 67

Figure 3.3 Chen Qing catches, selects and kills fish: in *Rainclouds over Wushan*

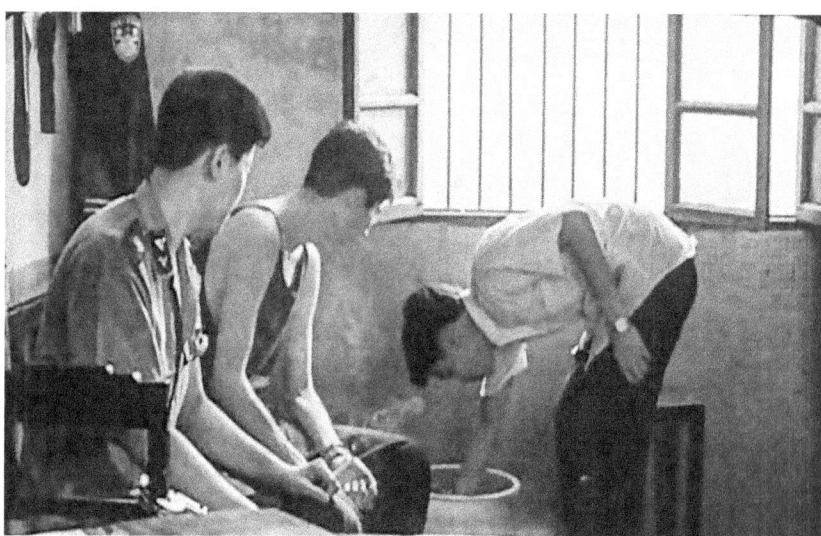

Figure 3.4 Wu Gang watches and catches fish: in *Rainclouds over Wushan*

as a symbol of special bond between people who may develop further connections in their lives. In the film, Mai Qiang eventually swims across the river to meet Chen Qing, the only initiative taken by Mai, which finally puts an end to the gossip triggered by the rape scandal. Fish can also be read as a sacrifice that is helplessly manipulated, mirroring the characters in the film who are forced to leave their home town and migrate to new places.

Living in a place threatened by the looming flood, where home and home town are about to become abstract concepts and historical records, the local people could only be 'in expectation'. Expecting a beautiful new house, a new relationship, even a new life can be every person's dream. But just like the ever-changing rain and clouds, there is no guarantee of a beautiful new life in a new place. The deep uncertainty about the future concerns everyone in the small town. Change is happening, while nobody knows for sure whether their expectation will be realised or not.

Why small town, why nobody?

In the 1990s, Chinese cities such as Beijing and Shanghai finally emerged from various power discourses after a long, long delay (Dai 2002: 93). Directors of the urban generation found an alternative cinematic style to articulate their understanding of Chinese identity and culture. They intentionally refused to showcase the spectacles of the endless yellow earth and grand historical narration, and began to look at the transforming cities. As Zhang Yingjin has observed:

> to a great extent, they consciously distinguish themselves from their fifth-generation predecessors. Whereas the latter are associated with rural landscape, traditional culture, ethnic spectacle, grand epic, historical reflection, allegorical framework, communal focus, and depths of emotion, the former are sided with a urban milieu, modern sensitivity, a narcissistic tendency, initiation tales, documentary effects, uncertain situation, individualistic perception, and precarious moods. For the new generation, their films are definitely more truthful to reality than the fifth generation's glamorisation of ethnicity, sexuality and history. (2004: 290)

In this way, rock and roll singers and newly released prisoners are represented as impulsive 'new' people, especially in some early works such as *Beijing Bastards* [*Beijing zazhong*] (Zhang Yuan, 1993), *Weekend Lover* [*Zhoumo qingren*] (Lou Ye, 1995) and *Black Snow* [*Benming nian*] (Xie Fei, 1990). These filmic characters roam around the dilapidated back alleys of some metropolis, existing in the grey area between the legal and the illegal, seeking and roaming, both vulnerable and ruthless (Dai 2002: 94). Both Zhang Yuan and Wang Xiaoshuai confirmed a personalised autobiographical perspective of exploring the urban spaces and psychological concerns of characters. Their works are like diaries or monologues that truthfully represent what has happened immediately around them (Chen 2005; Ni 1995). Nevertheless, the cinematic depiction of the desire and disillusionment of ruthless youth, especially young artists in big cities in the context of urbanisation, can hardly be identified with those from small hinterland towns, where modernisation may have partially changed the physical appearance of the space while leaving the residents' spiritual world intact. Moreover, directors such as Wang Xiaoshuai and Zhang Yuan, who tend to configure their personal diaries in films, cannot be said to represent the majority of the common Chinese.

In *Rainclouds over Wushan*, Zhang Ming leaves personal experiences behind and investigates his birthplace Wushan, a small town near Chongqing, and the lives of its people. Echoing Jia Zhangke's home town trilogy on a small northern town, Zhang Ming made a Wushan trilogy: *Rainclouds over Wushan*, *The Bride* [*Xinniang*] (2009) and *China Affair* [*Tamen de mingzi jiao hong*, lit. *They are called Hong*] (2013). The three films made an equally valuable and insightful reflection on the small southern town. The cinematic Wushan creates a heterotopia that appears like a counter-site, where the real sites and all the other similar places that can be found in the culture are simultaneously represented and contested (Soja 1996: 157). Wushan, to a certain degree, can represent an enormous number of small towns in southern China that lack cultural, historical or social significance in the context of urbanisation. They are omitted by mainstream media and overshadowed by those metropolises' achievements in modernisation and grand national images. Cinematic Wushan examines the dominated space where common people dwell, walk, desire and resist from a localised perspective, and hereby creates a bridge connecting the local reality of such a small town and the national modernisation project. Born and raised there, Zhang Ming develops a deep understanding and a wealth of experience about the peculiar ambience, the living conditions of the local people and their desires and values. In *Rainclouds over Wushan*, he explores how people's behaviour and perspectives are influenced by the small city characterised by impressive natural beauty and the pending inundation, and how the local dwellers confronted with the national project deal with the loss of home.

Filming *Rainclouds over Wushan*, according to Zhang Ming, was meant to fill the blank of cinematic representation of ordinary Chinese people's everyday life. The mass is the majority of Chinese. What they wish to do, and what they look for and hope for are the most urgent questions to address (Cheng and Xu 1996: 287), as the mundane everyday life, which is perceived by Lefebvre as a 'lived space', can be 'marked out materially and metaphorically in spatial praxis, the transformation of (spatial) knowledge into (spatial) action in a field of unevenly developed (spatial) power' (cited in Soja 1996: 31). Like Jia Zhangke's small town trilogy *The Pickpocket*,

Platform and *Unknown Pleasures*, Zhang Ming's *Rainclouds over Wushan* engages with an alternative intersection of space (the city per se and the natural landscape) and power (the national project of building the Three Gorges Dam) and knowledge (people's awareness and response to the impending inundation).

Subjective time

As witnesses to one of the most significant national construction projects in the reform era, the local population living near the Three Gorges are unexpectedly unenthusiastic towards the project. During the 1990s, the construction of Three Gorges Dam became one of the most monumental projects of the reform era, and it had been estimated that the project would greatly fuel the economic growth in the Yangtze River region. It became an emblem of realising modernisation, while for those ordinary individuals in *Rainclouds over Wushan* it was a symbol of national power, a future which related only remotely to their immediate daily concerns. The looming backdrop of the film, the flooding and the consequent forced migration, guarantee no promising future and stability for ordinary citizens. On the contrary, the lack of certainty traps the characters in inertia. While national news reports spread across the whole country, emphasising how this enormous project will benefit the region economically, the local people's living circumstances remained mysterious to the outside. *Rainclouds over Wushan* becomes a window for the outside world to look in. The slow-rhythmed narration and on-the-scene style of the film bring a 'personal, human dimension to a grand, impersonal process of dam building and national building' by representing people who act indifferently and passively towards the grand project (Lu 2012: 246). Some of the subjective and mysterious scenes are highly intriguing, making viewers wonder whether it is the protagonist's dream or reality.

Resonating with the humid, foggy and mysterious local landscape, the narrative often unfolds with ambivalence. Time is presented from a very subjective point of view. In one sequence, Chen sees a Daoist-dressing man standing at the threshold of the hotel and staring at her attentively. She is stunned, looking away immediately. After a moment when she raises her eyes cautiously, she only sees the familiar empty street. Another equally odd scene appears when Chen Qing sits behind the service desk, looking outside absent-mindedly. Then her eyes follow a man walking towards the hotel exit, while another four men are playing cards at a corner of the lobby. As the man walks out and disappears around the corner, the camera continues to follow Chen Qing's subjective view, spinning rightward, revealing the barber and her customer across the street, and a man in a white T-shirt walking to the receptionist desk to make a phone call, and finally shows the four men sitting in the lobby, who were playing cards moments ago, have now fallen asleep.

The entire sequence lasts for nearly ninety seconds. In the diegetic world, it is a short period of time for Chen Qing to conduct her duty as a receptionist. How could they fall asleep in such a short time? The two sequences entail a strong sense of illusion that breaks the mundane and still surface of the daily routine, stunning and bewildering Chen Qing. The street and hotel lobby sequences under Chen Qing's gaze create a strong sense of locality. Despite the pending inundation and the flows of tourists summoned by the media to catch the last glimpse of the natural beauty of the Three Gorges, the local populace does not show much sense of nostalgia for their disappearing home, or bother to envisage the possible future. They retain the stable and slow pace of their daily routines.

To further slow the sense of time down, various street scenes are repeatedly represented. For example, police officer Wu is walking for the first time through the block of the hotel where Chen Qing works; a wedding ceremony is taking place and a swarm of people are gathered around. But the next scene shows officer Wu walking the same path, which is now empty, quiet and messy. The juxtaposition of the two scenes creates a strong sense of estrangement and unreality. Another example is the repeated presence of a poster promoting a film entitled *In Expectation*. The poster indicates that the film is coming soon, but no exact date of release is provided. 'In Expectation' is also the alternative English title of *Rainclouds over Wushan*. This conveys an intricate intertextuality between Zhang Ming's debut, made and screened in real life, and the virtual film promoted through the poster within the film. The filmic characters have been clearly informed that they will be displaced and their homes will be flooded – the government has all the information about migration and the water level (175 metres) displayed on a white board on the busy street (Figure 3.5).

It takes only a little effort for the local administration to calculate these numbers and schedule the migration, while it is difficult to forecast the prospects of the migrants and the ecological consequences of the project on the local area. Common people's psychological and material concerns are marginalised by the mainstream news coverage in the film, they may well expect a new house and a new life, but with little passion and dynamism. Audiences who watch the film may expect some drama between characters and stark contrasts between old and new landscapes, and the changing urban environment evoked by the enormous national project of modernisation. However, all our expectations remain 'in expectation'

Figure 3.5 The white board: in *Rainclouds over Wushan*

and the appearance of streets and hotels are contingent on the characters' subjective sense of time. For better or for worse, the local people do not show an explicit stance or preference. With the trivial daily practices represented, the film casts a negative view on the project. The silence and passivity of the people represent silent resistance to the project. Grand pictures of an advanced modern state propagated by the mainstream media are too remote to relate to their immediate everyday concerns. The mundane, slow but serene and stable everyday life is what matters.

In the film, both Chen Qing and Mai Qiang are keen to look outside. Mai looks at the river and the other bank, and Chen Qing, laden with anxiety, often sits silently and looks outside of the hotel. Now and then, she hears someone calling her name, but when she turns to her son Liang'er for confirmation, she is merely given negative answers. Meanwhile, Mai Qiang tells his friend that he dreams of a woman, and when the policeman Wu Gang interrogates him about the rape case, he responds 'I might have met her before'. Is this woman Chen Qing in his dream? The film does not provide an answer. For the alleged rape case, Lao Mo perceives it as an unforgivable crime. Meanwhile, Mai's statement is, 'I slept with her', and he leaves almost all his salary for that month to Chen Qing. For Chen Qing, no matter how Wu Gang persuades her to state her opinion on the case, she does not perceive herself as a victim and refuses to provide any information. Without evidence and a 'victim', the case is soon closed and Mai Qiang gets released after several days of being locked up. It is difficult to confirm who the real sinister one is. Lao Mo has been having an affair with Chen Qing, while Mai Qiang's 'rape' case appears to be rather a consensual relationship. In the film, 'moral boundaries are blurred', and what audiences notice is quotidian daily routines and 'acts of contingency' in the ordinary citizens' lives (Lu 2012: 251).

Working at a fairly rundown police station in a small town, Wu Gang appears more interested in preparing for his wedding than solving cases. He is constantly distracted by irrelevant things during interrogation, and he never condescends to his interrogees, sitting bare chested and smoking with these potential criminals. The interrogation of Mai Qiang resembles a casual meeting with old acquaintances rather than a serious case investigation. What is more interesting is that when Mai Qiang is about to leave the police station, Wu Gang takes out hair clippers from a drawer and cuts Mai's hair. The above sequences show that the relationship between average people and 'the police as an instrument of state control' has shifted to a humanist one in the reform era (Shi 2007: 316). Distinguished from the police depicted in films of the 1950s, for instance, *This Life of Mine* [*Wo zhe yibeizi*] (Shi Hui, 1950), which conveyed strong socialist ideological messages: 'only socialism can save China' (*Zhiyou shehuizhuyi cai neng jiu zhongguo*), post-1990s cinematic representations are 'no longer odes to socialist utopia', and the new filmic narrations foreground the potential conflict between ordinary citizens and the 'People's Police as agents of the states rather than their harmonious coexistence' (Shi 2007: 323). In police-centred features such as *On the Beat* [*Minjing gushi*] (Ning Ying, 1995) and *Seventeen Years* [*Guonian huijia*] (Zhang Yuan, 1999), the police are demystified and occasionally find themselves impotent when dealing with new social problems and coping with suspects' questions and challenges. All films listed above are set in big cities where modernisation has transformed the urban spaces and people's way of life, but the accompanying problems brought by urbanisation cannot be solved by the existing regulations and rules; therefore, the police are caught in the dilemma of the state's high expectation for them to maintain justice and solve criminal cases and the masses' questioning and challenging of their authority. However, *Rainclouds over Wushan*, filmed in a southwestern small town where local residents relate to one another economically or socially, shows an alternative relation between the people and the police.

The town of Wushan is a place of legend, of marvellous natural landscapes and important cultural legacy, but all of this will disappear under the water. At the beginning of the 1990s, when the market economy had not yet utterly overthrown the planned economy, many places, in particular the remote western region of China, had one foot still deep in the state-owned economic system and the other just dipping into the market. However, the ambience in the eastern coastal area was quite different. In Mi Jiashan's *The Trouble Shooters* (1988), Beijing local residents actively join in the market, becoming private business owners; in *After Separation* [*Da sa ba*] (Xia Gang, 1992), the characters manage to go abroad; in *Shanghai Fever* [*Gu Feng*] (Li Guoli, 1994), the protagonists plunge into the stock market; in *A Beautiful New World* [*Meili xin shijie*] (Shi Runjiu, 1999), characters expect a new apartment in metropolitan Shanghai. While the nouveau riche and pioneers of the market economy from eastern cities embraced the new economic system and explored business opportunities, the majority of people from the western region lived in the same way as previous generations under the planned economy. The national project pushes the Three Gorges area into nationwide focus, and features, news reports and tourism promotion of the area relate the building of the Three Gorges Dam to national resurrection and modernisation. Radical spatial changes confront small towns like Wushan, and residents in the area have to deal with the disjuncture between their accustomed everyday practices shaped by the planned economy and their current circumstance oriented by the enormous national project. From the planned economy era (socialist era) to the present market-oriented reform era, central and local governments envisage, configure, arrange and rearrange the cityscape to produce new places, new ways of life and new values. Soja contends that 'city and state participate together in the more invisible processes or "normalisation" that pervade and sustain patriotic allegiance' (Soja 1996: 235). This process of normalising the massive relocation for the cause of national prosperity and modernisation is conducted 'invisibly' through a sense of nostalgia and a compliment to the local residents' sacrifices, which have been promoted by the mainstream media. In Zhang Ming's alternative representation of the national project, the city and its people withdraw from such a grand expectation of celebrating new life at relocated sites; instead, we are provided a *micro*-view examining the inertia and subjective dimension of the city. The film creates a heterotopia and Thirdspace by showing the street view of the urban space and everyday life related to emerging commercialism, and oppressed desire in a claustrophobic space.

Still Life: Expectation becomes Stillness from Wushan to Fengjie

Fengjie, another small town under the jurisdiction of the municipality of Chongqing, is the setting of *Still Life*. Similar to Wushan, the small town is also involved in the Three Gorges Dam project. The film pushes the construction of the Three Gorges Dam into the background, but foregrounds the ruins of Fengjie and those who make ruins, live in ruins, are exiled by ruins and even buried by ruins. Released ten years after *Rainclouds over Wushan* (1996), *Still Life* juxtaposes the dam and the accompanying construction of infrastructure with the ubiquitous ruins. If *Rainclouds over Wushan* displays the inertia of the place and its local residents before the impending inundation, *Still Life* shows the spatial and social consequence of building this tremendous landmark of modernisation and the ensuing large-scale migration. To represent the submerging of a town with valuable cultural and historical heritage, Jia adopts the style of magical realism to convey the dramatic changes underway in the physical space and the consequent traumatic experiences in the mental space of characters. If the dream-like sequences in *Rainclouds over Wushan* reflect the protagonists' subjective view of time and space, showing their desire for intimate relations and a better future, *Still Life* casts a strong impression of reality through two outsiders' calm observation of the ruined city. *Still Life* records and contemplates the lives of the migrating population, and the absurdity and 'unrealism' of the intensive spatial transformation taking place. The film works as a space of resistance by focusing on those marginalised people and their perseverance and dignity in the lived space.

Still Life reflects, according to Jia Zhangke, the material items and everyday concerns of common people, some of whom can be regarded as subaltern due to their unprivileged economic situations and low social status. When Jia first arrived at Fengjie with contemporary Chinese painter Liu Xiaodong, for whom he had planned to make a documentary titled *East [Dong]* (2006), he was astonished by the poorly furnished interior spaces and the lack of material possessions in the houses of local residents (Li et al. 2007: 12). The town is in a state of anticipation of flooding due to the construction of Three Gorges Dam, and the local people who remain at home are awaiting compensation for enforced migration. Such a historical time and space inspired Jia to record and reflect on the enormous changes underway, which resulted in the making of the feature *Still Life*. The film begins with a long take, from left to right, showing people entertaining or sitting in silence on a ferry. Accompanied by a deep bass soundtrack of a piece of Sichuanese opera – *Lin Chong's final fight* [*Lin Chong yeben*] – the spanning shot unfolds like a landscape scroll, revealing characters one by one.

The protagonist Han Sanming (Han Sanming), a coal mine worker from Shanxi Province, distances himself from the ragged or bare-chested men, sitting at the end of the ferry with a tired and confused face. He is travelling from Shanxi Province, a place well-known for its rich coal mines, to Fengjie, Sichuan Province, in search of his spouse and daughter who left home sixteen years ago. The other storyline follows Shen Hong Zhao Tao, also from Shanxi Province, a nurse who wishes to settle marital problems with her husband who left for Chongqing two years ago. The two outsiders roam around the ruins, trying to resume or bid farewell to their previous marriages. Coming all the way from northern China to this small town of southern China, they not only cross the border of provincial territory, but also the boundaries around cultural practices and everyday conduct. According to Soja, when 'borders are crossed, disturbed, contested, and so become a threat to order, hegemonic power acts to reinforce them: the boundaries around territory, nation, ethnicity, race, gender, sex, class, erotic practice, are trotted out and vigorously disciplined' (Soja 1996: 115). In the film, hegemonic power on the state level concretises itself in the construction of the gigantic hydropower station and the ensuing ruins which become the signature feature characterising the town and affecting local residents' lives. Meanwhile, on the individual level, the hegemonic power can be seen in the trivial cultural etiquette of giving cigarettes, alcohol, sugar and tea as gifts to relatives, or even strangers, with the intention of creating harmonious interpersonal relationships. However, Han Sanming finds this etiquette is invalid when he migrates from his Shanxi home town to Fengjie. He is confronted with constant rejection when presenting his carefully prepared gifts. Meanwhile, he is cornered by the firm hand of commercialisation. Following the opening sequences set on the ferry, Han Sanming is coerced by a man of obscure identity to a show staging magic tricks that turns white paper into bank notes, and is obliged to pay a fee for the performance in the end. The scenes foreground the bank notes and the threatening faces of the showmen who extract the fees from the audience, indicating the ruthless practices of commercialisation in daily life. The other form of overwhelming hegemonic power of commercialisation is reflected in Han Sanming's marriage. His wedding sixteen years ago was a commercial exchange (a possible human traffic case); now he wants to resume the marriage, but is asked to pay again to have his ex-wife back (she left Han after giving birth to a baby girl). In Shen Hong's case, it is her husband who is empowered by business success; he ditched her and in fact terminated their marriage years ago.

Ruins in Still Life

Ruins play an important role in many of Jia Zhangke's works. In his debut *Pickpocket*, set in Fenyang, Shanxi Province, the Chinese character *chai* (拆), which means demolition, appears ubiquitously on walls. *Chai* (拆) 'the act of tearing down . . . points not only to the physical demolition of the old cityscape but also, more profoundly, to the symbolic and psychological destruction of the social fabric of families and neighbourhoods' (Lu 2007b: 138). In *Unknown Pleasures*, the city of Datong, also in Shanxi Province, is depicted as a wasteland. Characters live alongside ruins, turning a blind eye to all the ruins across the city. In *Still Life*, ruins are shown in long takes and characters are dwarfed or even buried (in Xiaoma's case) by them. For instance, in one scene Han Sanming and his long-lost wife share a sweet moment in a half demolished building (Figure 3.6). They are squatting on the ground, turning back to the ruined side, persuading the other to have the only toffee. Suddenly, they are stunned by the explosion of a high-rise building not far away. They get up and turn around to watch the crashing down of the building. In this long shot, the couple is surrounded by ruins, and their sweet reunion is ruthlessly interrupted by the demolition.

Figure 3.6 Han Sanming and his wife: in *Still Life*

Ruins could be represented as the witness to personal or collective trauma, or serve as a metaphor of redemption in a number of films on wars or terror, as Mennel points out:

> Ruins can have two different functions, which are rooted in distinct traditions: on the one hand, they mark precise historical moments, for example in the rubble films of the immediate German post-war moment. In these films from 1946–48, Berlin in ruins becomes the site for negotiating guilt, redemption, and rebuilding in regard to the Holocaust and the Second World War. On the other hand, ruins as a postmodern cipher (code) invoke historical moments and iconic images but empty them of their historical geographical specificity in what I call the retro-rubble film. (Mennel 2008: 103–4)

Cinematic Berlin in ruins, either as a site of redemption and rebuilding immediately after the Second World War or as a space of 'empty' historical remembrance in the postmodern era, reflects the affinity between ruins and traumatic experiences. In the context of China, ruins in different historical periods register different meanings. During the Maoist era, ruins symbolised socialist progress as it was accepted that the old streets, architectures and walls should make way for new, socialist monuments and spaces. In the reform era, however, such representational meaning of ruins has been replaced by 'history, memory, trauma and social crisis' (Schultz 2016: 442). The shifting representation of ruins in Chinese films is a result of urban redevelopment under the discourse of modernisation, which arouses multiple social issues relating to social stratification, regional uneven resource distribution and economic development. In the film, the lower social classes, including migrant workers and the urban poor, make ruins, live with ruins and make a living in ruins (Figure 3.7).

Thus, *chai* (拆) and construction ruins are arguably themes of many urban films in contemporary China since the 1980s (Lu 2007b: 137). In an interview, Jia revealed that he had to race against the relentless pace of demolition to capture the disappearing cityscape in Fengjie, using long shots to show manual labourers striking walls and the dust spreading out as the walls collapse. Following Sanming's steps and views, spectators sense the apocalyptic atmosphere generated by ruins and misty weather. In addition, traces of private life and memory remain in the ruins, such as pieces of calligraphy, posters of a pop singer and certificates. These items occupy the domestic space of the previous residents, bearing witness and memorialising its inhabitants. These personal belongings are preserved by *Still Life*; they are 'resisting the force of *chai*' (Mello 2015: 145). Echoing the English title of the

Figure 3.7 Ruins, workers and death: in *Still Life*

film, *Still Life*, these small items bear 'the secret of life', as Jia has confirmed:

> Once I walked into someone's room by accident and saw dust-covered articles on the desk. Suddenly it seemed the secrets of still life fell upon me. The old furniture, the stationery on the desk, the bottles on the window sills and the decorations on the walls all took on an air of poetic sorrow. Still life presents a reality that has been overlooked by us. Although time has left deep marks on it, it still remains silent and holds the secrets of life. (Mello 2015: 145–6)

While the former residents move out of their homes, some migrant workers turn the unliveable place into their temporary home. They sleep there, cook there, entertain themselves there and even make a living there – several prostitutes work in a half-demolished room. Ruins in *Still Life* appear as a 'live space' that registers as 'a non-space that is neither public nor private, and caters to the basic physical and social need of the lower class' (Luo 2015: 165). Ultimately, the daily practices of the lowest class relate closely to ruins, as they have been hired to tear down existing constructions, therefore they make ruins, meanwhile, they take shelter in ruins, and make a living out of ruins. Ruins bear clear and indivisible class marks.

The cinematic spaces of *Still Life* teem with ruins and death brought by the hegemonic power of implementing the enormous national project. Consequently, spatial experiences of people from the marginalised group represented by Han Sanming are characterised by uncertainty, fragmentation and dislocation. To survive, they participate in the speeding up spatial transformation and social mobility, calmly dealing with changing circumstances and navigating between places (ruins). The construction of the Three Gorges Dam cannot be seen as merely reflecting the general anxiety of a society eager to realise modernisation and establish a distinct identity in the world; it stirs up individual anxiety triggered by social inequality and materialism. At this point, bodies, cities and cinematic representations serve as 'key sites of hegemonic and counter-hegemonic contestations' (cited in Soja 1996: 115). The plenitude of representations of ruins and dislocated populations and the still life left in the abandoned households become Jia's 'counter-hegemonic contestation' of the process of modernisation. To show such a large scale of construction and demolition under the hegemonic political power and the mixed responses of the people involved in this great transformation, Jia employs magical realism to illustrate the sense of real-and-imagined of the happenings in the area.

Magical realism

Realism is a slippery concept used to describe aesthetic works that 'truly' reflect social and natural realities. André Bazin's famous statement that 'realism in art can only be achieved in one way – through artifice' (2005a: 26) shows that no absolute reality exists in artistic works. The traditional Chinese aesthetic concept *zhen* (真) could be an equivalent term for realism, which 'would imply more a sense of authenticity or sincerity in art rather than a strictly mimetic relationship between representation and reality' (McGrath 2016: 20). These interpretations of realism resonate with Jia Zhangke's point of view on how he represents the complexity of Chinese reality through films:

> I have the impression that a surrealist atmosphere prevails in China today, because the entire society faces an enormous pressure to speed up. As a result, many strange and unimaginable events have occurred in reality. As they say: 'reality is more exceptional than fiction'. The surrealistic elements sound unbelievable to most of us, but they are part of reality. It is precisely because I tried to catch such an allegedly surrealistic atmosphere that I have decided to direct this film. (cited in Lu 2006: 126)

In *Still Life*, Jia represents the huge material disparity between the rich and the poor, and the ruins in an apocalyptic space through magical realism. As Jia explains in an interview:

> when taking the ferry through the Three Gorges, I had a strong sense that I was walking the same path that the ancient people walked, because the landscape remains the same as depicted in old brush and ink paintings, which made me feel so close to history, as if I had entered a different spatial-temporal. However, no sooner do I get to the shore than I was overwhelmed by the noisy and vulgar reality of the county, which made me bewildered and dislocated. (Jia et al. 2007: 20)

The natural beauty of the Three Gorges, the local history of the area and its culture, preserved in poems and paintings, co-exist with the noisy bustling everyday practices of the small town and stun those who visit the place. These intertwined realities mirror Jia's 'unimaginable', 'surrealistic' and 'magic' sense of reality. Therefore, magical realism is employed by him to catch 'the complexity of the real when the materialist depiction of things proves be to inadequate if conducted without a sharper attention to the spiritual undertones' (Bertozzi 2012: 165). China now is facing a highly heterogenetic post-socialist reality, as economic and social disparities sharply distinguish the rural and urban areas, and on a larger scale, western China and eastern coastal China. Despite the fact that contemporary Chinese post-socialism is often seen as the equivalent of postmodernism, it has its own specificity, which according to Sheldon Lu, 'consists of multiple temporalities superimposed on one another; that is, the pre-modern, modern, post-modern coexist at the same place and at the same time' (2001: 13). In this sense, magical realism is highly effective in capturing the tangled, transient and bewildered experiences and feelings triggered by the coexistence of the diverse facets of contemporary Chinese reality.

Jia has been classified as a 'Bazinian director' by critics as he frequently adopts cinematic techniques and ideas on neo-realism praised by André Bazin. His home town trilogy takes up Italian neorealism by letting marginalised characters speak in their own dialect and placing them into hopeless conditions. As Andrew contends, Jia Zhangke explores 'a China whose ambitious young people find themselves channelled into what are literal or figurative construction zones, where they live not only with diminished agency, but with diminished dreams' (Andrew 2018).

However, in *Still Life*, Jia deploys computer-generated images of a flying UFO and the launching of something resembling a spaceship, which 'problematises his early classification as a "Bazinian director"' (Ramos Monteiro et al. 2015: 107). The on-location shooting and these magic supernatural images create an innovative style that embodies the individual's subjective experience amid the catastrophic atmosphere enveloping the entire region.

In one sequence, Han Sanming roams around and sees a flying saucer moving across the sky and disappearing. At the same time, Shen Hong looks out at the foggy landscape, becoming the other witness to the unusual phenomenon. However, the two witnesses handle the rare phenomenon calmly and the UFO serves as the only link between the two protagonists. The two never know each other, although both of them come from Shanxi Province and both roam around this disappearing town for reconciliation with their spouses. Both have gone through a prolonged journey to find their spouses, as most addresses have either changed or been submerged under the water. Jia explained the reason why he utilised surreal phenomena in such a realistic work:

> One day, during the shooting, I was walking along the river when suddenly it started thundering and raining. The nature seems incredibly mysterious. I raised my head and wondered whether it would be possible for a UFO to cross the sky and see me. Because after the enormous changes we are witnessing, a lot of things that go beyond reality could happen, and they could partially change the reality as well. (Wu and Wang 2007)

The UFO symbolises the complicated and transient changes happening in contemporary China. The country is going through large scale construction

Figure 3.8 The tower hua (華) and its quiet launching: in *Still Life*

and demolition, destruction and creation. It may be unrealistic, magical and unbelievable for viewers to see a UFO, but the unrealistically huge dam, the unbelievable scale of migration, the magical lights that brighten the newly completed suspension bridge are occurring in real life.

In another surreal scene, a tower fashioned in the shape of the traditional character for China (*hua*, 華) launches into space at dawn (Figure 3.8). In reality, the tower, called 'Monument to the Three Gorges Migrants' [*Sanxia yimin jinianbei*], was built in 2003 by the local government to pay attribute to the grand project, but was demolished in November 2009 due to a shortage of funding (*Monument to the Three Gorges Migrants* [*Sanxia yimin jinianbei*] 2010). In the film, however, the tower disappears in a sublime and romantic manner. The launching of the structure 'could be interpreted as representing the uprooting of Chinese traditional culture in the process of China's modernisation' since the character *hua* (華) symbolises Chinese civilisation (Luo 2015: 163). In a different interpretation, Schultz perceives it as 'a space of the intangible future, and not the concrete present . . . the futuristic replacement is not only a sense of estrangement from place but also from time as well' (Schultz 2016: 455). However, both interpretations fail to recognise the practical function of this structure – whether it is a symbol of Chinese civilisation or a futuristic space, it was constructed by the local government to 'show off' its achievement in overcoming all kinds of difficulties, in particular, the migration problem, to contribute to the building of the Three Gorges Dam.

As a monument, its symbolic meaning greatly outweighs its practical function of being inhabited or lived. However, when it disappears into space in filmic representation – or is demolished due to the lack of funds in reality – it becomes an allegory revealing the problems hidden from the public in completing the hydropower project, such as the migrant problems and the local government's abuse of compensation funding distributed by the central government. Thus, the launching of the structure can also be interpreted as 'the dream of modernisation' that is irrelevant to the local people. The local population's indifference toward its existence and disappearance indicates that the dream remains out of the reach of the ordinary, especially the subaltern class whose immediate concern is to survive. The ambitions of political and social elites has little positive impact on the wellbeing and affluence of migrants. They can travel around the country to undertake certain types of job, making a living and wishing for a better future for their next generation. However, just like Han Sanming's daughter and the girl called Chunyu who wants to be a nanny in the big city, they have to set out on the same path their parents have taken. This group of people, including their descendants, are closely associated with ruins, whether of a coal mine, a construction site or a waste plant.

The hydropower construction project is a significant step toward modernity, a 'dream of a powerful state' and the 'ambition of the social elites' (Jia et al. 2007: 22). However, its construction drives a large population out of their home town, erasing their community and its emotional bond with the land, leaving them struggling to survive. Both the national modernisation project and the individual's material and emotional concerns are matters of social urgency. Despite the access to modern media (radio and TV) and technology (mobile phones), people like Han Sanming are still far from living a modern life. At the end of the film, the other protagonist, Shen Hong, boards a ferry setting out for Shanghai, and the radio broadcasts that construction of the Three Gorges Dam has been a dream of the central leaders for several generations. The mainstream message recognises the local people's contribution to the enormous project, but where have the migrants gone? What problems have they encountered in the process of migration? Why is there violent turmoil and how does it end? These problems, which are immediately relevant to each of the local individuals, are left unanswered by the mainstream news coverage. The voices of the ordinary and the specific sacrifices made by them are hidden from the public view.

Ten years ago, when those tourists flooded into Wushan in *Rainclouds over Wushan* to catch the final glimpse of the spectacular natural landscape of the Three Gorges, the local people appeared emotionless, but they were nevertheless expecting love, marriage and a new beginning. Ten years later, in *Still Life*, the tourists are gone – local residents and outsiders alike are leaving. It seems that they are able to move freely across the country; however, those who belong to the subaltern class or who live at the bottom of society can only realise that their lives have come to a point of stagnation. The state of being still for them does not mean they cannot travel from place to place; rather, it means that they are permanently stuck at the bottom in a highly mobile society, no matter where they are. As the ending of the film shows, in a long shot where Han Sanming and his colleagues set out to Shanxi Province to become coal miners, there is a man standing high above on a thin suspended rope, cautiously moving forward (Figure 3.9).

Calmly and silently, Sanming looks at the tightrope walker, who appears in silhouette, performing his dangerous feat. As audience to the spectacle, Sanming shows no enthusiasm, nor does he clap the performance. Instead,

Figure 3.9 The funambulist and Han Sanming: in *Still Life*

he walks away, back towards the camera, and disappears in the background. By juxtaposing the group of manual labourers and a man who risks his life for his performance, the sequence reveals a brutal truth: the aerial walking is associated with danger, uncertainty, vulnerability and risk to life, resonating with this group of lower class workers who live with danger and risk their lives mining coal. The performance contains no surprise for them, for they were, are and will be undertaking the same sort of work. The difference is that they do not have an audience.

PART III
CINEMATIC CHENGDU

CHAPTER 4

Spaces of Consumption Replace Spaces of Production

The cityscape of Chengdu before the reform era was divided by an array of socialist 'work units' – state-owned enterprises – that functioned as centripetal spaces, attracting talent, resources and capital. The spatial arrangement of work units characterised the socialist urban space; they were designed and built according to socialist ideals of uniformity and collectivism, and could be seen as the 'representations of power and ideology, of control and surveillance' (Soja 1996: 67). Such spatial arrangements, the attached power structure and values, and their disappearance are represented in Jia Zhangke's 2008 film *24 City*. This 'docufiction' demonstrates how and why such a socialist utopia was established and developed but has now disappeared. Generational gaps in consuming and appropriating social spaces, and the transition of the urban space from production space into consumption space, are unfolded in the narrative of different generations living in the city.

According to Soja, 'history defines the power of place' and 'by recovering and preserving the history of places and spaces, we can recover and preserve our collective selves much better than if we forget the past and repeat our mistakes and injustices' (Soja 1996: 192). In *24 City*, we are shown the history of a socialist state factory lasting over half a century. The dense social, cultural and historical narrative is presented spatially by framing the characters' different relations with the city through the generational gap in using the industrial space and the urban space. Accordingly, a minor and personal perspective emerges, adding to the grand history of reformation of the city since the 1980s.

Chengdu in Films

Cinematic representations of Chengdu and its nearby cities have two competing styles – either primitive or modern. Action thriller *Mysterious Grand Buddha* [*Shenmi de dafo*] (Zhang Huaxun, 1980), melodrama *The King of*

Masks [*Bian lian*] (Wu Tianming, 1995) and black humour allegory *Design of Death* [*Sha sheng*] (Guan Hu, 2012) show the distinctive natural beauty and primitive cultural landscapes of the area. Urban drama *A Narrow Lane Celebrity* [*Xiaoxiang mingliu*] (Cong Lianwen, 1985), set in a small Sichuanese town, alternates between a series of flashbacks of a neighbourhood's traumatic experiences during the Cultural Revolution and the lingering influence of devastating sufferings on characters' present situations. Feature film *Ripples across Stagnant Water* [*Kuang*, lit. *The Unrestrained*] (Ling Zifeng, 1992) focuses on consecutive conflicts between the common people, local secret societies (called *paoge*, brother gangster) and missionaries in the late nineteenth century (1894–1901). *Paoge*, also known as Sworn Brothers, are gangsters identified by their rough appearance and strange clothes, who 'established their turfs in the teahouses or other places and took responsibility for maintaining peace, resolving conflicts and protecting economic interests in the area' (Wang 1998a: 57). *Ripples across Stagnant Water* employs a panoramic view to show the flourishing domestic industrial and commercial culture in the context of the invasion of western capitalism at the end of the nineteenth century. During that time, Chengdu became the economic, cultural and political centre of the upper Yangtze River. It was noted that:

> Sichuan overlooks China, and Chengdu is the centre of Sichuan, with fertile lands, rich natural resources, high population density, well-developed production of silk, many historical sites, and beautiful scenery. It is the hub of transportation coming from or going to Shaanxi, Gansu, Hunan, Hubei, Yunnan, Guizhou, Qinghai, and Tibet. (Cited in Wang 1998a: 36)

Chengdu's significance in transportation and trade, in addition to its natural beauty and abundant resources, attracted large numbers of foreign visitors to this inland city. They agreed that the province was 'one of the fairest and richest corners of the Chinese Empire' (cited in Adshead 1984: 3). However, the city remained a conventional imperial city with little western impact during this period, maintaining its traditional lifestyle and culture more visibly than cities such as Shanghai and Beijing (cited in Wang 1998a: 36). Such a situation can be seen in *Ripples across Stagnant Water*, which shows the majority of Chinese people's suspicion of western medicine and hostility towards Christian churches and missionaries. As the title of the film indicates, the isolated hinterland area is like 'stagnant water' and the western influence can only stir up slight ripples.

Mysterious Grand Buddha is the first action film made after the establishment of the PRC in 1949. Set in Leshan, a small city two hours' drive from Chengdu, the film unfolds with a journey in search of the buried treasure that was raised for the maintenance of the Grand Buddha. The film was a box office hit with its dramatic plot and kinetic action sequences, and was regarded as the first commercial film in mainland China after the Cultural Revolution (Wang 1998b; Zhang 2004a). *The King of Masks*, also based in Leshan, depicts an aged 'face-changing' performer's difficult journey to secure a proper successor to whom he can pass down his techniques and talents. The film realistically showcases local street scenes and ordinary people's limited means of entertainment in the impoverished city, which was plagued by extreme sexism and corrupt local government during the 1920s. Face-changing is an essential magic trick in Sichuan opera, which also appears in *Mysterious Grand Buddha* as a startling addition to the plot. Both Leshan-based films deploy local legends, native arts (face-changing and fire-breathing) and the riverside Grand Buddha to depict an alternative cultural and natural landscape.

Design of Death (2012) is an allegorical story based in a Qiang community, an ethnic minority living south of Chengdu. It presents an enclosed living space under an autonomous administration. As a remote isolated kingdom, old traditions and practices remain influential in the small town. For instance, widows are compelled to be drowned as funeral sacrifices for their dead husbands, and impoverished people save every penny for a grand funeral ceremony. Yet one man stands against all these gruesome practices, and, as a result, he becomes a thorn in the flesh of the entire town. Meanwhile, the town is frequently struck by earthquakes, which symbolise the pressing and enormous exterior influence on the small kingdom. The exotic built space and allegorical narrative explicitly indicate certain obsolete traditions and practices that remain in China. The earthquake, a clear reminder of the catastrophic earthquake that occurred in Sichuan province in 2008, combined with these odd social practices, becomes a devastating force that threatens the existence of the small town.

Chengdu, in contrast, is presented as a highly modernised city characterised by local cuisine, mah-jongg, tea houses and a leisurely lifestyle. In 2003, Zhang Yimou made a short promotional video about contemporary Chengdu, of which he said, 'once you have been there, you won't want to leave'. In this video, Chengdu is presented as both modern and traditional, peaceful and dynamic. The extensive urbanisation does not destroy the leisurely atmosphere of the city. On the contrary, modernity and tradition co-exist harmoniously. Five years later, when the city was hit by the Wenchuan earthquake, the video was rediscovered online and satirised as 'a city once you have been there, you cannot escape from'. Despite the joke, the short video received more public attention from areas outside Chengdu. The third person point of view of the narration served more persuasively than official tourism promotion to attract tourists and investors, domestic and overseas, to this dynamic city.

After 2008, the distinctive natural landscape and cultural heritage of Chengdu and its nearby cities, especially the disaster-stricken area, drew greater attention from filmmakers. Documentaries such as *China's Unnatural Disaster: The Tears of Sichuan Province* [*Jiehou Tianfu zongheng lei*] (Jon Alpert and Matthew O' Neil, 2009), *Buried* [*Yanmai*] (Wang Libo, 2009) and *People First* [*Renmin zhishang*] (Chen Zhen, 2009) were made immediately after the earthquake. In the following years, more documentaries and films were released, exploring the ruins, heavy loss of life and local survivors' troubled situations wrought by the disaster. These films foregrounded the positive roles of local and central government in the process of reconstruction, and exposed and interrogated a series of problems such as corrupt officials and low-quality building construction. Overall, these cinematic representations tend to anticipate a fresh start for the affected towns and cities. *Fallen City* [*Shang Cheng*] (Zhao Qi, 2011) focuses on the journey of three earthquake survivors in search of identity and hope, while another documentary, *The Next Life* [*Huozhe*] (Fan Jian, 2011), features a couple who have lost their daughter in the earthquake and who try to conceive another baby to redeem themselves.

There are also feature films made on the disaster theme, such as *Aftershock* [*Tangshan da dizhen*] (Feng Xiaogang, 2010), which intertwines the two most devastating earthquakes in contemporary China – Tangshan in 1976 and Wenchuan in 2008. It shows how natural disasters traumatise individuals and families, and how common people facing such disasters struggle with moral dilemmas. *Frightening Moment* [*Jingtian dongdi*] (Wang Jia and Shen Dong, 2009) and *The Melody of Qiang Flute* [*Qiangdi youyou*] (Miao Yue, 2011) concentrate more on the rebuilding of the affected areas with assistance from all over China and on paying respect to the local survivors' hard work and optimism.

Apart from films engaging with the disaster directly, post-earthquake cinematic Chengdu becomes an optimal space for emotional remedy and contemplation on existence. There are a number of works that treat themes such as fate and faith, suffering and redemption: for example, romance *A Good Rain Knows* [*Haoyu shijie*] (Hur Jin-ho, 2009); science fiction film *Chengdu, I Love You* [*Guoqu weilai*] (Cui Jian and Fruit Chan, 2009); TV film *A Love Story in Chengdu* [*Qingyu Chengdu*] (You Xiaojin and Lü Gengxin, 2011); and *Buddha Mountain*. In most of these films, the earthquake, which was of almost unprecedented magnitude, becomes a lingering nightmare for the local people. It drives people to reflect on their own personal sufferings and the meaning of existence. More significantly, faith, the long-absent subject in contemporary China since the Cultural Revolution, begins to be touched upon, questioned and contested. An alternative representation of Chengdu is contributed by Jia Zhangke in *24 City*. Made and released before the earthquake, it seeks to preserve a disappearing socialist utopia built half a century ago in this hinterland city. It records an industrial Chengdu that is planned and designed in the service of national security under an enormous project – the Third Front (or Third Line).

In addition to Chengdu, adjacent areas of the city have also been increasingly presented on screen since 2008. Just like those people from the rural areas of Chongqing municipality who are determined to leave their home town for a better future, the rural Sichuanese are also eager to seek new opportunities in the coastal region and are devoted to bringing a decent life to their next generation and rural families. The documentary *Last Train Home* [*Guitu lieche*] (Fan Lixin, 2009) projects three different spaces used by the protagonists: a roaring factory, a crowded train station and a scenic rural home town. The modern city of Guangzhou is reduced to a busy plant where the migrant couple work, and a railway station where they have to queue up for days for tickets home for a family reunion during the spring festival. They are like migrant birds who travel between the major city and their remote home, working hard to provide better material conditions for the next generation, only to find, to their disappointment, that their daughter wishes to join them to work in the megacity when she comes of age. For the girl, living in the megacity would be a part of a 'playful-constructive behaviour' (Debord 1996b: 22); however, such an expectation of the city is completely different from her parents' experience, which is characterised by 'oppressive living conditions imposed through . . . technocratic city plans' (Andreotti 1996: 7). The documentary asks potent questions: when modernisation draws a great number of migrant workers to coastal cities to demolish, construct, produce and maintain the glistening urban spaces, what happens to their rural families? Will they eventually bring a bright future for their next generation? Ironically, as *Last Train Home* indicates, a better life does not necessarily come along with an exhausting job, and the next generation eventually takes the same path as their parents do.

Cinematic Chengdu, to a certain degree, is defined by unique Sichuanese elements such as hot pot cuisine, pandas, tea houses, mah-jongg and Sichuan operas, as they are immediately identifiable and distinguishable for Chinese people. However, for many years, its hinterland location and impoverished rural areas also made it an inaccessible and unpresentable site. Unlike contemporary filmic representations of Beijing and Shanghai, which have been recognised as models of modernisation since the 1980s, films set in Chengdu made it appear more like the dilapidated backyard of the highly urbanised eastern coastal region. After the earthquake, it became a place to lament the disaster and to contemplate the fast pace of urbanisation and the ultimate meaning of life. However, it retains some of the old spatial arrangement as visual cue of the socialist past – industrial buildings of work units, and values and conduct produced by the spatial structures that propagate collectivism, uniformity and stability.

24 City: Making Way for a Modern Space

24 City recounts the rise and fall of a state-owned enterprise by orchestrating stories of nine interviewees from across three different generations. The account of the past history of the enterprise alternates with the rapid demolition of the previous working spaces, creating a strong sense of melancholy and loss. The corporation, known as Chengfa Jituan (lit. Chengdu Engine Group), is usually referred to as Factory 420 by the workers (hereafter Factory 420), and used to employ nearly 30,000 workers and support around 100,000 dependent family members. The factory was built to produce and repair engines for military aircraft in 1958, but in the film, it undergoes a deconstruction and is juxtaposed with a rising commercial complex named 24 City. The name '24 City' derives from an old poem about Chengdu, which is fully written in white Chinese characters on the screen in the opening sequences of the film:

> The twenty-four city is brightened by hibiscus flowers, Jinguan has always been thriving [*Ershisi cheng furonghua, jinguan zixi cheng fanhua*].

The poem forms a picture of a prosperous and historical city. However, accompanied by an elegiac soundtrack, the opening sequences are inflected with melancholy.

Following the old poem about Chengdu is a long take tracing a running truck that carries a set of machines painted green, passing down a grey street. Bicycles, motorcycles, buses and sedans occupy the street, and identical buildings line one side, appearing dirty and ashy under the gloomy sky. Along with the melancholic soundtrack, two Chinese characters, Chengdu (成都), emerge in black on the misty grey background (Figure 4.1). The camera then moves inside Factory 420, zooming in for a close-up of a floor lamp and a meter that stand still in the steamy and empty factory. The spaces captured in the sequences include the front

SPACES OF CONSUMPTION REPLACE SPACES OF PRODUCTION   97

Figure 4.1 Street view of Chengdu: in *24 City*

gate, the major entrance of the corporation, the interior, heavy machinery, the gathering hall, the dim grey stairs, and the empty and abandoned rooms, all of which will soon be wiped out. Both the city and the state-owned factory are enveloped in a grimy and misty atmosphere. Contrasted with the dynamic and prosperous scenario conveyed by the poem, the city and its important production unit – the state-owned enterprise – appear bleak and mournful. Demolishing the material space may take only a couple of months, but the wrenching psychological disruption and vacuum can linger for generations.

24 City weaves nine interviewees' personal experiences into a complete narrative of the rise and fall of Factory 420 with its history of over half a century. Jia Zhangke selects five non-professional actors and four professional actors and combines the style of documentary and fictional narrative to create a 'docufiction' (Deppman 2014). Jia wishes 'to project over hundreds of people's memory onto several characters' and claims that 'history is always made by fiction and fact' (Liu 2008: 42). Therefore, this 'docufictional' feature experiments with interviewing workers from different generations about their memories and experiences in Factory 420 and synthesising hundreds of real-life stories. Utilising such a compound style with the strong impulse of the documentary form, Jia explains, is necessary:

> There have been changes in China in the past one or two years that have come so swiftly that if I don't film as fast as I can I will never be able to catch up. I feel the need to use documentary to record the changes we are experiencing right now . . . I must use documentary to tell my stories and prevent not only the disappearance of memories but also the disappearance of the architecture, the buildings, the disappearance of the whole generation of people after 1949. (Nochimson 2009: 421–13)

The reiterated word 'disappearance' in this interview emphasises the trademark process occurring in contemporary Chinese cities. The disappearance of material spaces and the generation of people who lived through the socialist era trigger a mournful nostalgia. In the film, the first generation, who were uprooted from their north-eastern home towns to come to Chengdu in the 1950s and 1960s, hold a strong collective view towards the state and individual life. They followed the central government's orders unconditionally and devoted their entire lives to constructing an industrial and military base for the country. As one retired worker states, they had to work extra hours because of the ongoing Korean War. The next generation followed in their footsteps, becoming workers in the same factory after high school, attaining various allocations from the central government as their parents did. The third generation, however, either refuses to wear the factory uniform that used to symbolise a decent social status and stable income, or has never entered the factory, not to mention working in it.

A socialist spatial design for working and living

24 City opens with a crowd of people riding bicycles and flooding into the factory. This routine was the most common sight across cities of China during the 1980s and 1990s. The bird's-eye view shows four Chinese characters in red, *Chengfa jituan* (lit. Chengdu Engine Group, 成发集团), that stand high on the top of the front gate. The workers on their bicycles look as small as ants. The small, dot-like figures suggest negated or exploited individual interest and compliance with the institutional, political, economic concerns of the state. The camera then cuts to workers in navy blue uniforms moving into a lobby, making their way up to a meeting hall. There, the chorus 'Ode to the Motherland' is performed by workers with solemn faces. This scene is then followed by an overview of the empty stairs of another building, where the first interviewee is captured walking upstairs slowly and then standing still in front of a broken window. His name is He Xikun, a worker in Factory 420. He plays himself in the feature, representing the majority of

SPACES OF CONSUMPTION REPLACE SPACES OF PRODUCTION   99

the workers like himself, who are silent, serious and laden with anxiety. Jia frames him in a spacious room, with pieces of broken glass on the window sill and dust-covered light bulbs. It is raining outside, and raindrops hit the windows regularly.

All the spatial details are evidence of an abandoned space and a sad man who is forced to leave the working space. In contrast to this gloomy scenario, the auditorium interview with Guan Fengjiu, the deputy secretary of the party committee of Factory 420, shows an upbeat picture of the factory. The backdrop of the auditorium stage shows a huge picture, with the Great Wall foregrounded and an array of missiles set symmetrically on each side, creating an arch down which rows of tanks ride deep in the background (Figure 4.2). The picture testifies 'not only to the military's strength and its weaponry, but also to its role as the aforementioned "Great Iron Wall"' (Schultz 2015: 53). Guan recalls the initiation of the state-owned enterprise. It was hastily built with the assistance of the well-established state-owned Factory 111 located in Shenyang, Liaoning Province (in the north-east). A large number of workers, along with heavy machinery, were moved to Chengdu, Sichuan Province (in the south-west) in 1958 as a result of Chairman Mao's concern with national security during the Cold War. It is one of thousands of industrial units built under a massive project – the Third Front.

Figure 4.2 The stage backdrop of the auditorium of Factory 420: in *24 City*

The Third Front was an enormous political and economic project carried out by the central government between the 1960s and 1980s, and the 'Great Iron Wall' was built to confront the complicated international situation following a deterioration in Sino-Soviet relations and the increased military involvement of the USA in Vietnam during the 1960s (Naughton 1988: 353). The PRC central government decided to move the existing industries, especially armament factories that were originally located in Beijing, Shanghai and the north-east, to the north-west and south-west to create 'a huge self-sufficient industrial base area to serve as a strategic reserve in the event of China being drawn into war' (Naughton 1988: 351). Geographically, provinces located in the remote hinterland have mountain ridges as natural barriers against military threats from the US and the Soviet Union. As a result, a significant number of industrial factories and armament units were transferred. The western region received unprecedented political and economic support under the Third Front Development project.

The massive project exerted far-reaching economic and social influence on western China. In particular, it brought clear changes to the spatial arrangement of the urban space where:

> residential segregation was unacceptable to the socialist regime and a neighbourhood concept was introduced to arrange the city into self-contained units (*danwei*) in which the workers lived and worked. These were often housing compounds attached to factories in which workers from the work unit lived. (Buck 1984: 5–26)

Neighbourhoods and communities were organised with factories side by side; hence, the urban space was divided into a number of industrial centres with attached dwelling and recreational spaces. Factory 420 was one of many examples of such an urban spatial arrangement at the time. It was hastily built on the outskirts of Chengdu in 1958. The workers, most of whom had migrated from the north-east, brought their lifestyle and customs to this hinterland city. Working and dwelling in the enclosed space created by Factory 420, they barely communicated with the city until the beginning of the reform era. In the film, as Song Weidong (Chen Jianbin) confirms in his narration, 'Factory 420 is an independent and self-reliant world.' He finishes primary and middle education in the factory-run school, and takes over his father's position immediately after graduating from high school. He consumes beverages produced by an auxiliary factory and entertains himself in the factory-owned cinema, playground and swimming pool. As Jia comments, 'birth, sickness, old age and death can all be done within the realm' (Jia 2009: 4). As Song recalls, his only connection with the city was fighting with the local kids from nearby suburbs. As for these fighting, the *danwei* kids always beat the local kids as he and his peers often outweighed their opponents in terms of the number of participants. The collective power of the state-owned enterprise separated the *danwei* kids from the local ones. *Danwei* people spoke their own dialect, cooked in a home-town style, refused to learn the Sichuan dialect and despised those who spoke that dialect.

However, after the market economy became fully established in the 1980s, although state interference persisted, private businesses began to spring up across the country and most of the state-owned enterprises were soon dismantled. Consequently, the working class, the most advanced and lauded group in the pre-reform era, gradually slipped from the top of the social ladder to the bottom of the social, economic and cultural strata in the reform era. The laid-off workers, represented by Hou Lijun (Jia Zhangke's third interviewee who was dismissed in 1994) in *24 City*, became the new poor in the urban area. However, the suffering of the urban 'new poor' in the 1980s and 1990s was 'officially described as "temporary pain" during economic reform, "historic sacrifice", part of the "process of progresses"' (Dai 2002: 228). This group of people correspond to Bao Shihong and his colleagues represented in *Crazy Stone* based in Chongqing. Both films reflect spatial transformations that result in the rise of commercialism. The state-owned factory undergoes demolition, and real estate developers take over the land, tear down the socialist factory designated principally for production, and turn it into residential and commercial complexes in the service of consumption.

A long take spanning over fifteen seconds shows workers dismantling the four red Chinese characters *Chengfa jituan* (成发集团). It takes place quietly and is followed by sequences where another group of workers are disposing of industrial appliances and transporting heavy machinery. The process proceeds slowly and solemnly, in contrast with the rapid installation of the new name, *Huarun Ershisi Cheng* (lit. Huarun Twenty-four City, 华润二十四城), on the top of the gate (Figure 4.3). Next to the gate is a cluster of half-completed high rises under construction, accompanied by a faint sound of building work (Figure 4.4). The scene 'situates precisely between the deterioration of the past and the incompleteness of the future, and thus offers the possibility of conceiving of both temporal directions simultaneously' (Pratt and Juan 2014: 46). In reality, the estate developer *Huarun*, one of the sub-branches of the China Resources Corporation, is one of the influential real estate companies in China. It invested one third of the funding for making and naming the film (Li 2009). The Corporation represents the power of capital that incorporates and demolishes the old urban space meant for production and establishes

Figure 4.3 Factory 420 becomes Huarun Twenty-four City: in *24 City*

SPACES OF CONSUMPTION REPLACE SPACES OF PRODUCTION 103

Figure 4.4 Construction sites next to Factory 420: in *24 City*

new urban spaces of consumption under the logic of market and capitalism. Jia displays the process of deconstruction at an intentionally slow pace, in contrast to the construction accompanied with sound and fury. He foregrounds the individuals' memories, the reflection of a utopian space that existed for over half a century, and the effects of the space that has been consciously organised on the emotions and behaviour of individuals (Debord 1996a: 18). Jia draws a psychogeographical map for his characters by interviewing and organising their stories in a lineated way, exposing explicit generational gaps between characters.

The vanishing socialist utopia in Chengdu

In *24 City*, just before Hou Lijun's interview, a dozen men walk across the street at night, heading to a bus station and carrying bags on their shoulders. They stop at the station and one of them looks at the metro information while Hou Lijun's bus is driving away. It is an interesting moment, when the old economic and social system represented by Hou – the proud working class of the pre-reform era, whose stable and decent social status has just been destroyed by economic reformation – is juxtaposed against the new economic system, which has brought its commercial/capital orientated labour force (the migrant workers) from the countryside to the urban areas. Such appropriation of spaces by social groups from both the rural and the urban areas shows the changing social conditions, especially the evolution of the long-established household registration system, the invisible wall between the rural and urban spaces before the implementation of reform and open policies. In the Chinese context, the spatial relations become increasingly complicated in the reform era, with the previous simplified division between the rural and the urban space declining as a result of the central government's loosening of its control over the 'household registration system' (*hukou* system). In the film, this loosening can be seen from the relaxation on the control over population mobility, in particular, the rural migrant workers moving to the urban area. The *hukou* system, introduced in 1958, is a legacy of Mao's socialist regime and has been undergoing rectification since the reform era. It classified Chinese people as either agricultural or non-agricultural (Cheng and Selden 1994: 662). The agricultural population, registered in local communes as 'the rural' [*nongmin*], earn their basic living from land but are excluded from state welfare benefits. The non-agricultural population, on the other hand, are recognised as 'the urban' [*shimin*] and are 'entitled to state provision of rationed food grain, cooking oils, employment, housing, education, medical care and other welfare benefits' (McGee et al. 2007: 35). Characters in

24 City represent 'the urban', as seen in the previous analysis, as those who live in allocated houses, usually constructed in a plain Soviet style. In the pre-reform era:

> hukou had functioned as an invisible yet effective 'wall' separating the urban from the rural society and prohibiting rural–urban migration because any unauthorized migrants in the city could hardly survive without the supply of food, jobs, housing, health care and other urban services that are all firmly controlled by the state. (Cited in McGee et al. 2007: 35)

The invisible 'wall' separating the agricultural and non-agricultural population works highly effectively in two aspects: first, it strictly controls population mobility, especially rural–urban migration; second, it guarantees the entitlement of the non-agricultural population access to social and economic benefits. Consequently, the agricultural population was excluded from the state welfare system that made it impossible for migrant workers to survive in the urban area in the pre-reform era. It is therefore a significant mechanism to control population mobility and distribute state welfare. It not only marks citizens' social status but also places different social groups in different spatial organisations.

The working unit, in addition to the *hukou* system, functioned effectively to maintain social and economic order in the urban area. Such socialist space of production can be seen as a 'moving cluster of points of intersection for manifold axes of power which cannot be reduced to a unified plane or organised into a single narrative' (cited in Soja 1996: 164). Employees from any state-owned enterprise such as Factory 420 were part of a privileged leading class in mainland China. Factory 420 was even superior to common state-owned factories as it related to military production during the Cold War. Even during the widespread severe famine period at the beginning of the 1960s, workers of Factory 420 were generously provided with all kinds of food supplies due to their significant role in military and political sections, as Hao Dali (Lü Liping), a model worker of Factory 420, confirmed. In its heyday, she could subsidise her relatives back in north-eastern China. The intertwined systems provided people with a clear vision of their future: what school they can enter, what job they will be undertaking and even what kind of spouse they will marry. Every turning point of life from birth to death was determined by this gigantic and omnipotent factory.

However, with the state retreating from political campaigns and military movements, from the 1980s it began to focus on economic growth, and military-related industry was no longer a priority for the central government. Consequently, the state-owned factory lost its political and economic advantage in the reform era, and struggled to adjust to the socialist market by producing household appliances. Working class people fell from their privileged position, both economically and socially. They became the subsidised ones, receiving help from relatives who had prospered by involvement in private business. As Hao Dali says sentimentally in her interview, her niece sends her 500 RMB to help her out. The switched roles of subsidiser and subsidised highlights the falling of the old system and the breaking down of the working classes, and engenders a strong sense of delusion with regard to Dali's current hand-to-mouth existence.

Having retired, Hao Dali lives alone in the apartment allocated by Factory 420. Her little son went missing during the journey from the north-east to Chengdu. When the ferry, which was carrying industrial crew and heavy machinery, resumed its journey after a short recess, Hao Dali found to her astonishment that her son was lost. She recalls that 'as the company was managed in a military fashion, workers were obliged to return to the ferry as soon as the bugle rang'. She never had an opportunity to search for her son afterwards. People like Dali and her husband, who were involved in a military-related state-owned company, had to leave familial and personal issues behind and devote themselves to the national unit. As noted by Chris Berry, characters in Chinese classical films love the Party, the nation, the People's Liberation Army, the workers, the peasants, Chairman Mao and the people, but rarely love their own family, nor do they value romantic love: 'even where love for family and romantic love do occur, they are subordinate to the larger didactic concerns' (2004: 100). The classic films in Berry's analysis are typically those made during the Cultural Revolution (1966–76), featuring larger than life characters, clear-cut class struggle, revolutionary stories and ideological propaganda. Hao Dali in *24 City* partially resonates with such a character type, but Jia discloses her hidden side by situating her in a doorway and slowly panning across the interior space that still has furniture and domestic decorations of a typical socialist style. She is alone, in bad health, poor and still mentally living in the socialist heyday. The sequences produce a sense of nostalgia through the outdated domestic furniture and the way Hao's face lights up when recalling her days of being a privileged model worker in the socialist era. It is a period that 'has conveniently come to signify values and ideals that are putatively absent today – idealism, egalitarianism, self-sacrifice, and innocence' (Lu 2007a: 131). In an examination of China's socialist era (1949–78), represented in cultural products in the post-socialist (1978–present) era, both Jason McGrath and Sheldon

Lu perceive that they convey a 'reflective' type of nostalgia rather than a 'restorative' type in the context of China (Lu 2007a; McGrath 2008). The filmic representation of the socialist past and the characters' recalling of or 'longing for' the period 'dwells on the ambivalences of human longing and belonging and does not shy away from the contradictions of modernity' (cited in Lu 2007a: 132). This group of people, now in their fifties or sixties, cannot integrate their past experience with the emerging new reality. For example, Hao Dali still dresses in a plain and socialist style, wearing no make-up and with her hair carefully tied up. Yet when she waits for someone in an office, realising that the girl sitting in the opposite seat is wearing make-up, she questions:

> Hao: You're allowed to put make-up at work nowadays?
> Girl: Yes, of course. If working in a company with foreign investments, you have to wear make-up. Otherwise, you are violating the office etiquette.
> Hao: Foreign company? Isn't this a state-owned company?

The girl then silently takes out a tissue and cleans her lipstick. Dress codes at work and office etiquette have changed over time, but Hao Dali still sticks to the old conventions. Hao's paranoid insistence on the socialist conventions shows how the affinity of memory and space varied from a city to a factory or even an office. Such place-based behaviour codes and heritage are often marketed as nostalgia (Pratt and Juan 2014: 116). In the context of contemporary China, 'it is a nostalgia of the past as duration rather than as a simple, quickly recognised snapshot', and reflects the 'multiple temporal frames of reference that actually coexist at any particular historical moment' (McGrath 2008: 152). The starkly contrasting situations that confront Hao before and after the reform era are displayed through her solitude in domestic space and her conflicts with the new generation. When the camera pans slowly over Hao's home interior, a melancholy tone and a strong sense of nostalgia arise. The fixed and slow motion of the camera invites viewers to reflect and recall the socialist history, and at the same time to ponder the present with a critical view on socialist and post-socialist history, personal memories and the future.

The transition from the socialist utopia's space of production to a post-socialist space of consumption illustrates the power and ideological reorientation in mainland China in the reform era. As the discourse of urbanisation and modernisation in the reform era are the '"dominating" spaces of regulatory and "ruly" discourse, these mental spaces, are thus the representations of power and ideology, of control and surveillance' (Soja 1996: 67). When state-owned working units transformed into self-dependent enterprises, they functioned no longer as units that shouldered the responsibilities of supplying employees and their families with schooling, work, housing and medical care. Rather, they became highly commercially oriented and provided only professional positions. Nowadays, divesting themselves of redundant employees and maximising each employee's value became common practice, and hiring cheaper labour and introducing more advanced machines became essential for a self-reliant company. Hence, the pressing contradiction between the demand for a cheap labour force in a modern market economy and the political limitations of population mobility stimulated the state to revise the household registration system (*hukou*) to facilitate economic development. The 1980s and 1990s saw a gradual relaxation in the rules governing population mobility, and a large portion of the rural population moved to towns and cities, becoming the major labour force in the socialist market.

Though the classifications of agricultural to non-agricultural status still persist in contemporary China, the *hukou* system has been undergoing constant amendments along with the changing economic and social landscape. For instance, significant progress has been made towards eliminating the gap between agricultural and non-agricultural *hukou*; the central state has 'abolished the *hukou* requirement in its hiring of new civil servants; presumably the positions are now open to all citizens, including rural residents, regardless of *hukou* status' in recent years (Wing Chan and Buckingham 2008: 601). The invisible wall has been 'lowered and the gates are opened more and wider. But to many, the dividing wall remains, so do the gates and locks' (Chan and Zhang 1999: 848).

According to *24 City*, as urban *hukou* holders, all workers from Factory 420 were granted state welfare benefits. Moreover, the thriving factory provided more material bonuses in its heyday than an urban *hukou* in the pre-reform era. Interviewees, including Hao Dali, Hou Lijun and Gu Minhua (Joan Chen), were the privileged ones in the previous era whose lives were fundamentally influenced by the peaks and troughs of the *danwei* in the reform era. They do not have to struggle with the barrier created by the 'invisible wall', but they do lose their advantages and the pride that comes with their urban status, especially after they are dismissed. They have to compete with an influx of agricultural people coming to the urban area for employment opportunities. In Hou Lijun's case, she encounters great difficulties finding a new job after being laid off. She has been an itinerant vendor, tailor and peddler. Some of them, like Hao Dali, still live in their allocated dormitory. The dormitory buildings are usually four or five stories high, with a dark grey façade and uniform in style. Such plain buildings can be found all across cities at different scales, from megacities like Beijing and Shanghai to small towns located deep in the remote hinterland. They are homogeneous socialist structures, representing the idealism of equality and uniformity. They reduce the individual workers to the role of a cog in the machine of national industrialisation and modernisation. Therefore, cinematic Chengdu is configured as a site dominantly shaped by national policies and political choices of the state at different historical periods. When studying the *Battleship Potemkin* (Sergei Eisenstein, 1925), Seremetakis concludes that the cinema screen not only enables audiences to see the protagonists and events, but '(through eidetic reduction) to "see" the idea of the unity of the revolutionary people, the collective sovereignty of the masses, the idea of international solidarity, the idea of revolution itself' (1996: 52). Hence, as Seremetakis continues, 'if the Soviet screen provided a prosthetic experience of collective power, the Hollywood screen provided a prosthetic experience of collective desire' (1996: 53). Here, Cinematic Chengdu provides a 'prosthetic experience' of a collective sense of loss and disillusion.

The first generation, as presented by Jia, includes He Xikun's master, Guan Fengjiu and Hao Dali, who were among those who established Factory 420 in the 1950s. Despite years of living in Chengdu, they still distinguish themselves from the local Chengdu by speaking their own dialect and retaining their home town cultural practices. Even the second generation, represented by Gu Minhua (nickname Xiao Hua, played by Joan Chen), Hou Lijun and Song Weidong, still hold firm to their respective customs. For example, Gu Minhua manages a Yue opera club that enables her and her friends to practice and perform the popular art form that originates in Yangtze River delta. Gu was born and brought up in Shanghai where the Yue opera is appreciated and well-received. This remaining cultural practice singles out Gu, as Chengdu has its own traditional Sichuan opera. People like Gu are floating between the local and the outsider. Like a drifter, her life trajectory has been a journey that is 'against the functionalist's idea of standardisation and rationalism' (Jorn 1996: 51). The third generation, born and brought up during the transitional period when the state-owned factory starts to decline, seek opportunities outside the all-inclusive space and assimilate into the city. They become buyers or journalists, and lead a totally different life from their parents. Due to globalisation, Chengdu has been transformed into a pluralist modern city that encourages difference and creativity. Uniformity and collectivism advocated in the socialist era have been discarded by the young generation. The factory is relocated to a nearby town, and workers in the newly built factory are recruited from across China. Chengdu, like other major cities of China, has become spaces dominated by commercialism and consumption.

Perceiving Chengdu as home town

The opening sequences of *24 City* show Chengdu in a depressing and grimy tone. It is neither modern nor primitive; rather, it appears as an in-between state that resonates with the current situation of Factory 420, which has lost its economic and political advantages along with the bygone planned economy. At the end of the film, Su Na (Zhao Tao) stands on the Panda TV Tower looking down at the city, which appears as a highly modernised urban area emerging from a haze. This is followed by a contemporary poem by Wan Xia:

> Chengdu even your faded face could brighten my whole life.
> [*Chengdu, jin ni xiaoshi de yimian, yi zuyi rang wo rongyao yisheng*]

It is both a summary and a retrospective of the interviews in which different generations' memories sit alongside the ongoing projects of demolition and construction, personal suffering and national policies, lingering with delusion, sorrow and more importantly, hope and pride.

Looking down at a city from up high is like reading the city as a text lying before one's eyes. Michel de Certeau describes 'looking down like a god' when he stands on the summit of the World Trade Centre, casting a 'solar Eye' towards New York City (Certeau 1984: 92). In *24 City*, Su Na takes the same perspective in observing Chengdu. She is a representative of Factory 420's third generation, who escapes from the confined space of the state-owned factory and expands her walking terrain far beyond the small realm. In the final scene, there is no trace of Factory 420 and only a panoramic view of Chengdu stretching to the horizon. It is a concrete forest, identical to Certeau's New York, where urbanisation as a compelling force overthrows the past and the present, forever looking at the future, while for the walkers who are taking an eye-level view of the city, it turns into a subject understood and appreciated through personal preference, memory and association. Walking in the city is not merely a physical action in a concrete space; rather, it 'acts out' the place spatially and links different positions together with 'pragmatic contracts', for the reason that one's acting out of space is characterised as 'present', 'discrete' and 'phatic', the person could enunciate various kinds of relations to particular spaces (Certeau 1984: 98). The two distinct manners of using space or 'acting out' concrete spaces can be seen in *24 City*.

In the film the use of space carries explicit generational characteristics that indicate different ideological and value systems. In other words, the space materialises the 'mode of existence of social relationships', as 'the social relations of production have a social existence to the extent that they had a spatial existence; they project themselves into a space, becoming inscribed there, and in the process producing the space itself' (cited in Soja 1996: 46). In *24 City*, the first generation is summoned by national policy to migrate to Chengdu. They value collectivism and the state's interests come before the individual's, and 'when they had chosen to work in the system, it was often a very idealistic choice, a very pure and human choice, because they wanted to change China, to remake the human being, to bring individuals happiness' (cited in Pratt and Juan 2014: 123). They are more conservative, cautious and passive in mobility than the third generation represented by Su Na and Zhao Gang (Zhao Gang), who, on the contrary, tend to be more open, self-centred and positive than their parents' generation. Su Na is a private buyer travelling between Hong Kong and Chengdu to purchase goods for her rich clients. The travelling experience exposes her to different cultures, people and business opportunities. For example, she is invited by a Malaysian friend to manage a luxury restaurant on the Chengdu Panda TV Tower, despite knowing little about running a restaurant. Zhao Gang was disillusioned by his apprenticeship experience in a similar state-owned factory in Jilin Province in north-eastern China during college, and now he works at Chengdu TV as a news reporter. When he started an internship in the 1990s, the uniform started to lose its 'magic' in the eyes of the younger generation. Zhao's parents view the uniform as a symbol of belonging to a well-established state-owned enterprise, a respectable social status and stable career, but for Zhao Gang, the uniform symbolises a lack of subjectivity and creativity.

Individualism has influenced the understanding of the dialectic relationship between state and individual, collectivism and self-value. Su Na weeps that the uniform makes her mother unrecognisable in a crowd of workers in the same grey-blue overalls. Zhao Gang equates the uniform to a boring and formulaic life. Both of them are descendants of the working class; however, compared with their parents who have been constrained within the all-inclusive factory, they are free to appropriate a much larger terrain, which can be out of Chengdu, maybe out of China. When Su Na stands at the summit of the TV Tower, director Jia puts her 'into distance' from the factory and from the city (Figure 4.5). This view 'transforms the bewitching world by which one was possessed into a text that lies before one's eyes. It allows one to read it' (Certeau 1984: 92). The city appears as 'a wave of verticals' amidst grey fog, stretching in front of both Su Na's and our eyes (Certeau 1984: 91). As the camera pans slowly to the left, the city unfolds like a landscape scroll, revealing itself inch by inch in front of Su Na and us, with sounds of bustling traffic and fragmented spatial appearance. The complexity and opaqueness of Chengdu is rendered

Figure 4.5 Panoramic view of Chengdu: in *24 City*

as a 'transparent text' in spite of the fog, in which districts, streets, and individual architecture stand out in planned areas with certain designated functions. The young generation, represented by Su Na and Zhao Gang, appear to have the confidence to understand and appropriate the different functional areas of the city.

24 City frames the two interviewees outside the factory, with Su Na in a variety of venues, such as a moving car, a field, a rundown classroom and on the top of the TV Tower, and Zhang Gang in a well-decorated anonymous location. Their career paths and daily routines connect more to the city than to the factory alone. Interviews with the first and second generations are juxtaposed with ruins and abandoned rooms with utilitarian half-green and half-whitewashed walls. Such walls are commonly seen in public spaces such as hospitals, schools, and government offices in socialist and post-socialist China. They are present in most of Jia's films, such as in *Still Life* (2006) and the home town trilogy. Dilapidated rooms with half-green walls are 'related to the director's own childhood memories of looking at green walls and connecting them with the idea of 'the system'. Thus, the green wall . . . is at once a personal memory and a collective memory' (Mello 2015: 145). Such personal and collective memories of green walls and uniforms belong to the generations before Su Na and Zhao Gang. Socialist spaces with the greenish tinge are disappearing, yet the bright glamourous modern structures have not entirely claimed the space. The two things stand for uniformity, exclusiveness and a recognition of the state's power and order. Yet such ideological consensus has disappeared in Su Na and Zhang Gang's perspectives.

Both Su and Zhao are able to choose a job they desire, live in a city that feels like home, and purchase an apartment in the city for themselves and their parents. They identify with the city Chengdu, not merely with Factory 420 as their parents do, for power of capital emancipates them from the confined small world created by the state-owned company. Their home (*guxiang*) is urban Chengdu, while for their parents, it is the Factory that makes them feel at home. Their parents' 'structure of feeling', the 'particular quality of social experience and relationship, historically distant from other particular qualities, which gives the sense of a generation or of a period' (Williams 1977: 131), has been formulated and nurtured by the factory. The first generation is uprooted from their home town and relocated to Chengdu; thus, the north-east home town dialect and home town flavour become their home. They have a more complicated 'structure of feeling' towards Chengdu, for home is 'more than a physical location' (Wu 2011: 16). Those in the second generation who have gone through the company's transition from military to household appliances production and unemployment are stuck in 'a sense of forever being in transition' and this 'involves a nostalgic longing for home, which in this case is a community of space and time' (p. 16). For the third generation represented by Su Na and Zhao Gang, they can either speak standard Mandarin or Chengdu dialect, and both have long discarded their sense of attachment to the home that lingers in their parents or grandparents' dreams. Instead, they have found their 'structure of feeling' in Chengdu and identified it as home.

Disconnection between the present and the past

24 City employs a series of old songs and film clips to create a socialist ambience and engage spectators with past space and time. Some songs and films become intertextual references to the characters' situations. As Cui reminds us, 'soundtracks work in conjunction with the visual realm to create a multifaceted aura that exemplifies not only a social-historical moment but also the trajectory of popular culture itself'

(Cui 2006: 118). Hao Dali keeps an attentive eye on a film about the Korean War, *Power Fighter in Vast Sky* [*Changkong xiongying*] (Wang Feng and Wang Yabiao, 1976), while having dinner alone at home. Gu Minhua watches *Little Flower* [*Xiaohua*] (Zhang Zheng and Huang Jianzhong, 1979) at the end of her interview. She has the nickname Xiaohua, identical with the female lead in the feature, due to her attractive appearance. In fact, Joan Chen is cast in both roles – Xiaohua in the eponymous film and Gu Minhua in *24 City*. But the young and passionate Xiaohua in *Little Flower*, made over two decades earlier, has aged and become frustrated in *24 City* by her impulsive choice of moving from Shanghai to Chengdu. For Gu Minhua, she recalls her bittersweet working and dating experiences in Factory 420, and her current situation is as wretched as that of Factory 420. Song Weidong's narration is accompanied by the theme music of a Japanese soap opera *Red Suspicion* [Japanese: *Akai giwaku*, Chinese: *Xue Yi*] (Segawa Masaharu, 1975) and Zhao Gang's youthful curiosity towards the outside world is illustrated through the pop song 'The World Outside' (1987) by Chyi Chin, a Taiwanese singer. The army bugle sound in the opening sequences has been a daily routine for the militarily managed factory and community; so has the man who rides a bicycle, holding a flashlight and conducting security checks every day. With advanced construction technology, the physical space of Factory 420 can quickly be demolished and will soon be replaced by luxury high-rise offices and an apartment complex. However, by making a documentary, and even pushing the boundary between documentary and fictional representation, Jia achieves his goal of authentically recording and reflecting a disappearing space and its users. The film records and represents these former workers' language (dialects), their homes and their current living conditions. As a marginalised and ageing group, their voices and images can hardly be heard and seen on screen. *24 City* provides a space for this silenced group and their subjectivity, identity, memory and disappearance.

Pop music, films and factory memos are carefully orchestrated into the narrative to proliferate the sense of reality. In Jia Zhangke's previous films:

> the media, particularly television news coverage, deliver the world into the living rooms of local Chinese. Yet access to and reception of the world news do not create engagement with the world: the gap between the world news and the local audience in terms of image and sound indicates the disconnection between the global and the local. (Cui 2006: 123)

However, news coverage on national and international current affairs are excluded from *24 City*; the only news broadcast in the film is related to the rising of the real estate named 24 City – a modern entertainment and residence complex – reported by Zhao Gang. All the music, films and news coverage and factory memos constitute the history of the factory; more importantly, all of them have been ascribed to individuals' memories and experiences. Together, the familiar spaces they use and consume form these characters' 'cognitive maps' that describe the 'mental images of space that . . . [they] carry with [them in their] daily lives' (Soja 1996: 79). *24 City* produces a space that preserves a detailed and micro history enriched by personal memories and sense of nostalgia.

Time passes slowly in the film, and at times it comes to stagnancy. Interviews are interrupted by still photographs and intermittent blackouts. Men and women, aged and young, are screened in photo poses (Figure 4.6). They are not identified by name nor do they fit into the narrative with or without uniforms; they represent 'the independence, individuality and subjectivity . . . they are seen as self-contained, free from the delimiting screen time that controls the audience's viewing experience, and from the clock time that regulates workers' cycle of life' (Deppman 2014: 201). The photos secure a cinematic space for those anonymous people, whose stories cannot be included in the film. They are the silent majority, whose experiences and voices can hardly be heard through mainstream media. However, it is their stories that structure an alternative history of the special time and space. By documenting ordinary workers' individual stories and orchestrating collective memories through fictional characters, Jia 'depoliticises and humanises socialism, and brings down grand ideologies to the level of the lives of ordinary people. It is the everyday, the quotidian, that structures the existence and aspirations of hundreds of millions of Chinese citizens in decades of socialist nation building' (Lu 2007a: 133). This film captures and preserves a memory for them, and adds a minor discourse to the grand history of reformation since the 1980s.

The generational gap in using the industrial space and the urban space in *24 City* illustrates that there is more than one city called Chengdu. As Iain Chambers concludes:

> the city exists as a series of doubles; it has official and hidden cultures; it is a real place and a site of imagination. Its elaborate network of streets, housing, public buildings, transport systems, parks, and shops is paralleled by a complex of attitudes, habits, customs, expectancies, and hopes that reside in us as urban subjects. We discover that urban 'reality' is not single but multiple, that inside the city there is always another city. (Cited in Soja 1996: 186)

Figure 4.6 Still photographs of anonymous people: in *24 City*

SPACES OF CONSUMPTION REPLACE SPACES OF PRODUCTION 117

As *24 City* has shown, the state-owned enterprise Factory 420 is the 'another city' inside Chengdu that represents the disappearing socialist space, and it was juxtaposed with a pre-modern Chengdu but is now disappearing in an increasingly metropolitan commercialised Chengdu. Correspondingly, the old generation who used to remain enclosed in the socialist space have declined in social status and are left disillusioned or impoverished. Meanwhile, the younger generation (grown up in the reform era), as urban subjects, have developed a complex of different attitudes, habits, expectancies and relationships with Chengdu. The feature *24 City* configures several different Chengdus for spectators to contextualise and decode the historical, economic and political reasons that dominate the transforming urban spaces of the city, and the changing geo-psychological landscape of the residents of the city.

CHAPTER 5

Natural Disaster and Trauma

The 2008 Wenchuan earthquake, which has become the watershed in cinematic representations of the area, creates a traumatic space (literally and metaphorically) to reflect the loss of life, home and community. Li Yu's 2011 feature *Buddha Mountain* juxtaposes this disaster with the disintegration of traditional family units and the consequent psychological vacuum in contemporary Chinese families in urban spaces. The ruins wrought by the Wenchuan earthquake symbolise the interior wasteland inhabited by film characters. Cinematic characters are shown as drifters, driven from place to place because of the trend of demolition and construction, and impacted by accidents, mobility and imposed spatial oppression associated with the unrestful urban space. The physical features of nature, the built environment and objects used by film characters are highly metaphorical, as they are often associated with psychological and emotional influences rather than their practical use.

Buddha Mountain tracks the urban *dérive* (drifting) of three disillusioned youths and a traumatised middle-aged woman and their attempts to reconcile with family and themselves. By drifting in the city to explore the urban space, the three young people are set against the imposing utility and function of urban spaces and social relations. The term *dérive* was perceived by the Situationist International (SI), founded in 1957, as an effective spatial practice that investigated the relation between urban spaces and mental space. Deeply influenced by avant-garde movements such as Dadaism and surrealism in the initial years of its foundation, the SI criticised the stifling functionalism and utilitarianism of the post-war urban space, and turned to the mental and psychological effects encapsulated in the urban spaces:

> as seen especially in the autocratic housing schemes built around Paris and other cities, which they felt curbed the individual's creative capacities. Against the oppressive living conditions imposed through such technocratic city plans, the SI sought to develop new forms of collective action and methods of agitation that would promote a free use and transformation of the urban environment. (Andreotti 1996: 7)

Functionalists hold the idea of standardisation and rationalism, believing that ideal and definitive forms of the different objects useful to people are possible. For them, spaces such as Haussmann's Paris were full of 'sound and fury' and concerned initially with allowing the rapid circulation of military troops and 'the use of artillery against insurrections', and the later post-war Paris developed to ensure an open space for the circulation of the increasing number of private automobiles (Debord 1996a: 18). The idea of utilitarianism conducted in the urban spaces in history – as shown in the above two examples – ensured the efficiency and operation of the modern city designed and developed under the discourse of rationalism and progress. However, the functionalists neglect the psychological effect of surroundings. The physical features of buildings and the appearance of objects that are used have a psychological and emotional influence that may have nothing to do their practical use (Jorn 1996: 51). By drifting in the city to explore the urban space, the drifters are set against the imposing utility and function.

As one of the exploratory modes of spatial practice and urban expression, the concept and practice of *dérive* is closely related to voyages of discovery and the acquiring of geographical knowledge. Furthermore, it is resistant to the power structures imposed by the definitive functionalist ideas of architecture and urbanism, celebrating the intangible but significant psychogeographical effect exerted by the physical space. The means of *dérive* and *détournement* (rerouting, hijacking) as manifestations of psychogeography, therefore, are strategies that can be deployed to critique and resist the rise of privatisation, commercialism and the decreasing pedestrian-friendly spaces in cities. Though the SI disbanded in 1972, the conception and practices of psychogeography have continued to reverberate in scholarship, urban planning and artistic fields, as it not only provides a form of spatial practice that aims at exploring the urban space, but also outlines 'a revolutionary project for overturning dominant social and spatial structures' (Pinder 2005a: 388).

The drifter's exploration of ambience and construction of situations is played out as a refusal of the 'categories and rhythms of capitalist urban life and its demands for discipline and utility as determined by structures of work' (Pinder 2005b: 150). The *dérive* is a strategy for drifters to undermine the fixed categories of work and leisure, or public and private, to fight against the 'city governed by principles of utility and efficient circulation' (p. 151), in other words, drifters' spatial practice aims at constructing a realm of freedom undergoing permanent transformation instead of a fixed and static space.

Buddha Mountain displays a chaotic and traumatic urban space where the young characters are confronted with broken families and their consequent exile experience in the city. Neither schools nor families provide young characters with a stable life or prospective future. Having failed the college entrance examination and suffered from family issues, Nan Feng (Fan Bingbing), Ding Bo (Chen Bolin) and Feizao (Fei Long) escape from their respective families and settle down in a small dilapidated room, undertaking some casual jobs and leading a seemingly freewheeling life in the city. They become drifters in the urban space. They work in a pub at the beginning of the film, but soon they are dismissed because of a violent incident caused by Nan Feng. The film then chases after the three strolling in the streets in Chengdu and wandering along crisscrossed railway lines and in the nearby mountains. Consciously or unconsciously, they escape from the urban space time after time, wandering around Buddha Mountain, sneaking into train carriages, and letting the train take them to unknown places. Their *dérive* 'entails [a] playful-constructive behaviour' (Debord 1996b: 22), namely, escaping from the urban space to nature becomes their strategy to undermine the anxiety and control imposed by their broken families and the fast-transforming modern city. After they are driven out of their previous room due to impending demolition, they rent Chang's apartment and start to share the domestic space with Chang, whom they believe to be highly irritated, sensitive and defensive. Meanwhile, Chang Yueqin (Zhang Aijia), who lost her son in a car crash a year ago, confines herself at home, struggling to adapt to the domestic space without her only son. The intertwined narration of Chang's traumatic experience, the youths' 'intrusion' into her domestic space and the growing bond between them composes a psychogeographical reflection of the imposed rules and structures of urban spaces, more importantly, shows how ordinary urbanites tactically handle the mobility and instability in the modern city.

Buddha Mountain opens with a long take showing Nan Feng putting on make-up in a narrow fitting room. With strong beat music and a poster of Elvis Presley, the most influential pop icon of the twentieth century, attached to the door, the opening sequences are imbued with a restless and disaffected atmosphere. Nan Feng is a singer in a nightclub where Ding Bo and Feizao work as bartenders. One night, microphone in hand, Nan Feng passionately sings and dances on the stage. Suddenly, the microphone somehow swings out of her hand and hits a male customer. The man seems badly hurt. He stumbles towards Nan Feng, cursing and screaming with pain, and threatening that there will be consequences. The tension is increased when Ding Bo rushes into the scene, breaking beer bottles and bluffing, making the situation more chaotic. Immediately after the disorder, the three sit down calmly, drinking beer and making fun of the accident and the injured man. Such a composed manner in facing the disturbingly violent event indicates their sophistication in dealing with instability and insecurity in the urban space. The opening sequences establish an urban space that is never static or fixed, but filled with instability, multiplicity, hybridity and contingencies (Soja 1996: 113). The youths' reaction to the 'never static or fixed' situation shows that they are psychologically well-equipped to handle such chaos. The urban space at first appears as a playground where they can dress up and sing, but it can suddenly transform into relentless jungle where accidents are common and the weak are bullied. Home, as the fixed image (space) of private security or refuge, however, is absent from the narration.

Buddha Mountain: Nature, a Railway Station and Religious Redemption

The name of the film refers to two specific spaces: a railway station and a mountain near Chengdu. As a railway station, it conjures up encounters and farewells; metaphorically, it is a station of life that brings people at different life stages together and enables them to encounter love, affection and to rediscover their lost selves (Ni 2011). Nevertheless, railway stations and trains usually function as a transitional, temporal space associated with impermanence and instability. The contrasting emotional and psychological meanings attached to railway stations and trains are represented and explored fully in the film, with the three youths frequently shown in a train thundering through urban and rural spaces. Parents and spiritual models (such as Feizao's idol Michael Jackson) in the film are either traumatised or dead. As a result, the youths find nowhere home, but rather exile themselves in the city and nature for consolation.

With its lush, green, natural location, Buddha Mountain provides a sense of serenity in contrast to the bustling urban space. For the youths, it is a sanctuary that allows them to escape from urban routines and anxiety, while for Chang Yueqin, it offers the potential opportunity for reconciling with herself. During one of their trips to Buddha Mountain, they stop at a ruined area that was destroyed by the 2008 Wenchuan earthquake (Figure 5.1). The images of destroyed blocks are crosscut with scenes of violent shaking, people screaming, collapsing buildings and injured people during the devastating earthquake. After arriving at the mountain, they find that the Buddha Temple and the statues of Buddha have also been destroyed in the earthquake. Human built spaces have become ruins but the mountain itself is still in good shape and still provides beautiful views and comfort for visitors. Nature here provides a sanctuary space that is healing, comforting and lasting. In contrast to the railway station, it stands for permanence and

Figure 5.1 The earthquake-affected area: in *Buddha Mountain*

stability, which are rare in the transient modern world but desired by the characters in *Buddha Mountain*.

In their last trip to the mountain, Chang makes a donation and devotes herself to rebuild the Buddha Temple with the youths and monks. She also becomes involved in painting the religious statues. To rebuild the temple and re-establish the statues of Buddha that were destroyed in the earthquake symbolises the re-establishment of faith in the ruined and transient world (Chen 2011; Tu 2011). The mountain and the temple act as a space empowered by healing effects that enable the youths to reflect on faith and relationships and escape from family issues and financial straits. Meanwhile, they are also spaces for Chang to converse with a monk about life and death, and to quest for the ultimate meaning of existence and suffering in the profane world. The destroyed temple and statues can be rebuilt within a short time, but Chang is unable to re-establish her shattered faith in life, nor can the religious conversation about life and death with the monk stop her from self-blame and depression. Accident and broken family are like a black hole that devours her maternal bond and social relations. Even though the religious sanctuary is supposed to provide consolation or spiritual comfort for characters stuck in broken and dysfunctional families,

Chang chooses to end her life on the mountain in order to be reconciled with herself. The earthquake rubble and collapsed Buddhas on the mountain represent unpleasant reality for Sichuan, and underline the heightened need for home and for national peace and harmony. The train station, the mountain and the temple symbolise the journey that must be taken to search for faith and the loss of it.

Dysfunctional and broken families in the urban landscape

Buddha Mountain displays four dysfunctional families in a transforming urban space. Family, as the basic fabric of society, has played an important role in maintaining a stable and harmonious social order. In both the occidental world and the oriental world, home has been recognised as 'a site of resistance' (Soja 1996: 103), as it is a space for assuring and defending one's identity, and for resisting oppression and discrimination imposed by the outside world. In contemporary China, Confucianism continues to reverberate in the ideals and conduct of Chinese families. Ideals such as filial piety, parental responsibility, loyalty, cohesion and harmony are valued and promoted; all help to form a communitarian and inclusive space (Teo 2013: 174–5). However, with the intrusion of modernisation and urbanisation, such values become increasingly challenged and questioned. In *Buddha Mountain*, Chang's family is destroyed by a car accident, and the three youths are also confronted with collapsing families.

Chang lived alone before the three young people moved in. She is a former Peking Opera performer. She still keeps her deceased son's residence registration (*hukou* – usually, after a man passes away, his death should be reported to the local police and his residence registration should be removed), psychologically denying the unacceptable reality. She also preserves the wrecked car, with its holes and cracks on the windshield, in the garage and pays regular visits to it. The car space is highly compartmentalised and private. In one sequence, the camera focuses on the broken windshield and Chang sitting in the driver's seat of the car. The myriad of breakages and cracks on the windshield are reflected on Chang's face and upper body, which makes her body seem covered in scars and injuries (Figure 5.2). The holes and breakages on the car materialise the psychological injuries she has suffered from the accident. The car is a secret and private space for her to let out suppressed emotions that she has to hide from others. The modern vehicle in Chang's eyes is associated with danger, accident and death, whilst it was freedom and dynamism for her son and his girlfriend. For the three young tenants, the car, though it is wrecked, is a useful tool to take a mountain trip.

NATURAL DISASTER AND TRAUMA 125

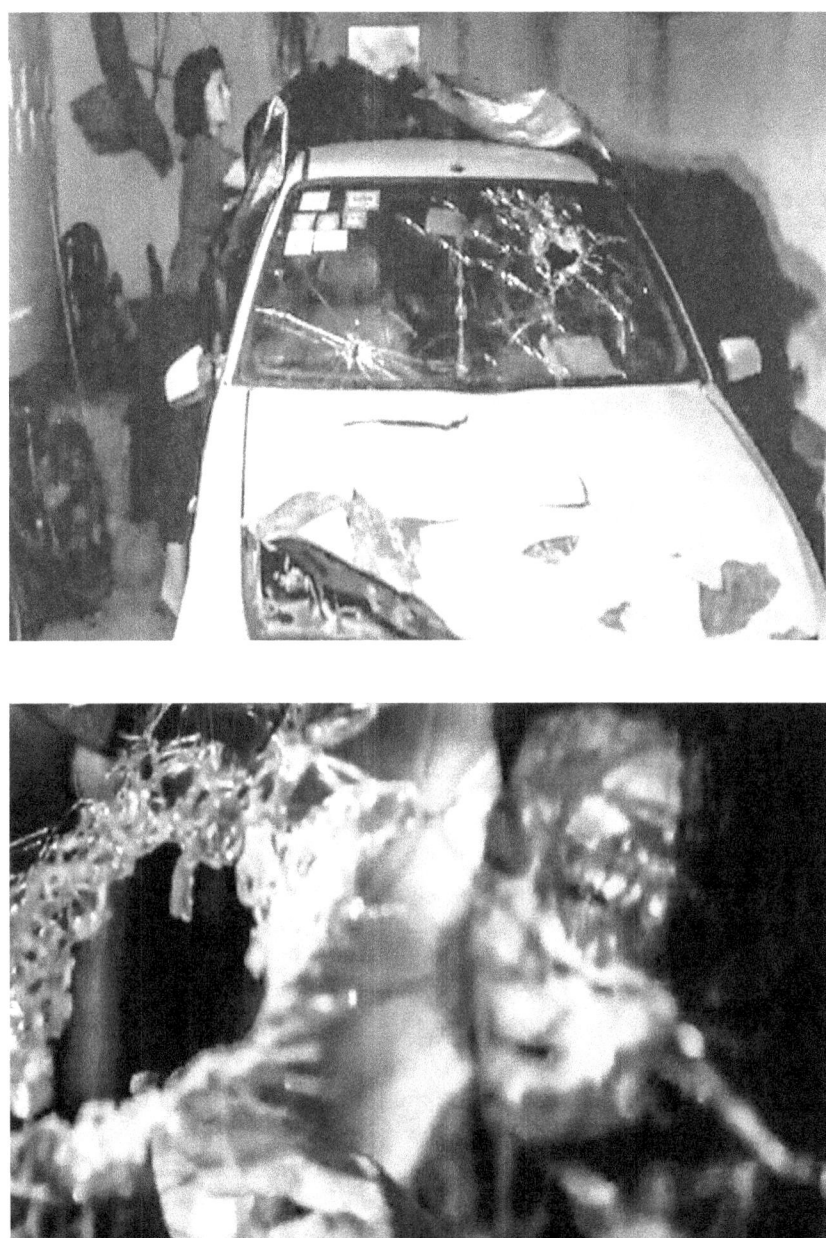

Figure 5.2 The wrecked car in the garage: in *Buddha Mountain*

Chang maintains the habit of practising Peking Opera in the early morning, and calligraphy is also a daily routine. The interior space of her flat looks crowded and packed with furniture and everyday appliances. There are pictures and tapestry on the walls, and newspapers and various kinds of items piled on the table, making the domestic space messy and cramped. She has confined herself within the domestic space since her son's death, and the role of father and husband is absent. It seems that she does not establish alternative circles of friends and contacts, nor 'establish a spatially separate sphere of existence' (Massey 1994: 209). After the three tenants move in, the room looks even more crowded and suffocating. Especially in the first few days, Chang and the three young tenants are in constant conflict due to their different living habits.

Chang's routine opera rehearsal at six o'clock in the morning wakes the youths, who stay up late, hanging out and drinking. The three ridicule Chang's boring and strange routines; they steal her savings to pay for the medical expense of the man who was accidentally hurt by Nan Feng; and they secretly drive Chang's broken car to Buddha Mountain. Nan Feng, coming from a town adjacent to Chengdu, is an independent and tough girl who can single-handedly challenge a group of young gangsters to get Feizao's robbed money back. Her father is an alcoholic and abuser, who eventually drinks himself into hospital. Ding Bo earns a living by transporting goods or passengers with a motorcycle. He blames his mother's death on his father's infidelity and irresponsibility. Their friend Feizao, a huge fan of Michael Jackson, is optimistic but cowardly. He turns to Nan Feng for help after being bullied by gangsters. Feizao's father, a gambler, beats him without cause every time he loses at gambling.

Despite petty conflicts between Chang and the three youths, the apartment offers both sides an opportunity to discover and establish a caring family bond. By saving Chang from suicide and taking care of her, the three come to understand her suffering and agitation. Mutual understanding and affection replace the previous hostility and indifference. They attain a temporary home, comprising a caring mother and three rebellious but self-reliant children. However, this home collapses soon with Chang's death. The sense of transience and impermanence, materialised through the car accident, bar incidents, earthquake and suicide, overwhelms and disturbs the characters in the film. These enemies of permanence and stability find their most brutal battlefield in the urban area that is essentially packed with instability and uncertainty because of the large population, mobility and urbanisation. The final sequences of *Buddha Mountain* capture the three youths sitting in a train carriage sobbing, with the train roaring through a series of tunnels and heading to a destination somewhere in the city. Yet this time the camera no longer gazes in the direction the train is travelling as on their previous upbeat train-rides. Instead, it focuses in the opposite direction, like a forced farewell to the briefly found familial bond and the bright prospect of life engendered from the quasi parent–children relationship. They are again thrown into the outside world without a stable and caring domestic shelter. Not only are the deep rooted traditional Chinese culture and values challenged and breached, but family members are traumatised and finally dead (in Chang Yueqin's case), addicted to alcohol (Nan Feng's father), or addicted to gambling and family abuse (Feizao's father).

Home in *Buddha Mountain* is presented as an example that challenges Ray Chow's view of home as a place of

> refuge from a tyrannical world. Because it functions as a refuge, this inside also tends to take on the import of a timeless, undifferentiated, and infinitely adaptable (interpersonal) time and space whereby conflicts ought to be resolved and opposites ought to be reconciled. (Chow 2007: 19)

Home should be a material space for basic shelter and an 'imagined inside' which could be intensified by sentiment (Chow 2007: 19). In the film, the original homes of the four protagonists are fragile, oppressive and unbearable. Ding Bo argues with his father in each of their meetings; he damages the wedding decorations in the room prepared for his father's upcoming second marriage, and insists on keeping the photo of his deceased mother in the wedding room. Nan Feng persuades her mother to divorce her alcoholic father. Home as a concrete space does not appear in Nan Feng and Feizao's cases. For Nan Feng, the family reunites in a hospital where Nan Feng tries to stop her father from drinking by pouring alcohol into herself in a self-destructive manner. Feizao mentions his chaotic family when chatting with Chang, without any resentment or agony. The only place that they can find peace is Chang's flat, where the four act as a loving mother and rebellious but good-willed children.

Meanwhile, the role of father in *Buddha Mountain* is shown as either absent or disappointing. Ding Bo is verbally and physically aggressive at his father's wedding ceremony; Nan Feng persuades her mother to divorce; Feizao avoids meeting with his father, as he gets beaten up without cause every time he stays home. The father, as the core of Chinese traditional families, is supposed to be the 'absolute authority to preserve order and maintain structure' (Zhou 2007: 63). Besides, the Confucian familial codes such as 'respect seniority' (*zun lao*) and 'filial piety' (*xiao*) require children to be completely obedient to their father. A child's position within the domestic space is low, even his/her marriage should be arranged by the elders of the family. Such ethical and moral requirements require children to be absolutely subordinate to their father on both 'domestic and social levels' (p. 63). Correspondingly, the family in a conventional sense should be the site of integrity and security for its children. However, in *Buddha Mountain*, such conventional family values have been abandoned by characters and their parents. Family as a cohesive sanctuary is in decline. The young generation plunges into the complicated urban space dominated by commercialisation that has been driven by political and capitalist discourses. Young subjects, drifting and seeking for their position and identity in the chaotic urban spaces, find their parents too busy putting their own businesses together to consider their struggles.

Failure of searching for home in an anonymous modern city

Urban Chengdu is presented as an anonymous city opressed by humid, hot and gloomy weather. *Buddha Mountain* traces the drifting of the characters on a restless 'bar street' (the street is lined with nightclubs) where the three work and hang out, a flyover where Ding Bo works as an itinerant transporter, and crisscrossing railways where the three often roam. Although 90 per cent of the scenes are shot in Chengdu (Du 2011), its outstanding landmarks are eliminated, and characters appear in close-ups and medium shots and unstable handheld follow shots. The film language emphasises the characters' emotional and spiritual dimensions. Framing the three characters in the mode of *dérive*, *Buddha Mountain* attends to the psychological and emotional influences of the urban spaces on people. Drifters are not just observant witnesses to the changing cityscapes and urban inhabitants' varied psychological-scapes, but doers who drift around consciously and construct situations to *détour* (tactics of hijacking, rerouting, or diversion), and loosen or transform the imposed rules of social space. Although the film's characters do not voluntarily take actions to loosen or transform the rules imposed by social space, for example, by constructing situations or organising activities to resist the functions or rigidity of certain urban spaces, they express their concerns, desires and expectations in a passive way, by escaping and by rebelling against irresponsible parents and traditional values such as filial piety.

The film foregrounds the emotional space of the characters, which encourages audiences to reflect on the dilemma confronting them, and in addition, questions the imposition of social rules, such as the bond of family and the policy that regulates private and public space. The intrusion of modernity and population mobility provide alternative ways of living for the young generation, who are exiled from family, to survive in a commercialised urban milieu. However, it also disconnects individuals and weakens the familial bond. The one-child policy that has been widely enforced since 1970 begot modern nuclear families in mainland China. Family size began to shrink, and traditional family values were gradually discarded. The basic social unit became quite fragile, vulnerable to accidents and disasters. Moreover, with the intrusion of modernity, notions of individualism and independence intruded into Chinese family space, and rendered the family a more 'dialectical and contested space' (Teo 2013: 174). In *Buddha Mountain*, the dysfunctional families as a universal phenomenon in modern China by no means undercut Chengdu's local imperatives in terms of the hovering melancholy and uncertainty enhanced by the 2008 Wenchuan earthquake. This natural disaster, that brought heavy loss of life and ruined space, corresponds to the film's car crash, which broke the family bond and disturbed domestic space. Psychologically, it is the almighty and unescapable natural force that devours lives, material spaces and affectivity. It traumatises characters' emotional space, and influences their perspective on life and death.

Nation, metaphorically, is seen as the extension of family. There is an old Chinese idiom says that prosperous and thriving circumstances are the result of a harmonious family. However, *Buddha Mountain* depicts four disintegrated families, showing the overall collapse of the most basic social blocks in modern society. Families, cities of various scales and even the country are discarding long-established values, with the intrusion of modernity and globalisation. Either the traumatised (in Chang's case) or the broken (in Ding Bo's case) domestic space, to a certain degree, corresponds with the increasingly divided and fragmented urban spaces shaped by the heavy hand of commercialisation and urbanisation.

Since her success with *Lost in Beijing*, Li Yu has begun to investigate more universal problems confronting the urban population from the perspective of female roles. Whether it is Beijing or Chengdu represented in her films, the stable and slow tempo of life has gone with urbanisation in recent decades. In investigating contemporary Beijing, Li contextualises the tragic story of rape and the baby-trade in a mundane setting where average people are 'boarding trains, selling pop-cultural posters of Mao, a grandmother wiping her grandson's face, pedestrians against the ice and snow', and reflecting a very personal perspective at the citizens of the city (Pugsley 2013: 103–4). In *Buddha Mountain*, it is about people shopping in markets and struggling with the urban management police for their confiscated motorcycles. Compared with more developed metropolitan Beijing, Chengdu's modernisation is much slower due to geographical barriers and economic backwardness. But it is no longer the enclosed world depicted in Li Bai's poem or Li Yu's early film *Dam Street*, in which the 1980s and 1990s saw a relatively estranged and isolated Sichuanese town.

PART IV
CINEMATIC XI'AN

CHAPTER 6

From an Enclosed Traditional Space to a Sprawling Urban Space

Cinematic Xi'an is best illustrated in Huang Jianxin's *Back to Back, Face to Face* (1994) (hereafter, *Back to Back*) and *Signal Left, Turn Right* (1996) (hereafter, *Signal Left*), two representative works from his second urban trilogy. The former captures the coexistence and hybridity of urban and rural conduct and values in an enclosed urban space, while the latter focuses on the centrifugal extension of the urban spaces and the obsolete political conduct in the reform era. Huang acts as a *flâneur* who strolls and observes the transforming urban space of Xi'an in the reform era, and analyses Chinese modernity in the urban space with an icy detachment. In *Back to Back*, Xi'an is depicted within layers of walls and 'guild halls', creating an enclosed space overwhelmed by traditional power structures and rural values, and enclosing its characters in a small space that overlooks them, dwarfs them, and constrains their vision, perspective and behaviour. In *Signal Left*, the urban space moves into the background, and a military-managed driving school located on the outskirt of the city becomes the main setting. The film foregrounds the speeding up of economic development in the inland city and its participation in transnational communication and investment in an increasingly globalised world.

Xi'an and Adjacent Area on Screen

Any consideration of Xi'an, the provincial capital of Shaanxi, in China's film industry and cinematic representation, cannot ignore the Xi'an Film Studio, as one of the principal studios in mainland China. The studio, founded in 1956, was just a 'medium-sized facility' that had a poor record in filmmaking in western China (Thompson 2003: 651) before Wu Tianming, the 'godfather of the Fifth Generation', was appointed as the head. Over a third of the Fifth Generation films were made at Xi'an during the 1980s (p. 650), and most of them represented rural landscapes, ambiguous themes and complex narratives. They became known as Chinese Westerns, which refers to a wider spatial and social terrain by including the cinematic representation of urban space in western China.

Huang Jianxin, who was working in the Studio, diverged from filming the rural landscape and communities, and contributed two urban trilogies that became the most intriguing and distinctive urban representation of western China between the 1980s and 1990s. His first trilogy, comprising *The Black Cannon Incident* (1986), *Dislocation* (1986) and *Samsara* [*Lunhui*] (1988), astutely depicts the conflicts between traditional ideological order and the processes of modernisation during the initial stage of China's reform. Zhang Zhen observes that 'the concrete mantles of the socialist economy and social order stayed mostly intact' despite the ideological reorientation propagating a 'march into the world attitude' in cultural production and popular consciousness' (Zhang 2007: 5). The intact socialist political consciousness and order during the ideological reorientation problematised the values and conduct of ordinary people who were thrown into a market-driven, technological-oriented society characterised by efficiency, speed and diversity. Urban spaces displayed in Huang's first trilogy appear as a 'given condition' that has realised industrialisation and modernisation; this is in contrast to the Urban Generation, who show urbanisation per se as a 'process' (Zhang 2007: 25). As a result, scenes such as the ubiquitous Chinese characters *chai* (lit. tear down, 拆), construction sites, ruins and immigrant workers are rarely represented in Huang's first urban trilogy.

In the 1990s, Huang turned from acute political criticism to urban life in another trilogy: *Stand Straight, Don't Bend Over* [*Zhanzhile, biepaxia*] (1993), *Back to Back, Face to Face* [*beikaobei, Lianduilian*] (1994) and *Signal Left, Turn Right* [*Hongdengting, lüdengxing*] (1996). Characters in the these films appropriate various spaces and walk in the city to establish 'relations among differentiated positions' (Certeau 1984: 97–8), as they locate themselves as observers, interpreters and negotiators with emerging social relations brought by urbanisation and modernisation. If political misconduct represented in the previous urban trilogy overshadows the immediate daily practice in anonymous urban spaces in the reform era, the new urban trilogy creates a 'strong sense of place' (Lai 2007: 218). The second urban trilogy marks Huang's 'self-proclaimed return from foreign-felling cities to genuine Chinese cites and from emphasising alienation to focusing on relationships and communal politics' (Kuoshu 2010: 47). Huang takes an eye-level view to observe the inland city and acutely captures the subtle and trivial daily practices of common people in the urban area. He acts as a *flâneur* who strolls and observes the transforming urban space, and who is 'self-assured in his role as a reflective critic (of his city), a close analyst (of its architecture), an archivist (of events, scenes, and images), interpreter (of impressions into texts), and all-encompassing observer and reader-decipherer' (Lai 2007: 217). Huang rejects emotional and melodramatic narration, rather tending to analyse Chinese modernity 'with an icy detachment that allows little room for sentiment' (Pickowicz 2012: 296). His observation of contemporary urban China stands for an alternative modernity that differentiates it from American and European concepts of modernity, which Pickowicz perceives as the 'post-socialist' reality (p. 296). During the 1980s and 1990s, Huang became one of the few filmmakers who projected attentive observation of the acceleration of industrialisation and urbanisation in major inland cities of China. His second urban trilogy carries more local characteristics of Xi'an, and meanwhile touches upon the conflicts between political conduct and economic development in the reform era.

Another Xi'an-based director is Wang Quan'an, who graduated from the Beijing Film Academy in 1991 and then worked at Xi'an Film Studio. Wang has made several Xi'an-based features. Family drama *The Story of Ermei* [*Jingzhe*] (2004) follows a tripartite structure with the protagonist Ermei travelling from rural home town to a nearby town and finally back to the rural home. In urban feature *Weaving Girl* [*Fangzhi guniang*] (2009), Xi'an is reduced to a state-owned textile plant and a run-down industrial district. Rural epic *White Deer Plain* [*Bailuyuan*] (2012), adapted from the eponymous novel by Chen Zhongshi, who co-authors the film with Wang, features two large families – Bai and Lu – who suffer from social upheavals and moral dilemmas during a restless historical period. The western region in Wang's depiction is characterised by endless wheat terraces, *yaodong* (lit. house cave, a unique type of dwelling space built in the earth which is the most common architectural form for people living on the Loess Plateau in the north-west), and zigzagging routes that divide the yellow earth into patches. Country people often appear superstitious, straightforward, persistent and impoverished. The setting and characterisation have been created and reinforced in a range of internationally acclaimed films including *Yellow Earth* [*Huang Tudi*] (Chen Kaige, 1984), *Old Well* [*Lao Jin*] (Wu Tianming, 1986), *Red Sorghum* [*Hong Gaoliang*] (Zhang Yimou, 1987) and *The Story of Qiu Ju* [*Qiu-Ju daguansi*] (Zhang Yimou, 1992). These filmic images have become stereotypes of the area and the people. Compared to the stereotypical portrayals, Huang Jianxin and Wang Quan'an's cinematic urban Xi'an provides an alternative and Under-represented observation of the region and explores the enduring complex relationship between urban and rural realities.

Apart from the two signature directors' cinematic representations of Xi'an and its adjacent area, there are a number of other films, with varied aesthetic styles and themes, that project the dynamics and stasis of Xi'an.

Gao Xing [*Gaoxing*, literally, means being happy] (Liu Xiaoguang, 2009), a comedy adopted from established local Shaanxi novelist Jia Pingwa's eponymous novel, provides a realistic display of the cityscape and urban life of Xi'an. It adopts the form of the Hollywood musical film, and shows how a group of migrant workers manage to survive and settle down in the city. The city does not look like a modern metropolis in the film, with main settings that include slum-like residential buildings, an abandoned factory and narrow back streets that provide the numerous immigrant workers represented by the protagonists with shelters and entertaining space. The ramshackle space reflects the underprivileged group's harsh living situations and bears witness to the cultural hybridity in an era of frequent social mobility, with characters speaking their home town dialects such as Cantonese, Mandarin and the local language of Shaanxi. Immigrant workers, street swindlers, prostitutes and the isolated elderly inhabit and walk in the city, creating their personal memories in the city's back alleys, plain streets and rundown residential buildings constructed during the 1970s and 1980s, showing a vernacular, subaltern but upbeat image of the city.

Designed as the national capital for thirteen dynasties in ancient China, Xi'an is readily recognisable in cinema with its abundant historical locations and cultural heritage. *Xi'an Incident* [*Xi'an shibian*] (Cheng Yin, 1981) focuses on the most important political and military turning point of China's Anti-Japanese War, which happened in Xi'an in 1936. The film settings switch between cities such as Nanjing (the capital of the Republic of China ruled by the Nationalist Party), Yanan (the revolutionary base of the Communist Party) and Xi'an (where the incident happened) with the main characters' shifting military and political purposes. Historical sites such as the Giant Wild Goose Pagoda, Drum Tower, Bell Tower, the City Wall and Mausoleum Site of the Emperor Qin Shihuang are briefly displayed. In the film, the ancient capital city is surrounded by the tremendous city wall that divides the rural space from the urban space, the site of political power and the site of students' demonstration. The historical fantasy *A Terracotta Warrior* [*Gujin dazhan qinyongqing*] (Chen Xiaodong, 1989) features Zhang Yimou, the most internationally established Chinese director and actor of the Fifth Generation, as Meng Tianfang, the general of Emperor Qin Shihuang (221–210 BC, the founder of the Qin dynasty and the first emperor of a unified China), and shows how he becomes immortal and able to travel in time to the 1930s and 1970s in mainland China. In the film, Xi'an is projected as a historical space of abundant archaeological discoveries and a space of power under the Qin Shihuang's brutal rule. Meanwhile, modern Xi'an is reduced to a space displaying the Terracotta Warriors that has turned into a tourist destination for foreign visitors.

In more recent cinematic representations, such as the family drama *The Marriage Certificate* [*Shui shuo wo buzaihu*] (Huang Jianxin, 2001) and *Einstein and Einstein* [*Gou Shisan*] (Cao Baoping, 2013), Xi'an appears as an anonymous urban space that contains modern middle-class families confronted with issues of family relationships and single parenting. *The Marriage Certificate* features a middle-class couple who are awarded a prize of 'model couple' but cannot find their marriage certificate to claim the prize. The missing certificate then triggers constant arguments between the couple, which turn the domestic space into a battlefield and threaten the model couple's marriage. The opening sequences of the film display a panoramic view of a modern city, accompanied by a teenage girl's narration: 'I grow up in China, and my home is located in a famous city of northern China'. Panning over the city, the camera reveals the skyline of a modern city defined by stylish high rises and construction cranes. Finally, the camera freezes at a well-lit square located in the foreground of the scene. Even though the city is not specified as Xi'an, scenes of the landmarks of the city such as the historical Bell Tower provide clues as to its identity. Similarly, in the coming-of-age film *Einstein and Einstein*, Xi'an appears as a featureless city where the sensitive teenage girl Li Wan (Zhang Xueying) resists invisible rules and conventions imposed by family, school and society, but finally learns to compromise with hypocrisy, lies and contradictions in reality. Family education and single-parenting issues became fiercely discussed after the film's public release in 2018. Xi'an, as the setting of the film, appears just like the conservative father: traditional, silent and stubborn.

Back to Back, Face to Face: The *Flâneur* Walking in an Enclosed Space

The concept of the *flâneur* originated in nineteenth-century Paris, where strolling around the city streets was perceived as a way to observe the rapid and unprecedented urbanisation. Charles Baudelaire's essay 'The Painter of Modern Life' gives the most original and comprehensive portrait of the *flâneur*:

> The crowd is his element, as the air is that of birds and water of fishes. His passion and his profession are to become one flesh with the crowd. For the perfect *flâneur*, for the passionate spectator, it is an immense joy to set up house in the heart of the multitude, amid the ebb and flow of movement, in the midst of the fugitive and the infinite. To be away from home and yet to feel oneself everywhere at home; to see the world, to be at the centre of the world, and yet to remain hidden from the world – such are a few of the slightest pleasures of those independent, passionate, impartial natures which the tongue can but clumsily define. (1978: 9)

Baudelaire perceived the *flâneur* as an enthusiastic observer of urban life. He was observant and acute in inferring attributes such as the class, character and profession of passers-by. The *flâneur* was an urbanite who read the city consciously to decode its mythical meanings. Similarly, the Parisian *flâneur* configured by Benjamin in the nineteenth century was also 'the passionate spectator, [and for him], it is an immense joy to set up house in the heart of the multitude, amid the ebb and flow of movement, in the midst of the fugitive and the infinite' (Benjamin 1999: 443). The *flâneur* emerged onto the Parisian boulevards at this time because of the genius of Baron Haussmann, the city planner who designed a new Paris, which Napoleon III turned into reality. Thus, the narrow and ancient Parisian streets were replaced with broad, straight avenues. Apart from military and political convenience, those streets were built to reconstruct Paris to facilitate the developing capitalism and provide traffic and accommodation for the benefit of the working class. Meanwhile, electric lighting and parks were also introduced to the city, which further enlarged the spaces for thriving commercial activities and public entertainment. This spatial transformation is embodied in both abstract and concrete spaces dominated by political and capitalist discourses, which according to Soja, shows humanity's historical, social and spatial attributes (1996: 46). Behind the new modern city blueprint is rationalism; however, it turns out that chaos, disorder, shocking experiences and irrationality ensue inevitably as the other facets of modernity. People from different social positions congregate in the city, walking in the streets, fulfilling obligations that society has imposed on them – working, attending business meetings, hanging out in the cafes and bars, shopping in the new department stores and arcades. Among them, the *flâneur* walks and keeps a distance from them, becoming the most valuable and insightful observer of the dramatic material and psychological change in the process of modernisation in Paris in the nineteenth century.

The primary aim of the *flâneur* is to transform the chaos and indeterminacy of the urban space into a legible, accessible and non-threatening version of itself, to demonstrate that the urban crowds are not as politically threatening and illegible as they appear to be in the bourgeois society (Brand 1991: 6). In a highly commercialised urban space, the experiences of the modern subject are often attended by anxiety and insecurity. The *flâneur* is entitled the authority and freedom to observe and interpret the wealth of the transient sights, sounds and smells of the urban space (particularly the arcades). Such observation and interpretation of the urban space entitled by the *flâneur*'s street-level walking transformed Paris from a well-planned rational city to a lived space of commercialisation, dynamism and labyrinth. On the one hand, the city was planned and organised by institutional bodies with the idea of rationality. On the other hand, it became a labyrinthine and enigmatic space created by extensive urban constructions (Benjamin 1999). In the latter-day interpretation, *flâneur* is not only an actual individual who is a detached observer of urban life strolling in the street and reaping 'aesthetic meaning and an individual kind of existential security from the spectacle of the teeming crowds' (Tester 1994: 2), but a literary and social archetype, or a concept adopted by contemporary writers and scholars as a paradigm of modernity, urbanisation and public mobility.

When the Chinese government launched its economic and social reform in the 1980s, Chinese *flâneurs* began to appear in streets that were subject to transformation and rebuilding for the realisation of 'Four-Modernity'. They are observers of the dramatic architectural and psychological changes occurring across contemporary mainland China. Huang Jianxin becomes one of the pioneer directors who observes and captures such radical changes occurring in Chinese cities. As a *flâneur* he attentively observes and appropriates the city spaces in the context of rapid urbanisation and modernisation. He provides a male-oriented observation of the urban space which, similar to nineteenth-century Paris, is characterised by mobility of the mass crowd and the rapid construction of separated commercial and residential spaces in 1990s China. However, unlike the Parisian's leisurely *flânerie* in the streets of the modern metropolis, which is a protest against the 'speeding up of circulation and time discipline' (Pinder 2005b: 152), the Chinese *flâneur*'s urban exploration (walking in the streets) is frequently impeded by intensive political and ideological control over nearly every aspect of social life. Huang Jianxin's urban exploration and street-level observation are a protest against the heavy hand of political interference in economic transformation. His two films – *Back to Back* and *Signal Left* – pointedly illustrate such protestation.

Back to Back portrays over ten characters, each of whom keeps 'walking' within their small world and craving maximum interest for themselves, during which, however, they stumble into awkward situations. The protagonist, Wang Shuangli (Niu Zhenhua), is a middle-aged mid-level bureaucrat working at the Culture Centre of a city. Niu Zhenhua has starred in every one of Huang Jianxin's second urban trilogy, and won the Best Actor award at the 1994 Tokyo International Film Festival for his powerful performance in *Back to Back*. The film also won the Golden Rooster Awards for Best Director and the Best Co-produced Film in 1995 in China. *Back to Back* unfolds with two storylines: the first is Wang Shuangli's failure to be promoted to the position of director of the local Culture Centre (a bureaucratic unit of the government); the other revolves around Wang's father's yearning for a grandson to carry on the family name. Having already had a granddaughter, Wang's father spares no effort to negotiate over the one child policy implemented in mainland China. The two lines eventually intertwine when Wang Shuangli and his father collaborate to fulfil their respective goals. Wang bribes a doctor who fabricates a document to prove that Wang's daughter has an incurable disease, which convinces the authority to allow the family to have another baby. Wang's father, in the meantime, schemes against Xiao Yan (Li Qiang), the newly appointed director, and ruins his reputation. Consequently, Xiao Yan is suspended from the position, and the director's position becomes vacant again. Wang is summoned at the end of the film, but will he finally be appointed?

With the principal scenes set in the Shanshaan Guild (located in Sheqi, Henan Province) (Figure 6.1) and the thick surrounding walls of Xi'an, the film encloses its characters in a small space that overlooks them, dwarfs them, and constrains their vision, perspective and behaviour. Guild halls, a distinctive architectural form that resembles Chinese traditional temple architecture in style and form, were established either by wealthy merchants or by government officials (Burgess 1930: 76). It is estimated that 70 per cent of guild halls were founded by government officials, and some of them were co-founded by powerful merchants and officials to provide accommodation and protection for their native townspeople (Wang 1996). Guilds are highly exclusive and regional, as eligibility for membership of such guild halls is often 'conferred by common geographical origin', which was the 'major bond – whether it was that of the same county, same group of counties, or same province' (Liu 1988: 9). They have existed for centuries since the Ming Dynasty and are not only found in Beijing, but in many provincial capital cities, minor cities and rural counties.

With significant political, economic and social functions, guild halls were usually built with delicate and refined decorations and on an extraordinary scale. These structures built by guilds were headquarters for 'meeting, theatrical representations, and as lodging-houses for high officials when travelling, and for scholars en route to metropolitan examinations' (cited in Braester and Chen 2011: 20). Therefore, the guild hall, in all ways, stands for power, whether political, commercial or religious. Power and 'the specifically cultural politics that arise from its workings', as Soja perceives, are 'contextualised and made concrete, like all social relations, in the (social) production of (social) space' (Soja 1996: 86–7). These enormous buildings and refined courtyards have become time capsules of imperial China. Today, the traditional, political and commercial influence borne by the architectures of hundreds of years of history seems obliterated by the assimilating force of globalisation. However, they can still exert powerful cultural and political control over people in modern society. In the film, characters are affected and manipulated by such cultural and political powers spatialised by the enclosed spaces.

FROM AN ENCLOSED SPACE TO A SPRAWLING URBAN SPACE 141

Figure 6.1 The guild hall: in *Back to Back*

Guild hall: the edifice of tradition and power

In the opening sequences, the Culture Centre is shrouded in morning mist like a solemn and enormous shadow (Figure 6.2). A parade of stylish and rising eaves and layered decorations on the roof soaring up to the sky mark the traditional building as a politically hierarchical and economically powerful space. As Huang Jianxin states, 'when looking from the top of the building, there are all roofs, no people! Merchant guild and temple share one attribute – that they sanctify the power' (Jia and Song 2011: 25).

In *Back to Back*, the guild hall serves as the workplace of the Culture Centre that is affiliated with the local Bureau of Culture. It no longer functions as a commercial or a religious space in the modern era, but as a cultural and political space in a given urbanised city. On the one hand, the Culture Centre is responsible for organising cultural activities such as photographic exhibitions and writing workshops and managing film screenings; on the other hand, it is a space of power conflict for Wang Shuangli and his competitors. The guild hall is an emblem of the imperial power structure that has been rooted in China for thousands of years. Chinese city planning and architectural structure during ancient times bore strong administrative and political imprints, as they were:

> conceived as part of a unitary hierarchy of country, department, prefectural, and provincial capitals all oriented toward the Son of Heaven in the imperial centre. This hierarchy was represented in bureaucratic chains of command, official rituals, and the successive levels of examination system. At every level, uniform systems of architectural, behavioural, and visual symbolism expressed the unity of the imperial system. (Esherick 2000: 6)

Such bureaucratic and official rituals and strict hierarchy not only orient the spatial arrangement of the city and architectural forms, but also affect the value and behaviour of people using such spaces. According to Soja, those who are spatially subjugated by the workings of the political power can 'either accept their imposed differentiation and division, making the best of it; or mobilise to resist, drawing upon their putative positioning, their assigned "otherness," to struggle against this power-filled imposition' (1996: 87). Spatially, to accept or to resist is often a complicated negotiation. In the case of Wang Shuangli, he has been stuck at the deputy position for around three years. He is capable, qualified and sophisticated enough to keep everything in the Culture Centre operating smoothly, and has established a solid network with some colleagues. Even though he accepts the imposed power structure, at the same time he struggles against the 'power-filled imposition' (Soja 1996: 87) by tactically dealing with the superior official and his competitors assigned by the superior official.

FROM AN ENCLOSED SPACE TO A SPRAWLING URBAN SPACE 143

Figure 6.2 The guild hall (the locus of the Culture Centre): in *Back to Back*

As a sophisticated government official involved in the complicated hierarchical power relations in the culture department, Wang employs a contingent and cunning way of negotiating with his superior, his peers and his competitors. To cater to the superior, he always says yes to the superior's demands. Meanwhile, he devotes himself to creating his image as an upright and capable leader who will not take bribes or pander to authority. Hence, when Leng (Ge Zhijun), the head of the local Cultural Bureau and Wang's immediate superior, requires Wang to arrange a proper position for his daughter, Leng Bingbing (Yu Nannan), at the Culture Centre, Wang insists that Leng Bingbing should go through the official procedure – public recruitment. Even though the public recruitment procedure is designated as a cover for taking Leng Bingbing into the position officially and decently, Leng (the father) feels he is being challenged and turns down Wang's promotion repeatedly despite his skills and qualification. By making the superior's goal come true in this 'open' and 'democratic' way, Wang establishes an image of decency and uprightness among his colleagues. His acceptance and familiarity with the structure and exercise of political power equips him with wiliness and techniques to survive in the game of power.

Back to Back opens with a poll conducted in the Culture Centre. The guild hall has lost its commercial functions in contemporary society, but it remains a space of power that operates within hierarchical political order and as a battlefield of the exercise and abuse of power. In the film, a serious-looking man announces: 'With the central government advocating democratic administration, a poll will be carried out to select the director of the Culture Centre as a case of such proposition.'

Wang hesitates for a while then puts his name down. He then hands in the paper with his name on it, walking out of the hall with confidence. Outside the hall, in a medium shot, an iron fence with sharp ends blocks the way out, while the overlapping eaves and pillars overwhelmingly occupy the exterior space. They resemble layered fences that block Wang's way to promotion. In addition, the man who inspects the poll stares at Wang with disdain and suspicion when he receives Wang's vote. He then stands with his back to the camera, watching Wang walking away.

Obviously, the superior's democratic conduct does not stretch to self-volunteered promotion; rather, it encourages a more traditional value – staying humble. Criticism of Wang's 'shameless' volunteering soon ensues, as the deputy-director of the local Cultural Department states, 'You are too young'. Here, being young does not necessarily refer to Wang's age; instead, it is his naïve understanding of 'democratic administration'. The authority system favours those who are not 'young'. Working in such an 'old' space that has borne witness to extensive social changes since the Ming dynasty, Wang should have known how tenacious the traditional ways can be and how difficult the alternation of power can be in a hierarchical power system. The centuries-old architecture, with its grand scale and distinguished style, is well preserved and retains a strong sense of authority. Traditional ways of administration have been equally preserved along with the architecture and the sophisticated 'old' officials tend to act accordingly. By choosing such a traditional space as the main setting for his characters, Huang juxtaposes tradition with modernity, setback with progress, people belonging to the past with those belonging to the contemporary world. They are not two divided groups; rather, they co-exist and affect one another.

The lobby of the guild complex is not only used to conduct the poll but also to interview candidates who apply for the position at the Culture Centre. In the film, an establishing shot of the public interview shows two plaques hanging up in the central area, respectively saying 'Fair and Square' and 'Awe-inspiring Righteousness', which creates heavy irony with the following sequences showing the public recruitment designated for Leng Bingbing, the daughter of the Head of the Cultural Department. No matter how qualified the rest of the candidates are, they will be excluded. From the poll to the public recruitment, democratic ways of administration have turned out to be formulated shows. Resonating with the regional and clan exclusiveness practised at guilds during imperial times, the contemporary Culture Centre is also highly exclusive concerning personnel appointments. Only those who have powerful connections can join.

Compared with the Western modern cities that initially developed in Europe, most cities in 1990s China, according to Huang Jianxin, cannot count as modern, especially his home town Xi'an:

> I grew up in Xi'an, a typical Chinese city. It looks more like a town with clear imprints of agricultural civilisation. Many of those who have been to Xi'an tend to perceive it as an 'urban village' since it retains traditional and ethical interpersonal relationships that are different from those in industrialised cities. (Jia and Song 2011: 23)

The social networks nurtured by agricultural civilisation distinguish Chinese cities from their western counterparts. Agricultural civilisation developed and became deep-rooted in China over the long course of imperial history. The guild hall represents a typical architectural form of the power and social relations that originated in imperial China and consequently inherited by the modern Culture Centre. Power is everywhere, and according to Lefebvre:

> it is omnipresent, assigned to Being . . . It is in everyday discourse and commonplace notions, as well as in police batons and armoured cars. It is in *objets d'art* as well as in missiles. It is in the diffuse preponderance of the 'visual,' as well as in institutions such as school or parliament. It is in things as well as in signs (the signs of objects and object-signs). (Cited in Soja 1996: 31)

As a space of power from ancient times until now, the Culture Centre set in this guild hall is the edifice of power and the space of the struggles of hierarchical power. In real life, it functions no longer as a clubhouse for merchants or government officials; instead, it increasingly serves as a cultural and temporal capsule of the grand traditional Chinese architectural achievement and symbolises the 'sprouts of capitalism' in the late imperial dynastic era (cited in Moll Murata 2008; Ying 2006). In *Back to Back*, the guild hall repeatedly appears as a space attached to solemnity, grandeur and feudal values, which displace the modern value of professionalism and frustrate the characters in the film.

From the rural to the urban: a zigzagging path to settling in

Wang's desired position is first taken by Lao Ma (Lei Kesheng) and then by Xiao Yan. Both of them are appointed by Leng, the Head of the Cultural Bureau. Lao Ma was the head of a village before being promoted to the director of the Culture Centre, while Xiao Yan was Leng's secretary before taking over the position. Wang's different ways of dealing with the two reflect his cunning and sophisticated practices dealing with rural–urban social relations.

When dealing with Lao Ma, Wang embarrasses him in public, schemes against him and finally drives him away from the position. Not only Wang but also clients working in the Culture Centre despise Lao Ma due to his previous humble position and rural origin. The first day Lao Ma comes to the Culture Centre, he should have been the focus of a welcome meeting. However, the camera projects this meeting from the back of the gathering hall at a low angle, showing rows of people's backs, which prevent spectators from seeing Lao Ma, the core figure of this meeting. When the camera finally concentrates on Lao Ma and pans around from his point of view, it shows people busy knitting, reading newspapers and whispering (Figure 6.3). Only a few people who have had conflicts with

FROM AN ENCLOSED SPACE TO A SPRAWLING URBAN SPACE 147

Figure 6.3 The welcome meeting for Lao Ma: in *Back to Back*

Wang enthusiastically applaud Lao Ma's entrance to the office. Wang's introduction of Lao Ma makes the awkward situation even worse:

> Lao Ma used to deal with peasants. He was skilful and capable of handling cremation and birth control, and supervising fertility and taxing grain were also his strengths. Now he is about to deal with you intellectuals, which I believe he will be good at too.

Wang's words trigger a burst of sneering laughter among colleagues.

Lao Ma's following inauguration speech is greeted with constant interruptions and one of his photographic works draws immediate negative comments. A clear gap between the rural and the urban emerges. Lao Ma's difficult road to settling into the position and urban life has just begun. His power and authority suffer from constant challenge and even neglect. He is appointed to manage finance and personnel. However, financial documents signed by him are invalid, simply because 'this is an urban bureaucratic unit, which operates differently from your village administration'. When he tries to persuade workers to clean up a construction site for the upcoming inspection of superior officials, he is again rebuked and refused. Being desperate and helpless, he loses his temper and threatens: 'If you don't clean it up now, I will withdraw the construction contract and transfer the project to another company!' Yet the threatening words fail to have the desired effect, only arousing further scorn from the construction workers. 'In this law-rule society, you will have to pay a high price for cancelling a signed contract.' Facing the 'law-rule' lecture, Lao Ma loses his power to think rationally. Concepts like law, legislation or jurisdiction are abstract and strange concepts for him. In the immediate daily practice of his humble power, he relies on simple rules to conduct administration, and one of them is the hierarchical political power that he believes can top everything else, including the law. That is why he can exclaim, 'If blamed by the higher official, there will be serious consequences.' Like his previous decisions that have been despised and denied, his threat only makes him seem more pathetic and is followed by further instruction on urban conduct. The urban spaces that he appropriates and tries to access are like glass walls – he can see though to the other side, but they offer no entrance for him to get in.

Xiao Yan is different from Lao Ma. He has complicated and powerful connections in the urban bureaucratic unit, which protects him from Wang's schemes. Consequently, Wang realises that all the tricks and schemes that he utilised against Lao Ma have been employed by Xiao Yan to humiliate and frame him. Competing with Xiao Yan, who has a more powerful political background, Wang becomes the object of bullying. Wang as the deputy, despite his rural origins, has settled down in the urban area long enough to be exempt from being despised by urbanites and intellectuals. While Lao Ma is a gullible rural man to be disdained, bullied and tricked, Xiao Yan has been working with Leng for several years, which provides security to him in the power conflict. The amount of social recourse, power and space that the three characters can appropriate is parallel with their origin, position and connections. Correspondingly, Wang has at least two spaces that he can comfortably use and inhabit. Lao Ma's apartment compares poorly with Wang's. It is intentionally damaged before he moves in, and he does not have proper furniture to decorate his domestic space. Xiao Yan's home is not shown in the film, but it is said to be located in the provincial capital city, testifying to his powerful connections and comfortable economic level.

Wang Shuangli and his father inhabit a hybrid space that includes modern and pre-modern constructions. However, mentally and spiritually, they belong to a socialist or even feudal space. The guild hall and cityscape enclosed by thick walls (Figure 6.4) and Wang Shuangli's household contextualise the characters' everyday practices, and have powerful influences on them. They stand for the complication of the time and the people, as 'the space enclosed by these architectures exert an invisible force upon people' (Jia and Song 2011). Moreover, characters are 'enclosed in these buildings just as their worldviews are set within the given cultural boundaries' (Kuoshu 2010: 61). Traditions motivate people to move around the law to bring political, economic and personal benefits, at the price of sacrificing those who are incapable of rebelling.

The last sequences see Wang briskly striding across the spacious courtyard that links an array of guildhalls. Wang is called to attend a conference summoned by the newly appointed Head of the Cultural Department. With the camera zooming out, Wang's figure keeps shrinking in a long shot of him walking. He appears dwarfed by the surrounding solemn constructions with their grandeur of scale and refined design. Wang's insignificance and his impotence in his fight against the space of tradition and power can be seen from the contrasted scenes. His long walk resembles the long journey through a frustrating and prolonged application for promotion. At last, he disappears from the corner of the frame, and the camera pans slowly up, revealing a parade of stylised roofs of the guild complex, leaving spectators to wonder if he will finally get the position he desires.

In *Back to Back*, there is no one who can see the whole picture of either the society they are in or their current situation. That is to say, none of them possesses an omniscient perspective on the whole story, instead, they are in a bustling city characterised by 'an opaque and blind mobility' (Certeau 1984: 93). Characters in *Back to Back* are enclosed in

Figure 6.4 Thick walls and forts that enclose the city: in *Back to Back*

a traditional space surrounded by layers and layers of heavy gates and thick walls, and those who attempt to break out will find themselves being constrained by traditional and bureaucratic conduct. The guild hall manifests such persistent values and conduct, becoming a barrier that prevents those capable 'volunteers' from moving forward. The film clearly illustrates how political and agricultural tradition and values persist and affect the practice of everyday life in the reform era; and how people holding onto such values tactically transgress moral and social rules and keep personal interests intact, as is reflected in the cases of both Wang Shuangli and his father. Wang drives his competitors away through cunning schemes, while his father tries to disable his granddaughter to get permission to have a grandson. The inertia and drawbacks of traditional values, customs and behaviour consequently impede the spread of new values and ways.

In his critically acclaimed work *Black Cannon*, Huang demonstrates the clash between China's economic ambition for modernisation by adopting capitalist market efficiencies and its Leninist–Maoist political mode that is 'historically rooted in class struggle and a paranoic fear of class enemies forever lurking in one's midst' (Silbergeld 1999: 239). *Back to Back* shifts to another clash between China's tendency of employing the democratic mode of administration and rigid power hierarchy that are historically imprinted in power struggles and rural–urban imbalances. Although characters like Wang Shuangli are social elites, they also struggle with the dilemma between personal ambitions and hierarchical social orders, prevailing consumerism and traditional thriftiness. Huang does not take a dialectic view of the centre and the periphery, the rural and the urban; rather, he captures the coexistence and hybridity of urban and rural conduct and values. His characters are often framed in multi-layered social realities, and in various circumstances take an ambivalent stance, which appears as an 'otherness', a 'thirding', a presentation of the city as a 'possibilities machine' (Soja 1996: 81) that provides people from various social classes with opportunities as well as disillusion.

Signal Left: *moving from an enclosed space to a sprawling urban space*

Unlike in *Back to Back*, in which characters are enclosed in a small world surrounded by layers of thick walls and ancient buildings, characters in *Signal Left* freely walk or drive in urban streets. Employing different vehicles, such as journalist Gou Yujia's (Niu Zhenhua) motorcycle, Headmaster Li's (Wang Gang) Jeep and Laochai's (Jü Hao) luxury Cadillac, characters in the film can approach distant places and travel to and from the vicinity of the city. The film represents a growing number of individuals engaging in private businesses and moving around in a more open and broader space, rather than being confined to an enclosed politicalised space. Spatially, the expanding urban space signifies a centrifugal spatial development that is in stark contrast to the long-established spatial configuration of the historical city.

As one of most ancient cities in China, Xi'an stands out with its remarkable city walls and numerous historical sites. During the Third Front Project launched in the 1960s (the military–industrial project aimed at establishing alternatives to east coastal industrial bases during the Cold War, and extending into the 1980s, as in Chengdu), dwelling spaces of workers were arranged close to work units, which reflected 'the concentrated nature of earlier population and employment pattern' (Walcott 2003: 633). This configuration of cityscape forms a centripetal spatial arrangement, as workplaces, dwelling spaces and commute distances were condensed within a conveniently accessible space. The limited transportation options and the administration control over population (*hukou*, the household registration) and in particular, the military–industrial state-owned factories contributed to the production of such a built environment. In reform era, within the old walled urban core, architecture from dynastic China is still erect while foreign fast food restaurants such as McDonald's and KFC also find their way into this increasingly commercialised historical city. In *Signal Left*, sequences of Cheng Fen (Ding Jiali) as a peddler running a night stand under the neon lights of KFC illustrate the vibrance of the old city. In reality, high-tech parks, universities, research institutes, billboards, apartment complexes are sprouting outside the walled urban core, which shows the modern façade of the ancient city. With Xi'an Hi-Tech Industry Development, one of the five national-level High Technology Zones designated in 1991, and Xi'an Business Incubation Centre established two years later, the urban morphology of the city has been drastically transformed. The low land cost and convenient access to freeways encourage new ventures to establish their business on the periphery of the city, attracting employees and residents to the newly developed urban extensions (Walcott 2003: 635). This spatial configuration and development display a centrifugal pattern, showing the power of marketisation and globalisation in terms of producing spaces. In the film, the main setting, a driving school, is located on the outskirts of the city, and the rehab clinic where Lü Dou (Wang Jinsong) is sent to deal with his drug addiction is also set in a suburban area. The sprawling cityscape represents the inland city's ambition of catching up with the eastern coastal counterparts regarding economy, and it is another case of the centrifugal spatial arrangement under the logic of capitalism.

Moreover, the centrifugal spatial pattern is not only shown in the sprawling urban spaces, but also in an array of changing attitudes and conduct. In the film, overseas study, transnational marriage and international cooperation and investment become available for individuals and private companies. Foreign fashions and lifestyles, in addition to ideas such as liberalism and privatisation, enlarge ordinary people's horizon and affect their behaviours. For instance, when Headmaster Li of the driving school announces the dress code of the school, a woman wearing sunglasses objects: 'Western women are allowed to wear dress and high heels while driving'; Laochai requests to be given priority to practise driving, as 'my international negotiation with foreigners would convene soon, which focuses on the housing reformation of the city, and the mayor will join me too'; Headmaster Li's son applies to the Tokyo Institute of Technology to further his studies; and at the end of the film, a Japanese delegation visits the driving school and decides on a big investment. All these instances illustrate the ubiquitous western influence on individuals' everyday practices, and show the inland city's participation in the world economy through the government-driven marketisation and internationalisation.

Meanwhile, the phantasms of the obsolete political views represented by the discourse of the Cultural Revolution continue to reverberate in the daily practices of the filmic characters. Now and then, we can hear characters express their political views about both domestic and international issues. Headmaster Li, for example, always appears in army uniform and strictly manages the police station owned driving school in a semimilitary fashion. In the opening sequences, such political expressions are exchanged between main characters. All students are required to introduce themselves in the first class, and Instructor Hou (Kang Aishi) starts with his pretentious statement:

> Instructor Hou: I am Hou Zhenfeng, a veteran and a party member as well, I will devote my whole life to train qualified drivers for my country!
> Headmaster Li: Could you say something tangible?
> Instructor Hou: Okay, but there is nothing fancy about it . . . If I don't work here, I have to go back to the countryside. The place is a poor mountainous area without enough water for irrigation.
> Journalist Gou: Does each of us have to confess?
> Assistant of Headmaster Li: This is called opening one's heart to the authority, and it is a tradition in the army!
> Journalist Gou: Well, my family name is Gou, male, and I am twenty-eight years old. I am 171 centimetres high and weigh ninety kilograms, and my blood group is O. I was born in a revolutionaries' family, and my household registration identity is

> student. I work as a photojournalist at the New Wave Daily . . . My purpose of learning to drive is to facilitate my work, and I aim to become an internationally well-known journalist.
>
> . . .
>
> Lüdou: I am Lüdou, nobody calls me by my real name. I don't know my blood group nor my family origin. Political status? No idea . . .
> Headmaster Li: Don't you have any political views?
> Lüdou: It's embarrassing to tell . . . Well, if I were born in the US, I would definitely be Bill Clinton. He always provokes disagreement with China, but his wife is fairly charming. If I were in Japan, I would stand against Cunshan fushi the long-brow (he refers to Murayama Tomiichi, the president of Japan (1994–6) and exclude him away from the Congress, as he makes the JPY (Japanese Yen) strengthened and our RMB (Renminbi) depreciated . . .

These lines effectively bring viewers back to the revolutionary era overwhelmed by a series of political campaigns, in particular, the Cultural Revolution that required individuals to make confessions and encouraged informants. However, such political discourse sounds pretentious and hollow in the reform era characterised by privatisation and marketisation. In the socialist era, the individual's private life was somewhat circumscribed owing to an array of collective movements and strict ideological control. The Party requested that an individual should not keep any secrets from the collective, and all private and personal problems were to be solved by 'opening one's heart to the Party' (Luo 2019: 134). However, such political expressions and behaviours provoke sarcasm in a group of students who represent a radically changing society in an out-of-date army-managed instruction (Kuoshu 2010: 62). The seemingly sublime words, especially those said by Journalist Gou and Instructor Hou, are in direct contradiction to their mutual distrust, antipathy and retaliation during the teaching–learning process.

Signal Left shows a dynamic and vibrant city that keeps expanding its urban boundary, and accordingly, characters are allowed to travel freely by various modes of transport. It demonstrates the most updated economic, social and cultural development of Xi'an in the 1990s by showing the centrifugal pattern of spatial arrangements and development. The configuration and production of space have changed along with the central government's reorientation in ideological and political focuses in the post-socialist era – from revolutionary struggles to economic development. Accordingly, urban space turns from a highly politicised space of production into a commercialised space of consumption.

CHAPTER 7

Female Space and Bodies

In contrast to Huang Jianxin's *flâneur* observations and appropriation of urban spaces, Wang Quan'an turns his camera on rural areas, the sprawling towns and industrial district in Xi'an and its adjacent areas, and outlines the contours and process of modernisation in the region. Wang Quan'an's cinematic Xi'an is represented as a capsule of rural inertia and socialist China in his 2004 *The Story of Ermei* and 2009 *Weaving Girl* respectively. In *The Story of Ermei*, Wang partially retains the symbols and cultural rituals of the area exhibited in films by Zhang Yimou and Chen Kaige, but he takes a female perspective. The film projects a town adjacent to Xi'an that serves as a conjuncture of the rural and urban areas, and examines the shifting boundary between rural and urban by showing the intrusion of commercial values into hinterland households who retain intact a culture of arranged marriage and parental power. In addition, it explores how women and girls in the area justify their positions and roles in different social spaces, and shows their vulnerability and strength in domestic and urban spaces. The female protagonist's rural–urban experiences and the limited physical spaces she can access display a complicated space–power relationship which is not only limited by gender but also social class and rural–urban disparities.

Weaving Girl explores female bodies and human suffering that resonate with grim anonymous industrial areas plagued with rundown factories and alienated streets and neighbourhoods. The cinematic image of Xi'an in this film is deprived of its heavy historical and cultural connections, and is associated with the fateful diseases suffered by female characters, which can be regarded as resonating with the collapse of the state-owned enterprise. The industrial district of the city is half-abandoned and lifeless, leaving the once respected proletariat in poverty or dying. In contrast to on-screen Beijing, the metropolitan hub, always appearing with dynamic and bustling comings and goings, cinematic Xi'an is represented as a self-enclosed place, remaining in the past and with bleak prospects for the future.

The Story of Ermei: Female Social Status in Rural and Urban Spaces

The Story of Ermei features Guan Ermei (Yu Nan) who escapes from her rural home to a nearby city to avoid an arranged marriage, but eventually returns home and accepts the marriage. The Chinese title of the film is *Jingzhe*, which means the third of the twenty-four solar terms in the traditional Chinese calendar. In agriculture-dominated time, Chinese people believed that the hibernating insects would be woken by a crash of thunder in spring, and this would be the sign of a new beginning or enlightenment. In the context of the film, *Jingzhe* signals the coming of the spring, and symbolises the female protagonist's awakening subjectivity and her act of walking out from the enclosed rural home. Escaping from the countryside, Ermei seems finally unchained from the roles and life arranged by her parents and imposed by the rural social order. However, can she establish her identity and subjectivity in an urban space characterised by fragmentation, instability, mobility, social stratification and gender oppression?

Feminist critic bell hooks, due to her identity as an African-American, locates herself in the margin as the departure point from which to criticise the oppressive gender, class and racial orders in America. She elaborates:

> living as we did – on the edge – we developed a particular way of seeing reality. We looked both from the outside in and from the inside out. We focused our attention on the centre as well as the margin. We understood both. This mode of seeing reminded us of the existence of a whole universe, a main body made up of both margin and centre . . . A mode of seeing unknown to most of our oppressors, that sustained us, aided us in our struggle to transcend poverty and despair, strengthened our sense of self and our solidarity. (Cited in Soja 1996: 100)

Such a mode of seeing from both sides, 'from the outside in and from the inside out' (Soja 1996: 100), provides bell hooks a vantage point from which to observe the complexities of the post-modern occidental world. In the Chinese context, specifically in *The Story of Ermei*, for rural females represented by Ermei, such a mode of seeing and experiencing both the rural and the urban, the public and private spaces, provides her with a comprehensive view from which to examine both social spaces and relations, and to develop her sense of self and subjectivity. The film opens with three men breaking into a sealed cave where a coffin has been preserved for years. Wang places his camera deep in the cave, showing the men checking the coffin and talking in local dialect in the shadows. The decayed coffin, made many years ago, is for Ermei's grandfather, who has been bedridden for a long time. At this moment, her grandfather is dying and a group of people gather to discuss and prepare for the coming funeral. Given that the coffin is damaged, the poor family now has to raise money for a new one. Meanwhile, Ermei is occupied by a variety of housework: fetching water from the well, feeding livestock and cooking. The decayed coffin, shadow-like male figures and grandfather's impending death cast a shadow on Ermei's life trajectory.

The Chinese title of the film and the opening sequences suggest a strong attachment to agrarian rituals and customs in rural China. The day of *Jingzhe* signifies the beginning of the spring cultivation, which is the most important event for people involved in agrarian work. The practice of preserving a good coffin for the dying has been perpetuated in rural areas, as it is widely regarded as a representation of filial piety and family decency. In the living room where the grandfather is lying on a *Kang* (a particular bed made of mud and heated by burning coal or hay, commonly seen in northern China), a group of people, mostly old ladies and males, are sitting or standing and talking. Ermei is excluded from the scene as she is preoccupied with all sorts of household duties. The living room as a private space is the most public space in the household, while a young woman such as Ermei, despite the flesh and blood bond between grandfather and grandchild, is not allowed to stay in the male-dominated space at home. Yet Ermei does not perceive herself as being excluded or ignored by the family. Rather, she takes it as natural and accepts the rituals, such as staying in her own space (a bedroom and kitchen) and eating after everyone else in the room. This age-old social etiquette remains rooted in rural areas up to the present time. Whether it is the Chinese traditional calendar or the taken for granted rituals, they have existed in proximity with primal natural elements and reserved ancestral rituals and life-sustaining skills in close connection with the ecosystem (Liu 2009: 219). Staying in accordance with the ecosystem, the traditional agrarian calendar and revering ancestral rituals, all this has been inscribed in the genes of the rural populace over many generations. Ermei and her family take all these values and behaviours for granted, seldom judging or thinking about them, far less rejecting or fighting against them. However, after being introduced to some modern items (Ermei's friend Mao Nü, working in the nearby town, brings some chocolate and a music card to her) and ideas (freedom of marriage and economic independence, illustrated by Mao Nü's personal experience in the town), Ermei is inspired to escape from the arranged marriage in the countryside, cross the rural–urban border and enter the nearby town to pursue a different life in the modern world. In the spaces of the borderlands, even though in Ermei's case it is only several hours distance by bus, there are 'two or more cultures [that] edge each other, where people of different [social or racial background] occupy the same territory, where under, lower, middle and upper classes touch' (cited in Soja 1996: 127). Such cultural contrasts – predominantly characterised by commercialism, rural and urban populations, class differences, and gender and sexual relations – all become a 'cultural shock' for Ermei. The bustling urban area appears as a larger village with no fancy modern structures or busy traffic. However, it is commercialised enough to shock the rural and illiterate Ermei when she is asked to pay for the use of a toilet. Without knowing the exact address of her close friend Mao Nü's (Shi Xiaoxia) hair salon, she gets lost in the city. Helpless and bewildered, Ermei asks numerous passers-by about the location of the hair salon called Dream Paris but is met by confused countenances. When she finally finds the hair salon, an amplifier repeats the words spoken by Mao Nü:

> Welcome to Dream Paris.
> You will have an extravagant experience here.
> We will make you confident, fashionable and younger.
> Do not hesitate,
> Dream Paris is waiting for you.

The repeated word 'Paris' represents their imagination of the modern foreign world, and shows their dream of escaping from the small claustrophobic rural spaces. When Mao Nü asks her why she did not call her in the first place, the innocent and ignorant Ermei bursts into tears. The hair salon is the only place Ermei knows in the city, and it is a place where she can let out the sorrow and tears she has held back all the way from her rural home to the town.

In the film, Ermei's urban experience is intensively related to her body and sensuality, specifically, the female body and sexuality are shown as sites watched, exploited and manipulated by masculine power. Attempting to settle down in the city, Ermei starts to work at Boss Yu's (Ma Zheng) restaurant. She is also convinced by Mao Nü to develop a relationship with a man to ensure her stay in the city. In the restaurant, a young adult colleague continuously harasses Ermei, and Boss Yu occasionally requires her to serve at the tables, even though she was originally hired to make buns. Beyond this, she has to deal with Boss Yu's unexpected visits at night. Mao Nü and her boyfriend Sanwa (Feng Jinlong) introduce Ermei to Qiao Liansheng (Liu Yanbing), who works at the radio station of a temple. The relationship lends her courage to fight back against the sexual harassment. When teased again by the young colleague, she yells at him for the first time, 'You're looking for trouble?' He then swiftly replies, 'You've got a boyfriend?' Both genders in the circumstance recognise the protective role of a male in the urban space. It makes a silent and marginalised woman fearless and provocative, and it protects her from being taken advantage of. As Chris Berry notes, 'even after over forty years of liberation, it is still commonly felt that a respectable woman should not be alone with any man other than a member of her family, a party representative, or a responsible government official' (1999: 210). As the time approaches the millennium, there are small steps of progress in female space and security: family members are no longer the only people who count, but a relationship can still protect a woman from harassment.

However, Ermei's courage and the happiness she derives from the relationship are soon shattered, when she unexpectedly finds a set of women's underwear in Qiao's bed. Distressed and disillusioned, she bursts into tears, striding out of the temple court to an open-air market. A two-minute long take tracks her struggling with Qiao who tries to stop Ermei and explain the situation. Ermei's wrestling with Qiao resembles her long tough journey in search of a position in the urban area, and shows that their relationship cannot ensure a stable and decent living in the town. The tangled relationships between Ermei and different men in the town unmask what might have happened to Mao Nü when she tried to settle into the urban space. Mao Nü had concealed the unpleasant side in her exciting account of city life in their conversation before Ermei escaped from her rural home.

Towards the end of the film, we see Sanwa standing on a truck in handcuffs, wearing a sign that says 'murderer' in Chinese. The scene catches Ermei's attention. Astonished, she hurries to the hair salon, only to find that a different couple has taken over. The amplifier still broadcasts the same slogan, and the radio is playing the same song that they sang together. Ermei learns that Mao Nü left long ago and has taken a train to Guangzhou (the south), the most desirable place for young people in hinterland China who want to realise dreams of prosperity, or to start a new life. The new owners also tell Ermei that Sanwa has been sentenced to death for killing Lao Wang (Bai Mang), the corrupt police commissioner. It turns out that Mao Nü and Sanwa were involved in a twisted relationship – Mao Nü worked as a prostitute to cater to Lao Wang, to whom Sanwa was connected through some shady deals. They may have been involved in a conflict of interest that somehow led to Sanwa's desperate action. The film takes no further interest in why Sanwa has murdered Lao Wang, foregrounding the labyrinthine characteristics of urban spaces and the complicated relations between urban residents.

As a privileged person, Lao Wang takes advantage of Mao Nü, Sanwa, Qiao Liansheng and Boss Yu. He abuses his power by using these people and forcing them to act in accordance with his own personal preferences.

These unprivileged ones either rely on Lao Wang for business reasons, like Mao Nü and Sanwa, or simply cater to his every whim to avoid trouble, like Qiao Liansheng and Boss Yu. Ermei realises that all the men who seemed strong and powerful before her behave in a cringing and ingratiating manner in Lao Wang's presence. This unbalanced and indecent situation reaches a climax when Lao Wang forces Qiao Liansheng to drink. After Qiao reluctantly finishes a whole glass of a mixture of beer and spirits (which Lao Wang calls a submarine), he is forced to drink another one. Lao Wang teases those who stop him and punishes them by forcing them to drink the same thing. Ermei ends this chaotic game by throwing a whole package of dead fish on the table and violently chopping them up. Startled, Lao Wang stands up, puts on his overcoat and refuses to pay the bill. Ermei's marginalised social position and uncertain prospect of settling down in the city free her from Lao Wang's manipulation. Lao Wang represents the dark and complicated side of the urban area, and more importantly, stands for the space of power.

In the final sequences, Ermei holds her son in her arms, riding on an electric train and wishing the boy will be able to go abroad one day. However, the everlasting circling of the train indicates the cruel reality that he may well repeat the life trajectory of other males in the countryside. Meanwhile, the blissful moment with her boy is accompanied by the music of *Qinqiang*, the representative Chinese opera popular in Shaanxi Province. The extreme high pitch and prolonged enchantment of *Qinqiang* singing is in contrast to the loving mother–son moment, which brings a sense of intensity and dislocation.

Female body as the medium of social representations

Human bodies as spatial existence register a physical occupation of certain spaces, yet more importantly, they embody the political, economic and cultural features of a given society. As Soja contends, the human body is a highly 'mediated space' that bears 'cultural interpretations and representations'; moreover, it is a 'social space' that involves the complex operation of power and knowledge, which shape and recognise it as 'a self, a subject or an identity' (Soja 1996: 114). In the Chinese context, the women's emancipation movement arose along with the social and cultural revolution that took place during the Republican era (1919–49). The establishment of the People's Republic of China furthered this movement due to Chairman Mao's official confirmation that 'women were upholders of half the sky'. This socialist government-propagated movement 'empowered women by promoting and institutionalising their political, social, and economic roles; nevertheless, it demanded women's self-sacrifice and identification with an implicitly masculine model' (Cui 2011: 17). In films such as Xie Jin's 1961 *The Red Detachment of Women*, women often appear wearing gender neutral uniforms and undertake exactly the same revolutionary tasks as men. Such asexual female images were reinforced in model plays during the Cultural Revolution, when the cinematic images of female characters were 'reduced to anonymous and faceless members of a large collective group identity – sisters of the proletarian class' (Zhou 2001: 7–8). Therefore, socialist cinematic female bodies become narrative sites for class oppression, national liberation and national trauma (Cui 2003: xi). Meanwhile, women's bodies, beauty and sexuality were watched and regulated under strict restrictions of 'Confucian patriarchy' before the 1980s (Zhou 2001: 11). Confucian tradition details requirements regarding women's attitude and manner, and sets strict limitations on female roles and conduct in both domestic and public spaces. One commonly practised tradition is arranged marriage, which is the case for Ermei in *The Story of Ermei*. However, the genderless politicisation and Confucian restriction of the female body have been challenged since the 1980s, especially in urban areas where urban youth tend towards a more liberal attitude towards gender, love and marriage (Zhou 2001: 9–10). Meanwhile, with the cultural and economic reorientation of the state, objectification, commodification and fetishisation of women replaced the previous asexual, politicised representation (Chow 2013). In *The Story of Ermei*, Ermei's urban experiences reflect such a transition in views on relationships and marriage, and show the bleak prospect for women from rural communities who try to settle down in the urban space, despite the fact that it has been two decades since women's emancipation was promoted in the 1980s. The situation of women in rural areas remains almost unchanged, as we can see in the Confucian values and practices to which Ermei's rural community adhere.

Before running away, Ermei lives in the crowded room of a *yaodong* (lit. house cave, described above). It is her bedroom and kitchen, and her time is filled with all sorts of housework. In these sequences, Wang frequently frames Ermei in long or medium shots and seldom represents her in close-up. She covers her hair with a scarf, often bends down, and scurries around carrying out her various errands. The audience cannot see her face clearly. All her private time and space are taken up with household chores, and she has no idea that a marriage has been arranged for her in exchange for the cost of a new coffin until her little brother discloses it to her.

Her friend Mao Nü (who may have suffered from the same arrangement at her rural home) finds an alternative route for life in the urban area, which encourages Ermei to escape from the countryside and pursue independence, freedom and the rosy urban life. In their conversation,

Mao Nü claims that her mother can be harsh to her, but cannot control her anymore, as she pays for everything in the household after she moves to the town and becomes economically independent. It seems that the parent–child relationship has been reduced to a purely economic relationship. Mao Nü buys herself freedom of marriage by covering all the expenditures of the family. Her freedom is based on economic independence, which motivates Ermei to leave for the city and realise hers by working and developing a relationship in the urban area.

When Ermei crosses the border between rural and urban, she comes to this strange society where her social status fluctuates along with the space that she is free to appropriate. In her countryside home, she is a marginalised, instrumental-oriented person, who has no privacy or agency. In the city, she has to cautiously deal with different men who purposefully approach her. The restaurant owner pays unexpected visits at night and her colleague keeps harassing her. If the domestic space back in the countryside deprives her of privacy and subjectivity, the urban space makes her insecure and anxious. She soon realises that gender alone may not be the cause of her sense of insecurity and instability, as both her ex-boyfriend and Boss Yu, who are constantly teased and rebuked by Lao Wang, appear helpless and servile. Men connected with her, either through a romantic relationship or employment, appear vulnerable and impotent before the powerful privileged class represented by Lao Wang. Therefore, the urban space teems with the exercising of power, imposing oppression and subordination on people stuck in sexually, socially or economically marginalised positions. Soja argues that feminism consists not in sexual difference alone, but rather a subject that is 'engendered in the experiencing of race and class, as well as sexual, relations; a subject, therefore, not unified but rather multiple, and not so much divided as contradicted' (Soja 1996: 111). In the film, exploitations suffered by Ermei are not caused by sexual difference alone, but rather engendered by social classes and urban–rural disparities. Ermei's eventual return to the countryside and marriage with Zhang Suo (Yan Li) are the compromises she makes after being frustrated by her urban experiences. To address existential problems and avoid being pressed by her parents, she has to marry someone. Consequently, marriage takes on a practical purpose rather than a romantic one. Economic development and utopian urban imagination appeal to rural women, making them venture to the urban area to pursue a better life. However, city life frequently brings them more frustration and disillusion than chances for personal growth and affluence. They eventually have to return to the rural village to marry for material reasons (Li 2013: 133).

Marrying Zhang Suo and becoming the mother of a boy, she ascends to a higher, more respected status in the domestic space; especially when the male–female roles are inverted in both domestic and public spaces, Ermei acquires autonomy and authority in the family. As Zhang Suo is an alcoholic, physically weak and emotionally dependent on his parents, his masculinity and patriarchal authority face constant challenges. The first day of their marriage sees the couple fighting, as Ermei refuses to have sex with him. When the lunar New Year arrives, Zhang Suo dresses as a female to perform in the local entertainment corps. His flamboyant dress and exaggerated feminine make-up arouse a sneer from the audience, making Ermei embarrassed and restless. This transformation in apparel registers Zhang Suo's lack of masculinity, which is then enhanced by a series of incidents following the New Year's celebration. The celebration offers a great opportunity for Zhang Suo to fill his glass and get drunk, but his son becomes ill in the night. Living in a remote village, a long way from the clinic in the town, Ermei manages to start up a tractor to take the child to the hospital. Zhang Suo, unconscious from drink, is dragged out of bed by family members and settled on the tractor to hold the child. Ermei drives the tractor all night and arrives at the town, where the child is checked and diagnosed. In this process, she takes on the responsibilities of a patriarch, while her husband remains unconscious and passive throughout. At the end of the film, when Ermei takes the child for a walk around a commercial square, Zhang Suo encounters a drinking mate in the street and 'reluctantly' joins him. Zhang's impotence in shouldering paternal responsibility and his drinking cause him to lose his patriarchal authority in the domestic space, and Ermei accordingly asserts her autonomy and authority.

The changing status to a certain degree reflects the uneven relationships between the rural and the urban. Away from the urban space infiltrated with power dynamics, social mobility and 'differences that are ascribed to gender, sexual practice . . . class, region etc., and their expression in social space and geohistorically uneven development' (Soja 1996: 88), Ermei assures her subjectivity by being a caring mother, a hard-working wife and a responsible daughter-in-law in the rural space. For Ermei, 'the domestic space turns into a contested space for both hegemonic (conservative, order-maintaining) and counter-hegemonic (resistant, order-transforming) cultural and identity politics' (Soja 1996: 87). In other words, the originally conservative and male-dominated domestic space is challenged by Ermei, with her resistance to male orders and acceptance of responsibilities. Ermei is a passive recipient of all sorts of suffering at the beginning, but can be strong-minded and rebellious in the face of unbearable and outrageous situations. She finally secures a stable life in the arranged marriage, which comes with the price of the inversion of her gender role and an exhausting household burden.

The train: trope of an alternative life

The train is repeatedly mentioned but never visualised in *The Story of Ermei*, apart from a toy train in the closing sequences. With excessive mobility and the crystallisation of technology, the train is the symbol of modern life, conveying a romantic and utopian aura for young people from the hinterland of China. Throughout the history of film, the parallel train tracks have always been a fascinating image. According to Kirby, 'the train is a mechanical double for the cinema and for the transport of the spectator into fiction, fantasy, and dream', as it is 'a machine of vision and an instrument for conquering space and time' (Kirby 1997: 2). In *The Story of Ermei*, neither Ermei nor Qiao Liansheng has a chance to board a train. At a rare romantic moment in their relationship, the train, as a metaphor of hope and access to an alternative life, adds a layer of romance to their trivial immediate daily routines. In other films, such as Jia Zhangke's 2000 *Platform*, the train functions as an important trope of hope and dreams for a troupe of singers and performers in Shanxi Province. As young as Ermei and Qiao, they cheer and shout at the sight of a train thundering from a distance. Like Ermei and Qiao, they have never had a chance to take a train, but yearn to go beyond their home town to see the world and experience a different way of life. In the reform era, young people from the geographically remote and economically marginalised Shanxi and Shaanxi provinces (both located in the northern hinterland area) have been longing to crossing provincial boundaries to the faraway south and east, but they would usually find themselves enclosed in the small village or town where they grew up.

The train, as a 'transitional dynamic space' and the mechanism that marks the urban space, keeps the urban space under constant transformation and brings massive population migration, has frequently been associated with the production of 'a fragmented and alienated social sphere' (Pratt and Juan 2014: 49–54). In films such as Dziga Vertov's 1929 *Man with a Movie Camera* and the Lumière brothers' short film *The Arrival of a Train at La Ciotat Station* (1896), the train represents 'limitless possibilities' and imparts shocking experiences to audiences. They are spaces that retain 'a history of industrialisation' and propose 'an urban space moving towards an uncertain future' (Pratt and Juan 2014: 54). The above examples show the affinity between the train and urban space, mechanisation and sense of time, speeding movement and modernity. In the context of Chinese urbanisation, the train has facilitated the rural–urban mobility of the Chinese population since the 1980s. However, young people from the hinterland area, especially the western regions, seem to be excluded from access to the train and the urbanised modern world at the other end of the track. Modernisation is too abstract for people like Ermei and Qiao to understand. For them, it means electronic devices such as radio and TV, and programs and pop music broadcast on TV, from which they learn what modern life looks like. Ermei can imagine and talk about places such as Germany, France and the US, but she may never be able to reach them (Zhu and Tu 2004: 21–2). Disillusioned and frustrated by her own urban experiences, Ermei still expects a bright and promising future for her son in different places overseas. Even though she has become aware that modern life represented on TV may never be part of her own daily life, distant modernisation nevertheless remains desirable and appealing. As the film approaches its end, Ermei learns that Mao Nü has gone to Guangzhou, the most developed and commercialised area in southern China, by train. 'By train', Ermei murmurs and repeats the words, holding her crying baby boy and trying to calm him down. Ermei reveals little concern about the probable adversities confronting Mao Nü in a distant and strange place. Rather, she seems more interested in the different life Mao Nü can lead. In the following sequences, she takes the boy to a toy train, picturing a grand blueprint for her son to travel as far as Germany, France and America. It seems that in Ermei's perception, life outside of the rural home town must be promising.

Ermei's escape and final return to the rural area is a compromise between individual freedom and a stable life. She grows from being a country girl with ambivalent will and voice into a strong woman who takes charge of the family. Crossing the boundary between the rural and the urban, she experiences the fluctuation in social status and realises the power structure behind gender and social class. Even though she returns to the countryside eventually, the city and foreign states still claim her imagination and expectation for the next generation. A stark contrast to this is found in *Weaving Girl* where the city is associated with disease and death, which comes to symbolise the end of a socialist utopia.

Weaving Girl: State-owned Enterprise and the Female Worker

Weaving Girl (2009) explores female bodies and human suffering in a grim anonymous industrial area plagued with rundown factories, alienated streets and dilapidated neighbourhoods. Li Li (Yu Nan) works in a state-owned textile plant and struggles with poor wages, disease and suffocating daily routines. The plant is on the verge of bankruptcy, and has hundreds of weaving girls like Li Li facing financial difficulties and bleak prospects. They wear uniforms, working between rows of textile machines roaring day and night. The factory and the workers in uniform are reminiscent of Jia Zhangke's 2008 *24 City* in which the state-owned factory is located in Chengdu and functions as a well-designed kingdom that provides all the infrastructure needed to satisfy the personal and public needs of the proletariat working and dwelling in the space. Related to military production and maintenance, the factory has thrived as an independent and all-inclusive utopia since its establishment. In contrast, the textile factory in *Weaving Girl* is far less influential in terms of its scale and production. It represents an unpleasant working space for Li Li and her colleagues and a company in disrepair that provides meagre wages. Sometimes workers' wages are withheld according to unreasonable 'rules', causing Li Li to lose her temper early in the film.

The film unfolds spatially by following the protagonist travelling between two different places. The first part is set in Xi'an, showing the tedious daily routines in Li Li's working and living spaces. She often appears absent-minded, upset and annoyed. The following part traces her trip to Beijing for a long-yearned-for answer from her first love who was assigned to another state-owned enterprise in Beijing ten years ago. Li Li's mundane life in Xi'an and her trip to Beijing cast a realistic comparison between the two cities, showing the uneven economic situations and different prospects of the two regions. The cinematic image of Xi'an in *Weaving Girl* is associated with critical illnesses suffered by female characters, which can be regarded as resonating with the collapse of the state-owned enterprise. The industrial district of the city is half-abandoned and lifeless, leaving the once respected proletariat in poverty or even dying. In contrast to the on-screen Beijing, the metropolitan hub packed with busy traffic, construction sites and large population, Xi'an is represented in film as a self-enclosed place, remaining in the socialist past and having no promising future for its citizens. The film portrays Li Li, a wayward girl who marries for revenge on her parents rather than for love, a mother who fails to establish intimate relations with her son, a weaving girl who has only a few months of life left, and a group of weaving girls struggling to survive after being laid-off.

Xi'an: a time capsule of socialist China

Weaving Girl opens with disturbing mechanical noises made by hundreds of textile machines in an enormous factory space. With her back to the camera, the protagonist Li Li walks quickly across rows of machines, complaining and cursing. A man is chasing after her with an envelope containing Li Li's wages in his hand, but he is challenged by Li Li's furious question: 'Why the hell withhold my salary?' The conflict ends with her returning to her position. A colleague comes over to enquire about the situation, which reveals the reason why Li Li's salary was partially deducted – she had fallen foul of the regulations of the enterprise by eating a meal in the working area. The colleague tells Li Li that her salary is also withheld for the same reason. The different reaction towards the same issue reveals Li Li's strong personality. Employees perceive the irrational rule as an excuse by the company to exploit workers. In the following sequences set in a public bathroom, another of Li Li's colleagues, who encounters the same situation, complains, 'Don't you know our factory? Whenever they raise our pay, they will find excuses to cut it short.' The sequences reveal the tangled relations between the company and the employees. The rule 'No food in the working space' is not highly demanding, but why do workers keep breaching it? Maybe there is no proper place provided for lunch; maybe there is, but workers find it difficult to squeeze time for eating and relaxation as well as completing their workload. The contradiction between company rules and workers' preferred dining space exposes the lack or dislocation of infrastructural and spatial supplements in this industrial complex.

The following sequences boldly display naked female bodies in a shower room. This is neither the socialist depiction of female as genderless and politicalised subject, nor the commercialised fetishism of female bodies. According to Ray Chow, in socialist Chinese cinema female images and bodies show a tendency to downplay the 'gendered or sexualised specifics of women's agency'. Since the 1980s, the female body has become a site of exhibition devoted to rediscovering 'the conventions of fetishism that had been evident in early Chinese filmmaking' (Chow 2013: 493–5). However, the public bathroom scene in *Weaving Girl* is represented in such a plain way that it avoids the spectacle of female bodies shown from an ethnographic perspective like that of the Fifth Generation veterans, as represented in Zhang Yimou's 1991 *Raise the Red Lantern*. Li Li even takes her toddler son into the bathroom. He is accustomed to being there and calmly plays with Li Li's colleagues. In this highly gendered space, Wang Quan'an filters the fetishism of the female body, showing it not as particularly beautiful or appealing; in fact, most of them have reached middle age. It is a secure space for them to take off their social masks, exchange true feelings and complain about the inhumane rules and regulations. It is a dreamlike space, enclosed, safe and free, indicating that there is no room outside this bathroom for women to protect them from violence and exploitation in society. Just like the innocent kid, they are powerless to change the outside world (Rashkin 1993: 114).

The image of Xi'an depicted in *Weaving Girl* does not bear the heavy historical and cultural weight associated with this ancient capital city with more than a thousand years of history. Instead, it appears as a grim anonymous industrial area, with rundown factories and alienated streets and neighbourhoods. When Li Li and her friends are taking a break outside the main building, the camera draws audience's attention to the redbrick wall of the structure. The wall, including window frames and windowsills, is covered by clumps of grey flock that have accumulated over the years (Figure 7.1). Seated under the windows, Li Li's friend Wujie (Shi Xiaoping) talks about her breast cancer and how it is a heavy blow to her family, and wonders why Li Li suddenly becomes so silent and cautious. Wujie despises a newly recruited young girl who is attracted to an accordionist, while Li Li takes a glimpse at the giggling girl without making any comment. The understated romance between the girl and the accordionist resonates with the romance between Li Li and Zhao Luhan (Zhao Luhan), who was Li Li's first love and used to work in the same factory long before the city was reduced to a silent and grey industrial site inhabited and appropriated by groups of laid-off workers.

The working space and bathroom have remained the same for decades, carrying on the socialist way of production and management. In addition, workers' entertainment activities have also passed down from generation to generation. On a snowy day, a group of female workers rehearse a chorus of a Soviet song 'Weaving Girl' on an outdoor stage. Li Li stands in the centre of the choir, but suddenly faints. There are red curtains hanging in the background of the stage and a five-star logo attached to the front wall of the stage, reminding us of past socialist decorations and routines of public life (Figure 7.2). The Soviet song was composed over half a century ago and the film illustrates how it is still practised and appreciated by the working class in the western hinterland area, while in Beijing, as shown in Zhao Luhan's case, such forms of amusement have long vanished. When the increasingly commercialised outside world infiltrates the domestic space through newspapers, magazines, TV and films, people who have been entrapped in the small kingdom grow increasingly dissatisfied but immobilised in a strong sense of impotence.

Li Li's home is located next to the industrial district with colossal chimneys emitting smoke day and night. Intertwined cables crisscross the neighbourhood, creating a typical scene of an industrial dwelling space and sense of unease. The harsh and freezing environment encapsulates this group of people in an old and slow-paced space where people sing the

FEMALE SPACE AND BODIES 169

Figure 7.1 Walls and window frames: in *Weaving Girl*

Figure 7.2 The Soviet style outdoor stage: in *Weaving Girl*

old songs, work on obsolete machines and live in rundown socialist-style buildings. The space is more like somebody's pale memory of an unpleasant past. Meanwhile, Beijing has already erased the old industrial traces imprinted by socialist China.

Both Jia Zhangke and Wang Quan'an record the disappearing state-owned socialist companies and the struggling workers emotionally trapped in the past and confronted with their miserable lives. The 'local items of the present and the here-and-now can be made to express and to designate the absent, unrepresentable totality' (Jameson 1992: 10). In *24 City*, the state-owned company is relocated to a nearby county, while in *Weaving Girl*, the factory is shut down on a grim snowy day. Its gate is shut tight, the yard is empty and a dark grey tone infiltrates the scene. Outside the gate, a peddler slowly passes the factory, followed by a motorised tricycle driving from the opposite direction and then disappearing (Figure 7.3). The scenario indicates the possible occupations that the workers may take after being dismissed. The factory used to provide a long-term stable career and an affluent life, but it has turned into a wasteland packed with stagnant and abandoned buildings. The camera gazes at the beige structure of the main entrance from a distance in long shots, indicating 'the jarring coexistence of the ordinary and the extraordinary, of the irreversible events of history and the repetitive small movements of everyday life' (Pratt and Juan 2014: 42). For the workers, the space was used to exhibit a respectable social status in the socialist era; however, the rundown factory and plain buildings that still stand in the reform era become undesired alternatives, since they represent neither the traditional and richly evocative world of agricultural China, nor a strong and affluent modern China. Moreover, the stagnant and abandoned industrial sites (Figure 7.4), present as a ruined space, embody the contradictions between political and economic power and the uncertain future of ordinary individuals.

Weaving Girl shows that the urban dissolution and rearrangement driven by the market are irresistible, and exposes a group of disappointed and debilitated people trapped in the previous spatial arrangement and social relations. The freezing and silent industrial city and the disease-ridden female characters become an intertextual signification. Li Li's leukaemia and Wujie's breast cancer are both severe and incurable diseases that threaten the well-being of themselves and their respective families. Family as the basic unit of society moves alongside the rise and fall of the enterprise. In Li Li's case, her disease impoverishes the family. Her husband sells their house before the New Year in order to raise enough money for Li Li's treatment. In Wujie's case, she is abandoned by her husband and child as the breast cancer financially exhausts the family. Living alone, she occupies herself with dancing in nightclubs. Neither of them reacts violently, but rather attempts to deal with the rest of their life, no matter how short or bad it is. As important subjects of a social discourse, disease-ridden bodies and unruly dangerous urban spaces are often juxtaposed to show the social fear of precarious situations (such as various contagions and pollution) and the obsessive desire to control them. As Barbara Hooper contends:

> desires for controlling and mastering [the unruly and haphazard situations become] the spatial practice of enclosing unruly elements within carefully guarded spaces. These acts of differentiation, separation, and enclosure involve material, symbolic, and lived spaces . . . bodies and cities and texts . . . and are practiced as a politics of difference, as segregation and separation. (Cited in Soja 1996:114)

In the film, the 'politics of difference' are practised through the separation of the working class (who are living in a dilapidated neighbourhood) from the emerging commercialised space. The fateful diseases suffered by the characters resonate with the collapse of the state-owned enterprise. Like the incurable diseases, the bankrupt factory cannot be restored. Both

Figure 7.3 A peddler passing by and a motorised tricycle: in *Weaving Girl*

FEMALE SPACE AND BODIES 173

Figure 7.4 Abandoned socialist factories: in *Weaving Girl*

of them stand for the 'the unruly' that the family and the state respectively try to 'bring under control'. The disease-ridden body and disintegrating factory will soon disappear from the terrain that massive and dynamic urbanisation claims. While the reform era bears witness to the fast pace of urbanisation and privatisation, it also drags the previously privileged working class down to a lower social position. Correspondingly, their working and living spaces are erased from the map of an advancing modern cityscape. That is, the space of production in the reform era has retreated into the background, making way for the post-socialist market-driven spaces of consumption. The social relations that were established around the previous social spaces also gradually melt away in a market-oriented context.

Beijing: a stark contrast to Xi'an

Li Li perceives Beidaihe (a coastal holiday resort near Beijing) and Beijing as an alternative ideal space for living, and more significantly, they are spaces of romance and hope. She still treasures the memory of her time with Zhao Luhan, who used to be an accordionist and passionately envisaged the beauty of Beidaihe when they were in a relationship a decade ago. Both places are far away from hinterland Xi'an, and set as a contrast in terms of physical appearance and emotional attachment. When Li Li first arrives in Beijing, she appears surprised and engaged by the stylish skyscrapers and the bustling traffic of the metropolitan space (Figure 7.5). She sees the CCTV Headquarters under construction (which indicates that the story is probably set around 2009). The monumental complex is an 'official site for remembering official history and simultaneously forgetting or erasing counterclaims to space; they are often dead zones that close off the possibilities for urban politics and contestation' (Pratt and Juan 2014: 105). As the political and propaganda centre of the state government, the tremendous CCTV structure signals the miraculous economic development of China and the official rhetoric overwhelmingly deafens the voices of underprivileged individuals. Ten years ago, Zhao Luhan left the textile factory in Xi'an and was reassigned to a dye factory in Beijing. The narration does not provide a specific reason why Zhao had to leave, but the state-owned enterprise, as representative of an enormous organisation, often appears as a space of power that can exercise operations across regions. Zhao's reassigned job can therefore be seen as a result of the omnipotent invisible hand of power that conducts its redistribution of resources and labour.

Figure 7.5 The cityscape of Beijing: in *Weaving Girl*

The modern street scenes of Beijing are soon followed by a massive site of ruins as Li Li comes to the old address of Zhao Luhan's working unit. The ruins, corresponding with the construction works that she saw on her way, show Beijing as a dynamic and estranged place. Beijing is on the path of a 'reconstructing urban space' where the character *chai* (拆) (which means to demolish or to tear down) has a ubiquitous presence. It is perceived by Sheldon Lu as the 'proper name for contemporary "China" as all Chinese cities have witnessed the destruction of old buildings and the construction of new structures' (2007b: 137). The ruins and the character *chai*, as noted in previous chapters in relation to *Still Life*, *24 City* and *Buddha Mountain*, display a transforming China where destruction is juxtaposed with construction, tradition with modernisation, optimism with trauma. In *Weaving Girl*, such colossal changes in the cityscape (Beijing) disturb the local residents and delay Li Li's searching for Zhao Luhan. When Li Li asks a passer-by about the dye factory, he replies briefly that he is not a native of Beijing. Li Li then turns to an old man who wanders around the ruins; he tells her that the factory was relocated ten years ago. The time neatly coincides with the time when Zhao moved to Beijing. From their conversation, we can visualise a dynamic Beijing that has constantly been in the process of deconstruction and reconstruction since the 1990s. The industrial area is first replaced by an accommodation area and now another round of urban transformation is underway. It is a space characterised by mobility, transience and dynamism. The presence of ruins in the narrative of Beijing (Figure 7.6), 'with all of its implications of past, present and future', reveals the uncertainties that surround the city (Pratt and Juan 2014: 43). Beijing is like a melting pot that encourages outsiders to venture and participate in multiple transformations, and allows the natives to wander around their old dwelling space with a sense of nostalgia.

Construction and demolition, mobility and nostalgia are juxtaposed in the everyday life of metropolitan Beijing. Landmarks are erected, modern constructions and skyscrapers continuously push the urban space further horizontally and vertically. In this extensive transformation, Beijing, as a highly integrated political, cultural, social and economic centre, has overwhelmed the individual under the grand narrative of national progress and economic miracles. The extraordinary process of urbanisation and modernisation silences and overshadows the voices and preferences of individuals. Zhao Luhan, the romanticised accordionist, has put away his instrument since he arrived in Beijing. When Li Li finds him, he is sitting

FEMALE SPACE AND BODIES 177

Figure 7.6 The character Chai (拆) and the ruins: in *Weaving Girl*

beside a large machine, leaning to one side with an exhausted expression on his face. After ten years, he appears more embarrassed than surprised at Li Li's unexpected arrival. When Li Li asks him why he has not replied to her letters over the past years, he pauses for a while, murmuring that he did not receive any letters from her. The hundreds of letters that have mysteriously evaporated signify the insignificant existence of the individual in the face of an overarching national discourse. Mysteriously, their private life is strongly affected by a grander narrative. The national political power, 'wielded by those in positions of authority, does not merely manipulate naively given differences between individuals and social groups', but it 'actively produces and reproduces difference as a key strategy to create and maintain modes of social and spatial division that are advantageous to its continued empowerment and authority' (Soja 1996: 87). In this film, such spatial and social division is imposed on scales from personal life to regional disparities.

At the end of the film, Zhao takes out the dust-covered accordion, playing the song he once sang and appreciated with Li Li. The melancholy tone fits with Li Li's current situation. She is lying unconscious in a hospital in Xi'an before the medical equipment beside her emits subtle sounds that indicate that Li Li has died. The cityscape of Xi'an appears static and stagnant, while Beijing appears dynamic and advancing. In Beijing, large scale demolition erases the neighbourhood and community, and produces debris and rubble, but the space promises a new life characterised by modernity and a promising future. There is a Maoist saying that '*Bu po bu li*' [there is no construction without destruction] (cited in Schultz 2016: 440). However, Xi'an's representation in *Weaving Girl* shows a scene of no destruction, therefore no construction.

PART V
CINEMATIC LANZHOU

CHAPTER 8

Contrast between the Urban and the Rural Regarding Mental and Social Space

Lanzhou, the capital city of Gansu province, often makes an 'absent presence' in films, as it often appears as the reference to modernity and a future destination in the eyes of film characters from the adjacent areas. Compared to the other three cinematic cities in western China, Lanzhou has the least exposure on the big screen. The city and its adjacent areas have been frequently associated with environmental pollution, a fragile ecosystem and deteriorating land. Urbanisation and modernisation have exacerbated the inherently fragile environment of the area, and films about the region, directly or indirectly, reflect such ecological and geographical changes, and the consequent economic, social and environmental issues. The frontier landscape outside Lanzhou provides a similar setting to the American Western, and has attracted many Chinese filmmakers to utilise the vast wild canvas to visualise their contemplation of the contemporary Chinese western reality and national modernity. Chen Jianbin's directorial debut *A Fool* (2014) displays such a 'absent presence' of the provincial capital city by introducing an in-between space of a small town located between Lanzhou and the rural area. The cinematic town creates a space of 'thirding' that breaks the mainstream representation of the area, either as the Chinese Western genre featuring vast expanses of desert, galloping horses and thrilling gunfights, or minority films characterised by the exotic costumes and mysterious religious rituals of ethnic minorities. I will then extend this idea of thirding the representation of the region by introducing a minority film River Road (Li Ruijun, 2015) to enhance the awareness of an evolving and fluid image of the area and the people.

The Cinematic City as an Absent Presence

Filmic Lanzhou remains mostly focused on the countryside and the vast barren desert. Lanzhou itself appears either in contrast to the rural area or as a space of banal everyday life. *The Red Awn* [*Hongse kangbaiyin*]

(Cai Shangjun, 2007), set in the Hexi corridor area, depicts a broken family and a troubled father–son relationship. Lanzhou appears as a controversial space for rural people: on the one hand, it appeals to innocent countrymen with plenty of opportunities for work, proper education and a promise of a better life; on the other hand, it takes a toll on their health, exploits them economically and diminishes them socially. *Up to the Mountain, Overlooking the Running River* [*Shangqu gaoshan wang pingchuan*] (Wang Fanqin, 2013) ambitiously covers issues including rural education, immigration and the construction of Lanzhou New Area, a state-level special economic zone to the north of Lanzhou established in 2012 (*China approves new state-level SEZ in Gansu* 2012). It shows the deteriorating rural environment and complicated rural immigration issues, and praises the new life in the newly developed area. Mountains and hundreds of villages have been bulldozed to make way for the building of the New Area, the fifth state-level special free trade zone after Shanghai's Pudong, Tianjin's Binhai, Chongqing's Liangjiang and Zhejiang's Zhoushan. However, outside the film, the designated area undergoing construction is perceived as a 'ghost city' by the locals of Lanzhou and visitors from outside the province, as it is empty and lacks vitality (Phillips 2017).

Another film, *The Missing Sheep* [*Diu yang*] (Wang Xiaoping, 2016), based in a subsidiary town of Lanzhou, features a shepherd who loses four sheep and eventually receives compensation for his loss from superior administration executives. The film's straightforward, almost banal premise exposes the local government officials' misconduct and corruption and reflects the difficulties an underprivileged shepherd can encounter at different levels of administration in the process of acquiring justice. However, the ending shows that government misconduct can be corrected and justice will prevail with the arrival of an upright superior official. *Hearing Implant* [*Erwo*] (Fang Junliang, 2015) is one of the few films set in urban Lanzhou and is based on a true story about a common family's twisted journey in search of a lost cochlear implant that costs 280,000 RMB. Unfolding like newsreels, the film displays the cityscape in detail by following the family members walking through vibrant city streets occupied by peddlers, imposters, trash pickers and pedestrians. In search of the expensive hearing implant, with grandmother becoming the victim of fraud and grandfather's health condition deteriorating, the already impoverished family slips into desperation. The film features warm-hearted citizens and responsible media workers in Lanzhou who provide assistance in the process. In the above films, the city itself does not necessarily present an advanced and glossy metropolitan appearance.

Instead, it is frequently referred to as 'the provincial capital' without being specifically named. Even though *Hearing Implant* is shot on location, the street scenes of Lanzhou do not stand out from any of the nearby towns in Gansu province. Rather, the city and its adjacent areas are frequently associated with desert, barren land, drought and environmental issues.

Cinematically, the barren land near Lanzhou is represented not only as a place of challenging natural conditions, but also a space of isolation, disorder, poverty and backwardness. Moreover, the isolated and wild desert serves as a sanctuary for criminals and a battlefield between order and disorder, the official and the non-official, as can be seen in Gao Qunshu's 2010 *Wind Blast*. The geographical and meteorological conditions of the land are suited to a nomadic way of living. Sheep, horse, camel or cattle herding become the overt images of the area, with protagonists in films often accompanied or symbolised by these animals, which can be seen in films such as *The Missing Sheep* (2016) and *A Fool* (2014). The brutal natural conditions of the area yield not only particular ways of production, poverty and misery, but constrain the development of education, traffic and business infrastructure. Cinematic works such as *Pretty Big Feet* [*Meili de dajiao*] (Yang Yazhou, 2002), set in the barren desert, show the lack of staff and basic facilities for teaching and learning in an elementary school. Similarly, *The Call of Maiji Mountain* [*Maiji shan de huhuan*] (Li Jialun, 2011) features two university graduates who voluntarily join a primary school in rural Tianshui, located three hours away from Lanzhou, imparting knowledge to students from the rural village and enlightening them by introducing new technology and new musical instruments. As one of the most remote regions in contemporary China, different levels of administration of the north-west face a shortage of educational resources such as school facilities, campus infrastructure and educational talents. Scenes of yellow earth and poorly equipped country schools dominate these films, while the provincial capital Lanzhou appears to have numerous education and job opportunities, and its 'developed' economy signifies a utopian space for the confined rural populace.

Such fascination with utopian urban space is absent in Li Ruijun's cinematic representation of his home town of rural Gaotai, one of the small cities located in the Hexi corridor. Similar to Jia Zhangke, who represented his home town Fenyang in a trilogy, Li Ruijun films Gaotai and the adjacent places in an array of works including *The Old Donkey* [*Lao lü tou*] (2010), *Fly with the Crane* [*Gaosu tamen, wo cheng baihe qule*, lit. *Tell them, I flew away with the crane*] (2012) and *River Road* [*Jia zai shuicao fengmao de difang*, lit. *Home located in a lush green place*] (2015). Adopting a realistic style, Li touches upon the most concerning problems triggered by urbanisation and environmental deterioration in the north-west Gansu province. *The Old Donkey* revolves around a seventy-three-year-old man who fights to preserve his farmland and ancestral graves on the edge of the desert. Serious desertification drives farmers and herdsmen away from home to urban areas or distant fertile lands, leaving behind children and the elderly. The small village becomes an ageing and abandoned place. In *Fly with the Crane*, the same old man stubbornly resists cremation advocated by the local government, as he and his generation cannot accept the concept and practice of being burned to ashes after death. He asks his grandson to bury him alive on the bank of a river, and to tell his family that he has flown away with the crane. Traditionally, 'flying with the crane' is a figurative expression indicating death, in particular, an elegant and decent death. Conventionally, the older generation prefers to be buried in a red coffin with painted cranes, clouds and pine trees, since they believe in an afterlife and reincarnation. To be buried instead of being burned means a proper passing and a possible afterlife. The direct conflicts between village people and the government units in enforcing the new funeral policy reflect a tangled situation between tenacious traditions and government's social and environmental concerns. *River Road* emphasises the environmental problems by representing two young brothers' long desert journey on camelback. Drought and desertification wipe out the necessary resources for living, driving the nomadic people from one place to another. Home becomes a mobilised, unstable and separated space in such circumstances.

Countryside dominates the cinematic representations of the region, and protagonists in the above films often have various kinds of disease, such as a father who suffers sever lumbar vertebrae damage in *The Red Awn*, a deaf girl and her grandfather with Alzheimer's disease in *Hearing Implant* and a disease-ridden grandfather and mother in *River Road*. The human suffering resonates with the barren land. The lush green lands that nurtured herds of healthy sheep and camels in ancient times no longer provide necessary conditions for grazing and living. When the tide of urbanisation assimilates the appearance of cities across China, the north-western cities are often overshadowed by their southern and eastern coastal counterparts, since the vulnerable ecosystem and remote geographical location of the area impede the development of the economy.

The contrast between the urban and the rural in terms of physical space

The black comedy *A Fool* was Chen Jianbin's directorial debut and he was awarded both the Best New Director and Best Actor at the 2014 Golden

Horse Awards in Taipei. Chen Jianbin is a veteran actor in Chinese TV shows, and he is both the director and the male lead in *A Fool*. The Chinese title of the film, *Yige shaozi*, literally means 'one spoon', which figuratively refers to a fool or someone insane in Xinjiang and Gansu dialects. It features Latiaozi (the nickname of Chen's character, whose real name is Ma Ji), a shepherd in a small town near Lanzhou who bumps into Shaozi (the fool, Jin Shijia), and is then followed by the fool and becomes a fool himself at the end. The protagonist's name – Latiaozi – the first and maybe the most important sign and reference to a person in the film, suggests subaltern. Latiaozi is his nickname, which has been used throughout the film, while his real name – Ma Ji – is barely used. Literally, Latiaozi refers to a type of noodle popular in north-western China. The vernacularism conveyed in his name enhances the locality of the film, and also creates a strong sense of the mundaneness and insignificance of the character. Latiaozi and his wife Jinzhizi (Jiang Qinqin) live in the small village of Caowotan. Their son is sentenced to six years' imprisonment (no specific reasons or crimes are given in the film). They borrow a large sum of money and consign it to Li Datou (Wang Xuebing) in expectation of having their imprisoned son's sentence commuted. Datou, literally means 'Big Head', but Li's head in the film appears not particularly big, so the name conveys the sarcastic meaning of Li's cunning in dealing with social relations and accumulating wealth. As a wealthy businessman, Li has connections to local officials and promises to help Latiaozi by bribing relevant institutional bodies. Latiaozi addresses Li Datou as Brother Datou throughout the film, even though he may not necessarily be younger than Li. Latiaozi's humbleness reflects that Li is socially and economically superior to him. Having handed over the sum of money, Latiaozi finds that his son's sentence remains the same. Li claims he has done what he can, but the case has been stalled beyond his control. Latiaozi sets out on a prolonged and frustrating journey of tracing the money back, travelling between the village and the nearby city to negotiate with Li. During one of his fruitless trips to the city, he kindly offers some food to a homeless man, but the filthy mentally handicapped man recognised by Latiaozi as Shaozi begins to follow him everywhere. In order to help Shaozi to find his family, Latiaozi spreads posters around the town appealing for Shaozi's family members to contact him, but this triggers series of absurdities and frauds.

In *A Fool*, Latiaozi comes from a walled village separated by a vast expanse of barren land from the nearby small city (Figure 8.1). In reality, Chen Jianbin grows up in a similar north-western circumstance before being taken to a megacity at the age of seven. Accordingly Chen sets the story in an adjacent town near Lanzhou to represent an authentic

Figure 8.1 Latiaozi's home town and surroundings: in *A Fool*

north-western rural place remembered from childhood (Chen et al. 2015: 63). To achieve 'a real touch of the local reality', he rents a shepherd's house in the village and borrows clothes from the local people to reproduce a realistic picture of an ignored and poverty-ridden rural place, portrayed without any beautification (Chen et al. 2015: 64). The location shooting invariably captures the material ambience of the place, and the employment of contrasts and vibrant colour, local accents and characters' rough mannerisms further enhance the local colour of the narration, which is reminiscent of Zhang Yimou's acclaimed realist work *The Story of Qiu Ju*.

Both Chen and Zhang's films feature frumpy farmers with red cheeks travelling between the countryside and city, attempting to solve confusion and pursue justice, but finding themselves disappointed and frustrated time after time in their confrontations with the urban social space. Both films contain images of mud-constructed houses and narrow lanes in the rural area, which provide a stark contrast to the bustling urban streets. However, the countryside in *The Story of Qiu Ju* appears more than a freezing and underprivileged place, it has an idyllic and picturesque side. Strings of dried chilli hang from eaves and walls, not only brightening the plain yard, but explaining the source of the family income. The passionate redness of the chilli and Qiu Ju's red clothes also show her unshakeable determination for pursuing justice. In the village, people maintain humane relationships, displaying simple, close and warm-hearted social relations with each other despite getting involved in disputes. The realistic techniques, such as shooting on location and using untrained actors and hidden cameras, employed by Zhang Yimou in filming *The Story of Qiu Ju* 'helped to set a new standard for realist techniques in Chinese fiction filmmaking' and contributed to realistic criticism of social issues, as it depicted 'the life struggles of the marginal and powerless' (McGrath 2008: 135). However, in *A Fool*, the warm-hearted kindnesses between common people, the idyllic country life and upright bureaucrats in the urban area are gone.

A Fool inherits the cinematic technical devices and the 'critical realism' tradition set by Zhang's work, and creates a space of 'indirect resistance' to the intrusion of commercialism and urbanisation. By saying 'indirect resistance', I mean that ordinary people in such films do not have access to the means of directly expressing their complaints and difficulties in public. Accordingly, such films do not serve as direct critiques of mainstream ideology or social injustices, but are tactically 'exposing rather than opposing', which 'rests on the belief that social contradictions are apparent in everyday life but elided in mainstream representation' (McGrath 2008: 136). The rural space represented in both films provides the characters with dwelling space and the basic ground for their simple social relationships. However, in the interaction with the urban space, their backward rural homes and marginalised social status (in comparison with people in the urban area) work as 'a central location for the production of a counter-hegemonic discourse that is not just found in words but in habits of being and the way one lives ... marginality as position and place of resistance' (Soja 1996: 98). This can be seen when Qiu Ju acquires her justice at the end of the film, though in a way she does not expect; and, in Latiaozi's case, when he finally gets his money back after a prolonged journey of negotiation with Li, he comes to be regarded as a fool.

Latiaozi's home, in a tiny village enclosed by a wall and towered fortress, appears as an isolated and sparsely populated space, which bears witness to his struggle between agrarian moralities and sophisticated urban conduct. The enormous height and magnitude of the thick walls that enclose the half-abandoned village dwarf the human inhabitants. Outside the wall is a vast expanse of desert scattered with drought-tolerant plants and broken stones, reminiscent of the landscape in Chen Kaige's 1984 *Yellow Earth*, in which the same inhospitable landscape becomes a permanent and stagnant space that blocks the characters' way out. In *A Fool*, however, the village is isolated by the surrounding desert but connected to the modern urban area by a tunnel and a busy highway (Figure 8.2). The tunnel is the boundary that divides the urban area and the countryside, and, at the same time, it is a boundary of social conduct between the urban and the rural. In reality, the small village was built in 1608 in the Ming Dynasty for military purposes. However, it has been eroded by cruel environmental degradation over 400 years. The shortage of drinkable water and the desertification in recent years drive the residents away to nearby cities, leaving the broken village to decay in harsh conditions (Song 2010).

A Fool opens with a live show in a bustling street in the town. Sounds of traffic and music create a lively and dynamic sense of the place. A local show is on, and the stage is surrounded by a group of light-hearted people watching the ongoing performance. The street scene, which is filmed on location, 'with its diversity, unpredictability and transience ... [not only shows the] physicality of urban space, [but displays] the uncertainties of modern urban life' (Pratt and Juan 2014: 19). In the film, the uncertainties soon appear with Shaozi's unexpected presence as he stalks Latiaozi.

Under the stage, Latiaozi squats on the ground, sharing a piece of pancake with a baby lamb kept in his satchel (Figure 8.3). The space under the stage is neatly covered by blue, red and white plastic tents. Shaozi walks to the back of Latiaozi, reaching out his hand from the outside of the tent for food. Contrary to the on-stage boisterous performance, the under-stage space appears lonely and grimy. The usually concealed under-stage space

URBAN AND RURAL MENTAL AND SOCIAL SPACE 189

Figure 8.2 A street scene in the town and the tunnel: in *A Fool*

Figure 8.3 The space under the stage and Latiaozi encounters Shaozi: in *A Fool*

is represented, and the announcement from the stage creates a contradictory sense: 'this is a new age when farmers don't have to plough with bulls, people don't have to light their house with oil and the Internet reaches every household'. The words praising the material progress achieved in the urban area contrast with the under-stage scene where the homeless man is wandering around begging for food.

The representation of Latiaozi huddling under the stage and his encounter with homeless Shaozi shows the alternative side of China's great economic miracle and glamorous social progress. The mainstream representation of contemporary China can be regarded as the on-stage show, proclaiming miraculous economic progress and massive transformation in cityscapes. *A Fool* peeps into the concealed and Underrepresented offstage world to reveal an alternative happening in China. Latiaozi, as a shepherd in a drought-ridden area, is left behind by society. His position and appropriation of social space indicate the disparity between the city and the countryside. For him, the countryside provides a harmonious family, a submissive wife and a herd of sheep that provides the source of the family income. It is a stable and safe place for him to relax and rule, whereas the city, with its appealing and abundant commodities, generates fraud, scams and indifference. In the interaction with Li and three groups of imposters, Latiaozi is like hapless prey hunted and exploited by vultures.

From the 1930s when Shanghai, the economic centre of mainland China, was frequently represented from the critical perspective of prostitutes' daily practice and bourgeois extravagant life, the urban space became the equivalent of moral decadence and social inequality. In leftist films of the 1930s, metropolitan cities and various urban spaces of industry, commercial exchange and residency were set in opposition to the tranquil and innocent countryside. As Zhang Yingjin contends: 'a fundamental suspicion of the moral implications of the modern city – in particular its power of penetrating, eroding, and subverting the foundations of Chinese tradition – is firmly rooted in a wide range of cultural configurations of the city' (Zhang 1996: 5). In films, the urban space represented moral decadence, chaos and adversities for rural people, while the rural space, despite its poverty and backwardness, was a sanctuary of human merit and virtues. This division can also be seen in works of the Fourth Generation, who often framed the urban and the rural into a clear-cut contrast to deal with characters' spiritual and moral dilemmas (Dai 2016). However, cinematic representation of the rural–urban relationship has been undergoing transformation since the 1980s. The countryside gradually fades into the background of a rapidly modernising China. The moral condemnation of metropolises is gradually being replaced by the celebration of the thriving market and transforming cityscape. Anxiety and disillusion wrought by economic and social inequality and class stratification replace the moral merits and idyllic lifestyles of the rural space. Meanwhile, urbanisation and modernisation intrude into the countryside, disturbing the stability, conventional values and conduct preserved in the isolated rural space. In an increasingly globalised context,

> as local stabilities break down, it is as if, no longer fixed by a circumscribed community, tactics wander out of orbit, making consumers into immigrants in a system too vast to be their own, too tightly woven for them to escape from it. (Certeau 1984: xx)

With modern traffic and technology, the impact of the urban area can easily reach the remote regions. Therefore, the simple-minded and straightforward countrymen are confused, fooled and cheated. The compelling urban influence is displayed through Latiaozi's interaction with Li and three groups of fraudsters. Such kinds of intrusion and destabilisation can be seen in *A Fool*, from every aspect of the protagonist's surroundings and his social connections.

Figure 8.4 The rear-view mirror scenes: in *A Fool*

URBAN AND RURAL MENTAL AND SOCIAL SPACE 193

Rear-view mirror and visual doorbell: the twisted gaze from the urban

In *A Fool*, Lanzhou makes an absent presence. It claims its influence through the licence plate of Li, who owns an automobile shop and a lamb shop in the city. He never shows up without his luxurious car when dealing with Latiaozi. All conversations between them occur in the car, and Latiaozi is taken to wherever it heads to without being given a chance to name his destination. In contrast, as a poor shepherd, Latiaozi has to walk between the countryside and the nearby city. The disparate mobility between a vehicle owner and a walker indicates the different paces of life in the urban area and the rural area. Director Chen employs various cinematic techniques to illustrate Latiaozi's isolation in the urban space.

Their communication always ends in deadlock as Li claims that he can do nothing about the current situation and there is no chance to get the money back. By claiming that 'I make a living by connections', Li frankly admits that he will not disturb his superior connections with Latiaozi's case. Latiaozi does not know the social connections that Li respects and depends on, just as he does not understand why three groups of imposters break into his home, claiming that the useless fool is their relative. Latiaozi is ousted from Li's car several times, left helpless and confused on the street. In Li's rear-view mirror, Latiaozi can be seen standing at the side of the street, staring in the direction of the car, getting smaller and smaller as the car drives away (Figure 8.4).

Moreover, when Latiaozi visits the well-guarded community where Li lives, he is often dismissed by Li's wife before he can enter. She arrogantly looks down upon Latiaozi's twisted face on the doorbell screen and impatiently sends him away with random excuses. It highlights the economic gap between two social classes – Latiaozi represents the underprivileged who are left behind by the economic leap in the reform era, while Li stands for those who catch up with the booming economy. Latiaozi's image, either a small point in Li's rear-view mirror, or a twisted face projected in the visual doorbell, reflects his low social status and passive reaction towards bullies and pressures from the privileged social class.

Li appears frequently in profile and with sunglasses throughout the film, and his appearance, domestic space, shops and connections remain a mystery for Latiaozi and the audience. In contrast, Latiaozi and his wife are framed frequently in close-ups that emphasise their confusion, anger and anxiety in dealing with Li and the imposters. Latiaozi's household and his way of making a living are frankly represented, just like the barren land that can hardly hide anything. Although living near to the city, he knows little about the city people and events happening in the urban space. This uneven knowledge and power is embedded in the interactions between Latiaozi and Li. Consciously or unconsciously, the two enter into a space where 'power has extended its domain right into the interior of each individual, to the roots of consciousness, to the "topias" hidden in the folds of subjectivity' (cited in Soja 1996: 32). Despite Li's arrogance and scorn, Latiaozi trusts him and regards him as an omnipotent person in the urban space. As a result, he turns to Li whenever he encounters problems and confusion. Their interactions, therefore, enhance their uneven social status and further define their respective subjectivity – the ignorant subaltern and the cunning rich.

The contrast between the urban and the rural in terms of mental and social space

In Latiaozi's interactions with Li (the representative of the urbanite) and the fraudsters (representatives of mysterious modern strangers and danger) we can see that these people's cognition of the same space and events can be wildly different, as 'the poor have highly localised mental maps in contrast to the wealthy, whose mental maps come close to reproducing a good road map from the gas station' (Soja 1996: 79). Even though this statement may generalise the fragmented, diversified and pluralised mental images of space or 'cognitive maps' (Soja 1996: 79) of those in similar circumstances, it is fairly true in the case of Latiaozi and his encounters in travelling between the rural and urban spaces.

There are three groups of imposters who come into Latiaozi's house claiming that they are relatives of Shaozi. The first group comes in one evening with Li. Wearing a bitter-sweet face, a man states that he is the elder brother of Shaozi and leaves some money with Latiaozi as a reward for taking care of his little brother. Without even asking for any evidence of the family connection, Latiaozi stands aside, watching Shaozi being taken away. The second group of fraudsters (a couple) arrives a few weeks later. With their faces covered with masks, they question Latiaozi about the location of Shaozi. Learning that Latiaozi took money (the reward money) from the previous group of imposters, the couple interprets it as an act of human trafficking. No matter how Latiaozi tries to defend himself against the slander, the couple insists that Latiaozi is involved in human trafficking, threatening him with consequences if he fails to bring Shaozi back. During the interaction, Latiaozi stands in the middle of the room, confused and frustrated, while the couple sit with their backs to the camera, hiding their appearances and identity from Latiaozi and the viewer.

Sometime later, the village officer shows up at the threshold of the sheep shed where Latiaozi passes the night, blaming Latiaozi for having abused his trust and becoming involved in human trafficking. Meanwhile, Latiaozi, dreaming of being killed, cries out like a bleating sheep. The sheep shed confrontation between the village officer and Latiaozi is a turning point in Latiaozi's journey to find Shaozi a proper shelter – searching for Shaozi's relatives, losing Shaozi to the first group of fraudsters and giving out flyers for Shaozi's whereabouts after being questioned and threatened by the aforementioned second groups of fraudsters. Before these twists and turns, Latiaozi proposed to the village officer to send Shaozi to a refuge and asked police officer Yang on behalf of Shaozi for a place to stay. However, the two local authorities refused to handle the issue, and they interpreted Latiaozi's intention as taking advantage of welfare benefits. The sheep shed scene is highly metaphorical with its cross-cuttings between the village officer's fierce verbal abuse and Latiaozi's dreadful dream of being murdered, which shows a space that is: 'simultaneously objective and subjective, material and metaphorical' (Soja 1996: 45). Materially, Latiaozi uses the sheep shed as a temporary shelter to spend the night, because he was shut out by his furious wife Jinzhizi due to the unending struggle triggered by Shaozi's presence and absence. Metaphorically, sleeping like livestock in the sheep shed becomes a metaphor for his suffering and his final ending. Just like the dumb and submissive sheep, Latiaozi's negotiation with the village officer, the police officer and Li Datou show him as a helpless sheep treated condescendingly and made to run around in circles. The opening sequences showing him carrying a little sheep also illustrate the equation between his sufferings in the city and the innocent animal. His dream of killing himself in the sheep shed indicates his change of identity, which is shown at the end of the film. He puts on the outfit previously belonging to Shaozi, looking through the tattered sun hat, seeing a group of children hit him with snowballs. The director uses this specific space to configure a sheep-like man's suffering and transformation after leaving the familiar sheep shed in the rural space and breaking into the strange urban space.

From the village official, who refuses to help Latiaozi find a proper shelter for Shaozi, to the police officer of the town, who refuses to take on the case because 'he is only a fool', Latiaozi is confronted with successive refusals from the officials who could have provided a solution for Shaozi, a social outcast. Latiaozi's experience 'reveals that the daily disposition of civil law remains much as it always has: opaque, bureaucratically ensnarled, and ever-tilted in favour of the state and its functionaries' (Silbergeld 1999: 90).

Latiaozi is left alone to take care of Shaozi, and what he does is partially out of humanity. On the one hand, he is afraid of Shaozi being frozen to death in the icy weather. On the other hand, if Shaozi accidentally freezes to death in his yard, he will be inevitably interrogated by the police. To avoid legal problems and the protest of his conscience, he cannot leave Shaozi unattended. Taken in by fraudsters, he and his wife blame themselves for giving Shaozi into the wrong hands. They decide to borrow some money to compensate the couple who claim they will come back again for Shaozi. However, there is no way to prove that he is innocent, and nobody believes his good intentions, as the compensation makes Latiaozi appear more suspicious and further deepens the misunderstanding. When the third group of imposters breaks in, Latiaozi and his wife still take their words seriously, rather than perceiving them as fraudsters. Despite being threatened and blackmailed, they tend to consider 'what a fool can be used for' instead of reporting the case to the police. The three groups of fraudsters come one by one to this rural isolated village, speaking wildly different dialects to fool the gullible couple.

Theoretically, Jinzhizi has been aware of the possible endings of people like Shaozi as there are TV programmes concerning such subjects. It is reported that mentally handicapped people will be targets for organ harvesting and free labour in illegal coal mines. Malicious scammers may capture people like Shaozi, make them physically handicapped and throw them in the streets to beg. Any of these scenarios will put Shaozi's life at risk. Tortured by guilt, Latiaozi eventually sets out to report to the police, and turns to Li for an explanation of why people keep coming for a fool. The peripheral people represented by Latiaozi, who have been invisible in mainstream representations, appear on the big screen with humility and gullibility. The three groups either show up at night or equip themselves with masks to conceal their identity and real purpose. The silent small village witnesses these outsiders come and go in a swirl of dust, leaving the honest couple bewildered. The urban area in *A Fool* is more accessible than the bustling urban regions represented in *The Story of Qiu Ju*, set in a similar rural space a decade earlier, but *A Fool* displays an urban space pervaded by more chaos, confusion and controversy for those from rural areas. When problems arise, both Qiu Ju and Latiaozi are caught in the predicament of solving the problem by negotiating with government inaction and enduring grievances and frustrations of their own. Just as Zhang Yimou points out:

> this is a very ordinary story [referring to Qiu Ju's case] that happens all the time in China. One never knows who to talk to, what to do, where to go. Most problems are not so bad to start with, they only become so because of the working of the

bureaucratic system and the ordeals you have to go through. In China, you have to try twenty times, spend years in order to solve the most minor problems. Officials don't make any mistakes really, but in the end, there's never any answer. (Cited in Silbergeld 1999: 129)

Two decades after Qiu Ju's case, Latiaozi is going through exactly the same frustration and confusion. The modern urban world shown in *A Fool* appears as an opaque space operating in a complicated way. It is pervaded by vehicles, carefully locked doors and cautiously covered faces. A clear boundary between the countryside and the urban area is established by the huge gap of living environment, material possessions and disparate behaviour and manners. The difference, first of all, is reflected in the physical spaces of the respective areas. Latiaozi as a sheep farmer lives in an enclosed rundown village, while Li has several households and is involved in the businesses of livestock and automobiles in the urban area. In the interaction with Li, Latiaozi is always on foot, whereas Li appears in his car and ditches Latiaozi wherever and whenever he wants to. The first meeting between Latiaozi and Li in the film is a near miss car accident. Latiaozi squats down in front of Li's luxurious car, scrubbing the bumper, while Li starts the car, almost running him over. The extremely high angle from which Li looks down from his car in search of Latiaozi indicates the unequal social positions between the two. Latiaozi's lack of knowledge about urban conduct and his weak social connections are amplified in the urban space. Due to the fragmented and labyrinthine urban space, Latiaozi is able to disorient Shaozi and get rid of him. Meanwhile, the mobility and unpredictability of the urban space bring groups of fraudsters to Latiaozi's house and leave him bewildered and lost. He is unconsciously involved in the 'mythical' and 'demonic' side of urban space, experiencing all the frauds, lies, blame, sneers and misunderstandings while asking his simple and straightforward question: 'Why do people come for a useless fool?' Mentally, Latiaozi and his wife still hold on to traditional social conduct and manners, which can be seen in the differing manner of receiving guests. They open their household wide to welcome anyone who visits. Whether they know the people or not, the wife will hurry out to buy bottles of wine, cigarettes and snacks to offer hospitality to visitors. Li's wife, on the other hand, cautiously communicates with visitors through a screen and never lets strangers into the house.

Latiaozi's particular way of receiving visitors is inherited from the agrarian norm similarly represented in *The Story of Qiu Ju*. In that film, even though there is conflict between Qiu Ju and the village officer – she even sues the officer for his misconduct – she still visits the village officer and receives kind salutations from the family. In an enclosed small village, where everyone is related to everyone else socially and economically in one way or another, the social network is relatively simple and warm-hearted. However, the straightforward and innocent social relations make these people gullible in sophisticated commercialised surroundings. Compared to Qiu Ju, who finally retained her countryside innocence and happiness after interacting with the urban surroundings, Latiaozi is overwhelmed, bewildered and transformed into a fool in his interaction with urban society, and in the end becomes identified as an outsider to modern society.

In the prolonged and frustrating process of negotiating with Li and the fraudsters, Latiaozi never doubts their statements. He trusts the urbanites unconditionally and indiscriminately. The inequality in economic terms, social status and inadequate knowledge and information about the urban space produces a gullible and fallible group of people. Spatially, this group of people reside in a rather small and backward social space that isolates them from the outside world and leaves them behind in time. It is a time when frauds are ubiquitous in the urban area and a time when urban people keep a suspicious eye on things they see and listen for overtones. The tiny villages, enclosed by thick walls and the vast barren land outside, are in contrast to the divided and fragmented urban spaces – one requires no effort to know and understand, while the other is too dynamic and opaque to see through.

At the end of the film, Latiaozi puts on the battered red sun hat left by Shaozi, and looks through it, seeing a group of local folk dancers walking towards him (Figure 8.5). The dancers, in flamboyant coloured costumes, drag their instruments, appearing fatigued and bored. Yet in the previous sequences, the same group of people staged a lively performance. In mainstream representation, we generally see what is on the stage. *A Fool* directs spectators to see what is under the stage and what it looks like after the performance. At the end, a group of children corner Latiaozi and hit him with snowballs, shouting 'hit the fool, hit the fool . . .' at the top of their lungs, just as they had done to Shaozi in a previous scene. Yet on that occasion Latiaozi was there to protect Shaozi and drove the children away. This time, now that Latiaozi himself has become a fool, he does not fight back. He remains silent and stands still, dumbly waiting for the snowballs to hit him. With his identity transformed, he might finally find the answer to his enquiry about the value of being a fool. However, as Jinzhizi has explained, he might also risk his life in the journey of figuring out the answer. The negotiation between Latiaozi and all those from the urban area is the interaction between the remote and enclosed small village and the dynamic urban space. In the prolonged and agitated process, the director portrays how a simple-minded and good-natured individual is deceived, cheated and exiled by the commercialised and mercenary urban world.

Figure 8.5 Latiaozi becomes Shaozi: in *A Fool*

Latiaozi represents the group of people in contemporary China called 'the grassroots'. His simple, rough and bewildering way of existence constitutes 'the rare picture of another type of the so-called "original eco-state of life" that lies locally beneath and beyond the glaring glamour of globalisation in China today' (Zhang 2009: 144). With urbanisation fast advancing, Chinese rural areas have seen unprecedented intrusion and infiltration of urban influence. The shortened distance between rural and urban areas in *A Fool* indicates the speed and overwhelming impact of the urban world on rural traditions and ways of living. Villages are decaying, with villagers bewildered and tricked by urban conduct and imposters. Chen's carefully designed on-location shooting anchors the 'filmic experience in the real world, sustain[s] documentary claims to truthfulness, and position[s] the viewer as witness to (and not simply passive spectator of) events' (Pratt and Juan 2014: 55). The 'making of a fool' reflects the sprawling urban influence and the power of capital and knowledge that transforms rural life and squeezes the rural living space. In another film, *River Road*, such transforming power appears more dramatic, with the inhabitants deprived of health, traditional ways of production and home.

Modernisation and environmental concerns

The rural feature *River Road*, based in the Hexi corridor where towns and villages have been devoured by the encroaching desert, provides the perspective of two little boys who are left behind by their parents and strive for a better life in a distant place. It exposes the disappearance of home and community, mode of production, ethnic cultural heritage and diversity of culture, which is caused by environmental degradation and ecological destruction. The disappearing spaces are archived and preserved by films as a virtual space that becomes a 'Thirdspace', 'which is differentiated and estranged from both the traditional space and the modern space, and projects a resistant space on screen to recollect the past while questioning and challenging the present and the future' (Nie 2009: 203). Mysterious religious rituals in previous representative minority films disappear in *River Road*, and people in traditional costumes are only present at the end of the school semester when parents come to pick up their children and at grandfather's funeral.

Similarly, *Tuya's Marriage*, set in the Inner Mongolian steppe grassland, tells the story of a female and familial predicament in the face of desertification and water shortage. The film makes 'a direct and severe questioning and critique, if not an indictment, of the nation's political, cultural and economic policies, by presenting the devastation afflicted upon the Mongolians resulting from overheated economic development and its ensuing problems in contemporary China' (Li 2013: 134). Minority religious rituals and spectacles of ethnic singing and dancing, as the most recognisable features of the minority group, are also absent in this film. Stripped of all these traditional characteristics of the minority subject, Li Ruijun portrays a disappearing nomadic lifestyle. On the one hand, the nomads have been assimilated into the Han-centred culture, while still preserving their own particular economic, social and cultural practices in the long course of history; on the other hand, an increasingly similar way of production and living is engendered under the pressing urbanisation and vanishing steppe. With traditional nomadic communities destabilised by intruding industrialisation and a deteriorating environment, local communities' attachment to land, home and space are accordingly confronted with deconstruction. The new mode of production generated by the discourse of industrialisation and modernisation produces new material spaces and a new sense of place. As Soja points out, 'the great modernist narratives that connected "fixed" community (whether identified by class, race-ethnicity, gender, or mere propinquity) with emancipation (if not revolution) are shattered (1996: 116). The extended barren land in both *River Road* and *Tuya's Marriage* becomes a serious existential threat, and the 'fixed' community is shattered due to the sprawling urban spaces and social practices. In a macro view, the land turns into a demonised space that devours the ethnic people's native culture and future development. In the new millennium, the protagonists of minority films become women and small children, instead of adult men, as in the films of the previous decades. Female characters, such as Tuya and her sister-in-law in *Tuya's Marriage* have to carry out all sorts of manual labour normally seen as masculine activities in minority communities after their male partner either becomes handicapped or dies. Such an inversion of gender roles in domestic space and the workplace becomes an unavoidable choice for the women. In *River Road*, little children are forced to be mature at a young age, as the deteriorating environment educates them to survive. They are left at home or put into boarding school, and have to deal with a family member's death alone and take a long journey to reach 'home'. The tight economic situation of the family makes them accept unpleasant situations and even death. The masculine and paternal roles in both films are either damaged or absent, which can be seen as the loosening of the central administrative power on minority subjects. The political and ideological urge of the state to maintain an image of ethnic minority solidarity and national harmony has been replaced by the economic and ecological concerns wrought by industrialisation.

Cinematic Lanzhou, more precisely, cinematic Gansu, does not provide a rich reservoir of urban images. Instead, deserts and small towns play an important role in branding the area. In many films, people undertake sheep or camel herding jobs, facing threats from the population mobility and environmental damage engendered by industrialisation and modernisation. They used to be economically, emotionally and spiritually attached to the land, which offers food and shelter, and symbolically, the land is home, representing a sense of belonging and identity. However, the space allowed for nomadic production is shrinking and disappearing with the implementation of the 'myopic ideology of modernisation' in the reform era (Mi 2009: 19). The film is a critique of such imprudent modernisation that leads to severe environmental deterioration and social reality characterised by 'displacement, anomie, estrangement, dysfunctionality, malaise and homelessness' (Mi 2009: 19).

River Road elegizes the loss of home in an ecologically fragile environment in the face of industrialisation and modernisation. Forty years after implementing the reform policy, under a deep-rooted discourse which proclaims that 'the city represented constant reformation, openness, science, education, and civilisation; the countryside stood for the inertia of history, closure, ignorance, and antihuman attitude and decay' (Kuoshu 2010: 3), rural and nomadic China is decaying and disappearing.

PART VI
CONCLUSION

CHAPTER 9

Cinematic Western China: An Open Space for Spatial Imagination

Cinematic western China, specifically the cinematic representations of the four provincial capital cities located in western China, have been accumulating in the reform era. Cinematic representations of the region and relevant scholarship have long been marginalised, either because of the power of Beijing and Shanghai cinema, or because of the authors' focus on Chinese national cinema which sometimes touches on China's west, but rarely moves beyond the praising of particular filmmakers. This 'on the periphery' position indicates the complicated and imbalanced economic, social and cultural development across mainland China, and in particular, shows the political discourses and workings of power in the production of space. Spatiality is not just an innocent dimension of contemporary society and how we exist and conceive the material and mental world; it is closely associated with history and society. As Soja puts it, 'we are first and always historical-social-spatial beings, actively participating individually and collectively in the construction/production – the "becoming" – of histories, geographies, societies' (Soja 1996: 73). The operation of power has always materialised through complicated interactions between the spatial-temporal-social.

Cinematic western China is represented as a space of demolition and construction, a disappearing space of living and production, a space for the cinematic subaltern as well as the ordinary citizens who use and consume various spaces in their daily lives, forming their 'space of enunciation' by walking in the city (Certeau 1984: 98). As either *flâneur* or drifter, these cinematic characters are voluntarily exploring or being compelled to explore, negotiate or *détour* (tactics of hijacking, rerouting, or diversion) the transient urban spaces of the four cities in western China. Through all the different modes of spatial exploration, cinematic characters' emotional and mental space are presented along with cinematic spaces of 'fragmentary and inward-turning histories, pasts that others are not allowed to read, accumulated times that can be unfolded' (Certeau 1984: 108). In the most mundane everyday practices, the marginalised and ordinary citizens represented in the films in question in previous chapters are given an opportunity to speak and act, which then reveals the enigmatic and Under-represented side of China's modernisation. As Soja perceives, it configures a space that allows the subaltern to speak (Soja 1996: 126).

The overall modernisation project carried out since the 1980s has wiped out many old spaces such as the traditional extended household, home town and socialist unit, and wrought large-scale transformations on cityscapes. In films such as *Crazy Stone*, *24 City* and *Weaving Girl*, the socialist unit, the representation of a socialist China, disappears and is being – or will be – replaced by modern commercial or residential complexes. In this modernisation process, with the demolition of the socialist urban space characterised by soviet-style grey low buildings and enormous factory spaces, the cityscape has been defined and redefined by emerging high-rises. Meanwhile, in *Rainclouds over Wushan*, *Still Life* and *River Road*, the home town disappears, the first two due to the construction of the Three Gorges Dam launched by the central government in 1992, and the last due to industrialisation, urbanisation and desertification. The construction of the world's largest hydro-power station represents the level and scale of Chinese modernisation, while for the people whose home town will be flooded, with themselves being dislocated and dispersed to various areas, the value of this enormous modernisation project seems questionable. *River Road*, ironically, shows a place devastated by drought and expanding desert due to the sprawling urban spaces in the process of urbanisation. The disappearing spaces of the socialist unit, home town and individual household correspond with the disease-ridden and dying characters featured in these films; and they in turn correspond with Soja's recognition of 'the body as the most intimate of personal-and-political spaces, an affective microcosm for all other spatialities' (Soja 1996: 112).

On a smaller scale, the domestic space in modern cities also faces crisis. In *Buddha Mountain*, modern Chinese families are confronted with disintegration, as the mobility and instability in the urban space destabilises the family, and previous family values and conduct become incompatible with the transforming family structure. Modernisation and urbanisation appear in a monstrous and devastating form when dealing with human existence in such a revolutionarily changing era. Those who struggle and survive in the process, especially those from the countryside who are eager to enter the urbanised spaces, as exemplified in *Curiosity Kills the Cat*, *Still Life*, *Story of Ermei* and *A Fool*, find a hostile urban space that refuses to communicate with them. The rural residents in these films would find their access to the urban area greatly increase, meanwhile they are often manipulated and bewildered by urban spaces. They are merely the spectators of the urban spectacle and the constructers of the modern facets of the urban space, while they themselves are excluded from the carnival of urbanisation. When they finally have to leave the city and return to their rural home after years of painstaking manual labour, they find that their homes have been transformed too, and they themselves have lost health and youth. The key words for these filmic representations of western China are chaos, danger, predicament, disappearance and death.

The rural–urban relationship has been transformed over the decades from a clear boundary between the two spaces to the urban space intruding the rural area with a powerful and sweeping force, as represented in films such as *A Fool* and *Story of Ermei*. In *Back to Back, Face to Face*, characters who have been living in the urban area for years find it hard to deal with the conflict between the rural and the urban. This is further complicated by the political power struggle for those who strive to attain power. In *Signal Left, Turn Right*, the ever-expanding cityscape corresponds with individuals' growing social mobility.

The twelve films examined in previous chapters mainly focus on ordinary citizens' urban experiences, and some of them feature the marginalised or the subaltern in a realistic style. These films configure a 'Thirdspace' of resistance that ultimately breaks the dichotomies of modernity–tradition, urban–rural, rich–poor, submission–domination, and establishes a space to observe and interpret the modernisation process of contemporary China in a globalising context. Cinematic western China creates an outlet to 'prioritise the voices of the weak who are straining to be heard over the voices of globalism that erase both people and places' (Zhang 2010a: 6). The people who are left behind by state-driven economic and social reform do not appear in the dichotomy-type representation that can be overwhelmingly observed in mainstream media – poor, sentimental and in agony. They are aware of all the ongoing changes, but, with powerful traditional inertia and persistence of existence, they remain in the marginalised and peripheral zone of society – just as bell hooks has chosen. Their mode of seeing society is like that described by bell hooks: seeing outside from inside, and inside from the outside (cited in Soja 1996: 100). It empowers them as they know both sides of living, and they choose to stay there, as a space of reflection and a space of home. It is a Thirdspace of resistance that can be used 'as a strategic location for exploring postmodern culture and seeking political community among all those oppressively peripherised by their race, class, gender, erotic preference, age, nation, region, and colonial status' (Soja 1996: 106). Directors of cinematic western China reflect on China's modernisation, look into the space, creating texts that enable mainstream audiences to peep into the lives and the mental spaces of the marginalised or subaltern groups that dwell in the disappearing space, so as to critique the current situations of Chinese urbanisation and modernisation.

The affinity between cinema and the city can be explored from two sides: film in space and space in film (Shiel 2001). This book provides an intensive exploration of the 'space in film' that focuses on specific places and locality represented in particular films. The space in film regards films as cultural and ideological products that are inevitably imprinted with authentic local cultural conduct, national identity and collective trauma and memory. On the other hand, 'film in space' means the national and transnational conditions of capital, resources, talents that are involved in film production, distribution and reception. For instance, Hollywood, as the centre of filmmaking, exerts a compelling force upon Los Angeles regarding political agenda, uneven economic development and everyday life of the city. The 'film in space' in the context of contemporary mainland China deserves an in-depth interrogation. The Chinese film industry (annual box office revenue grew from $1.47 billion in 2010 to $9.2 billion in 2019, and it has the largest movie production complex) seems to register a huge potential to counterbalance the global film industry dominated by Hollywood. In addition, China and the Belt and Road countries have signed an array of agreements on film co-production, exhibition, screening and awards, which provides a significant platform – The Belt and Road International Film Festival Alliance – to promote national and transnational cooperation in developing the Chinese film industry and to enhance China's cultural soft power. The Belt and Road countries as a term derives from the enormous project the Belt and Road Initiative. This international economic cooperation programme aims at promoting the overall development of China's western area and enhancing cooperation with neighbouring countries along the ancient overland corridor of the Silk Road and maritime routes. China's western region, therefore, will anticipate a myriad of opportunities as well challenges with the impetus of the enormous project.

Apart from the state-endorsed Film Festival Alliance, cities of western China also increasingly participate in the development of the Chinese film industry. For instance, the Xining First International Film Festival (hereafter, the FIRST), held annually in Xining, Qinghai province since 2011, aiming at discovering and promoting emerging filmmakers and their early career works, has become an important impetus for China's film industry. The local government of Xining has endorsed the FIRST by allocating resources to facilitate the operation of the festival and coordinating different levels of administration departments to promote and assist the film exhibition. The annual FIRST decorates Xining with billboards advertising films, information about the exhibition and outdoor movie theatres. The FIRST as a significant site of 'film in space' has contributed to the Chinese film industry with its embracing and encouragement of originality and creativity in aesthetic and thematic expressions. Meanwhile, awarded features such as *Deep in the Heart* [*Xin migong*] (Xin Yukun, 2014), *The Summer is Gone* [*Bayue*, lit., *The August*] (Zhang Dalei, 2016) and *Old Beast* [*Lao shou*] (Zhou Ziyang, 2017) represent a contemporary China by attaching intensive attention to local characteristics, the dynamics and stasis of places, social mobilities and individuals' predicaments in modernised spaces. The filmic images of different cities with distinguished local features add alternative cinematic places to the Chinese cinema landscape.

Xining, together with the other provincial capital cities in western China, used to be a space where national projects such as the Third Front Plan (1950s to 1980s), the Three Gorges Dam project (1990s to 2010) and China Western Development (1990s to present) played out. These state-driven projects demonstrate the state's sustained effort of realising an overall economic and social development across the western and eastern coastal regions. Under the great force of transformation carried by these projects, cityscapes, daily practices and people's conduct and values have accordingly changed. The area nowadays is increasingly associated with emerging metropolises, in addition to its geographical and cultural ties to neighbouring countries along the Silk Road and its diversity in culture and ethnicity (as the area includes the Xinjiang Uygur Autonomous Region and Tibet Autonomous Region), which makes the area a focal centre of cinematic representations.

As an increasingly popular setting for the genres of thrillers, action comedies, martial arts films as well as urban features, the image and voice of western China is seen and heard by a growing number of people, domestically and internationally. How do the exotic legends and history of western China blend with these different genre films and mirror the social concerns and intellectual reflection of contemporary China? For the minority groups who inhabit the area and negotiate with the majority Han, and who are experiencing the influence of expanding urbanisation, will their cultural and ethnic identities disappear, or will they be assimilated and transformed? Such enquiries are quite beyond the scope of this book, but these two questions should be flagged for future examinations on cinematic representations of western China. Perceiving the cinematic western China as Thirdspace, this book configures an alternative image of contemporary China, which is full of traditional inertia and economic dynamism, destruction and construction, and sense of nostalgia and loss. By focusing on the urban spaces of the region represented in films, the long-standing ethnographical stereotypes of western China have been reconfigured. Whether it is an agrarian ethnographical representation or an urban subaltern configuration, western China on screen can be seen as a Thirdspace that is radically open and contains a limitless scope of spatial imagination.

Filmography

After Separation 1992, Xia, G, Beijing Film Studio, China
Aftershock 2010, Feng, X, Huayi Brothers, China
Amélie 2001, Jeunet, J-P, UGC-Fox Distribution, France
The Arrival of a Train at La Ciotat Station 1896, Lumière, A and Lumière, L, Société Lumière, France
Back to Back, Face to Face 1994, Huang, J, Xi'an Film Studio, China
Backlight 1982, Ding, Y, Zhujiang Film Studio, China
Balzac and the Little Chinese Seamstress 2002, Dai, S, Les Productions Internationales Le Film, France and China
Battleship Potemkin 1925, Eisenstein, S, Mosfilm, Soviet Union
A Beautiful New World 1999, Shi, R, Imar Film and Xi'an Film Studio, China
Beijing Bicycle 2001, Wang, X, Beijing Film Studio, China
Berlin: Symphony of a Great City 1927, Ruttmann, W, Deutsche Vereins-Film and Les Productions Fox Europa, Weimar Republic
Bicycle Thieves 1948, Sica, V De, PD Sica, Italy
Big Shot's Funeral 2001, Feng, X, China Film Group, China
The Black Cannon Incident 1985, Huang, J, Xi'an Film Studio, China
Blade Runner 1982, Scott, R, The Ladd Company, United States
The Bride 2009, Zhang, M (Production company unknown), China
Buddha Mountain 2011, Li, Y, Laurel Films, China
Bumming in Beijing: The Last Dreamers 1990, Wu, W, (production company unknown), China
Buried 2009, Wang, L, Beijing Guangmo Films, China
The Call of Maiji Mountain 2011, Li, J, Tianjin Aimei Film Coporation, China
Candyman 1992, Rose, B, Propaganda Films and PolyGram Filmed Entertainment, United States
Cell Phone 2003, Feng, X, Beijing Film Studio China Film Group, China
Chengdu, I Love You 2009, Cui, J and Chan, F, Beijing Zhongbo Shiji Media Ltd., China
China Affair 2013, Zhang, M, Xi'an Jiafang Motion Picture, China
China's Unnatural Disaster: The Tears of Sichuan Province 2009, O'Neill, JAM, Downtown Community, United States and China
Chongqing Blues 2010, Wang, X, Beijing Bona Film and Television Culture Co., China
Chongqing Hot Pot 2016, Yang, Q, Wanda Pictures, China

A Corner in the City 1982, Teng, W, Xi'an Film Studio, China
Crazy Stone 2006, Ning, H, Beijing Frontline Production, China
The Crossroads 1937, Shen, X, Mingxing (Star) Film Company, China
Curiosity Kills the Cat 2006, Zhang, Y, China Vision Group (Beijing), China
Deadly Delicious 2008, Zhao, T, Megajoy Pictures, China
Defend Our Land 1938, Shi, D, Hankou China Motion Picture Studio, China
Design of Death 2012, Guan, H, Stellar Mega Films, China
Dislocation 1986, Huang, J, Xi'an Film Studio, China
Distant Thunder 2010, Zhang, J, Beijing Ruitang Film and Video Culture Co. Ltd and Beijing Xingshi Union Film and Video Culture Co. Ltd, China
East 2006, Jia, Z, Generate Films, China
Eleven Flowers 2012, Wang, X, Beijing Dongchun Culture Communication Co., Ltd., China
Ermo 1994, Zhou, X, Shanghai Film Studios and Ocean Film (II), China and Hong Kong
Evening Rain 1980, Wu, Y and Wu, Y, Shanghai Film Studio, China
Fallen City 2011, Zhao, Q, NHK, China and Japan
Farewell My Concubine 1993, Chen, K, Beijing Film Studio, China
Fate of Graduates 1934, Ying, Y, Diantong Film Company, China
Fly with the Crane 2012, Li, R, Heaven Pictures (Beijing) Culture and Media Co., Ltd., China
A Fool 2014, Chen, J, Shandong Jiabo Entertainment, China
Forgetting to Know You 2014, Quan, L, Xstream Pictures and Hansen Media, China
Frightening Moment 2009, Wang, J and Shen, D, August 1st Film Studio, China
Good Husband 1939, Shi, D, Chongqing China Motion Picture Studio, China
A Good Rain Knows 2009, Hur, J-h, Pancinema, China and South Korea
Hearing Implant 2015, Fang, J, Gansu Fengxing Film Company, China
Hero 2002, Zhang, Y, Beijing New Picture Film, China
High Noon 1952, Zinnemann, F, United Artists, United States
Horse Thief 1986, Tian, Z, Xi'an Film Studio, China
I Love Beijng 2001, Ning, Y, Eurasia Communications and Happy Village, China
In the Heat of the Sun 1994, Jiang, W, China Film Co-Production Corporation, China
In the Wild Mountains 1986, Yan, X, Xi'an Film Studio, China
Ju Dou 1990, Zhang, Y, China Film Co-Production Corporation, China
King of the Children 1987, Chen, K, Xi'an Film Studio, China
The King of Masks 1995, Wu, T, Youth Film Studio of Beijing Film Academy and Shaw Brothers (Hong Kong), China
Last Train Home 2009, Fan, L, EyeSteel Film, Canada
The Last Emperor 1987, Bertolucci, B, Columbia Pictures, Italy and United Kingdom
Life 1984, Wu, T, Xi'an Film Studio, China
Life Show 2002, Huo, J, China Film Group, China
Little Flower 1976, Zhang, Z and Huang, J, Beijing Film Studio, China
Living Forever in Burning Flames 1965, Shui, H, Beijing Film Studio, China

A Love Story in Chengdu 2011, You, X and Lü, G, China Movie Channel, China
Lost, Indulgence 2008, Zhang, Y, Filmko Film, China
Man with a Movie Camera 1929, Vertov, D, VUFKU, Soviet Union
March of Victory 1940, Shi, D, Chongqing China Motion Picture Studio, China
The Melody of Qiang Flute 2011, Miao, Y, Emei Film Studio, China
The Missing Sheep 2016, Wang, X, Lanzhou Literature Association and Lanzhou Haofa Motion Picture Company, China
Mission Impossible 1996, Palma, B De, Paramount Pictures, United States
My Homeland 1945, Shi, D, Chongqing China Motion Picture Studio, China
My Memories of Old Beijing 1983, Wu, Y, Shanghai Film Studio, China
Mysterious Grand Buddha 1980, Zhang, H, Beijing Film Studio, China
A Narrow Lane Celebrity 1985, Cong, L, Emei Film Studio, China
The Next Life 2011, Fan, J, Al Jazeera English, Japan and China and UK
No Man's Land 2013, Ning, H, China Film Co., Ltd., China
Ocean's Eleven 2001, Soderbergh, S, Village Roadshow Pictures, United States
The Old Donkey 2010, Li, R, Li Ruijun Film Studio and Indie Workshop, China
Old Well 1986, Wu, T, Xi'an Film Studio, China
On the Beat 1995, Ning, Y, Beijing Film Studio, China
Once a Thief 1991, Woo, J, Golden Princess Film Production Limited and Milestone Films, Hong Kong
Orphan Rescues Grandfather 1923, Zhang, S, Mingxing (Star) Film Company, China
People First 2009, Chen, Z, Central News and Documentary Film Studio, China
The Pickpocket 1998, Jia, Z, Hu Tong Communications and Radiant Advertising, China
Platform 2000, Jia, Z, Hu Tong Communication, China
Power Fighter in Vast Sky 1976, Wang, F and Wang, Y, Changchun Film Studio, China
Pretty Big Feet 2002, Yang, Y, Xi'an Film Studio, China
Rainclouds over Wushan 1996, Zhang, M, Beijing Film Studio, China
The Red Awn 2007, Cai, S, Wan Ji Communications, China
Red Sorghum 1987, Zhang, Y, Xi'an Film Studio, China
Rickshaw Boy 1982, Ling, Z, Beijing Film Studio, China
Ripples Across Stagnant Water 1992, Ling, Z, Beijing Film Studio, China
River Road 2015, Li, R, Laurel Films, China
Rock 'n' Roll Kids 1988, Tian, Z, Beijing Film Studio, China
Roman Holiday 1953, Wyler, W, Paramount Pictures, United States
Samsara 1988, Huang, J, Xi'an Film Studio, China
Sentinels under the Neon Light 1964, Wang, P and Ge, X, Shanghai Film Studio, China
Seven Swords 2005, Hark, T, Film Workshop, Hong Kong
Seventeen Years 1999, Zhang, Y, Xi'an Film Studio, China
Shane 1953, Stevens, G, G Stevens, Paramount Pictures, United States
Shanghai Fever 1994, Li, G, Xiaoxiang Film Studio and Impact Films Investment Ltd (Hong Kong), China

Sherlock Holmes 2009, Ritchie, G, J Silver, L Wigram, S Downey and D Lin, Warner Bros Pictures, United States
Signal Left, Turn Right 1996, Huang, J, Xi'an Film Studio, China
Sister Jiang 1978, Huang, Z and Fan, L, Shanghai Film Studio, China
Stagecoach 1939, Ford, J, United Artists, United States
Stand Straight, Don't Bend Over 1993, Huang, J, Xi'an Film Studio, China
Still Life 2006, Jia, Z, Shanghai Film Studio and Xstream Pictures (Beijing), China
Storm on the Border 1940, Ying, Y, China Motion Picture Studio, China
The Story of Ermei 2004, Wang, Qa, Xi'an Film Studio, China
The Story of Qiu Ju 1992, Zhang, Y, Yindu Orgnisation, China
Street Angel 1937, Yuan, M, Mingxing (Star) Film Company, China
Taxi Driver 1976, Scorsese, M, Columbia Pictures, United States
The Third Man 1949, Reed, C, London Films, United Kingdom
This Life of Mine 1950, Shi, H, Wenhua Film Company, China
Time until the Mountain Leaves 1980, Yu, B and Tang, H, Shanghai Film Studio, China
Troubled Laughter 1979, Yang, Y and Deng, Y, Shanghai Film Studio, China
The Trouble Shooters 1988, Mi, J, Ermei Film Studio, China
Tuya's Marriage 2006, Wang, Qa, Maxyeecul True Industry Co., Ltd and Xi'an Motion-Picture Co., Ltd, China
24 City 2008, Jia, Z, Shanghai Film Group (Shanghai Film Studio), China
Unknown Pleasures 2002, Jia, Z, Hu Tong Communication, China
Up to the Mountain, Overlooking the Running River 2013, Wang, F, Lanzhou Broadcast TV Station, China
Weaving Girl 2009, Wang, Qa, Xi'an Qujiang Film Ltd., China
White Deer Plain 2012, Wang, Qa, Western Film Group Corporation, China
Wind Blast 2010, Gao, Q, Beijing United Power Films, China
A Woman, a Gun and a Noodle Shop 2009, Yimou, Z, Beijing New Picture Co., China
Woman Sesame Oil Maker 1993, Xie, F, Changchun Film Studio and Tianjin Film Studio, China
The World 2004, Jia, Z, Shanghai Film Group, China
Yamaha Fish Stall 1984, Zhang, L, Zhujiang Film Studio, China
Yan Ruisheng 1921, Ren, P, China Film Research Society and Commercial Press Motion Picture Section, China
Yellow Earth 1984, Chen, K, Guangxi Film Studio, China

Bibliography

Adshead, S. A. M. (1984), *Province and Politics in Late Imperial China: Viceregal Government in Szechwan, 1898–1911*, London: Curzon Press.
Andreotti, L. (1996), 'Theory of the derive and other situationist writings on the city', in L. Andreotti and X. Costa (eds), *Theory of the Derive and Other Situationist Writings on the City*, Barcelona: Museu d'Art Contemporani de Barcelona.
Andrew, D. (2018), 'The absent subject of *The World*', *Journal of Chinese Cinemas*, vol. 12, no. 1, pp. 59–73.
Baudelaire, C. (1978), *The Painter of Modern Life and Other Essays*, trans. J Mayne, New York: Garland.
Bazin, A. (2005a), 'An aesthetic of reality: neorealism: (cinematic realism and the Italian school of the liberation)', in *What is Cinema?*, Berkeley, CA: University of California Press, vol. II, pp. 16–40.
Bazin, A. (2005b), 'The Western: or the American film par excellence', in *What is cinema?*, berkeley, CA: University of California Press, vol. II, pp. 140–8.
Benjamin, W. (1999), *The Arcade Project*, trans. H Eiland and K McLaughlin, Cambridge, MA: Belknap Press.
Berry, C. (1999), 'Representing Chinese women: researching women in the Chinese cinema', in A. Finnane and A. E. McLaren (eds), *Dress, Sex and Text in Chinese Culture*, Clayton: Monash Asia Institute.
Berry, C. (2004), *Postsocialist Cinema in Post-Mao China: The Cultural Revolution after the Cultural Revolution*, New York: Routledge.
Berry, C., X. Lü and L. Rofel (2010), *The New Chinese Documentary Film Movement: For the Public Record*, Hong Kong: Hong Kong University Press.
Bertozzi, E. (2012), 'A still life of the wildest things: magic(al) realism in contemporary Chinese cinema and the reconfiguration of the *jishizhuyi* style', *Journal of Chinese Cinemas*, vol. 6, no. 2, pp. 153–72.
Braester, Y. (2007), 'Tracing the city's scars: demolition and the limits of the documentary impulse in the new urban cinema', in Z. Zhang (ed.), *The Urban Generation: Chinese Cinema and Society at the Turn of the Twenty-first Century*, Durham, NC: Duke University Press, pp. 161–80.
Braester, Y. (2012), 'From urban films to urban cinema: the emergence of a critical concept', in Y. Zhang (ed.), *A Companion to Chinese Cinema*, Malden, MA: Wiley-Blackwell, pp. 346–58.

Braester, Y. and T. M. Chen (2011), 'From 'The Life of Wu Xun' to the 'Career of Song Jingshi' – crisis and adaptation of private studio film-making legacy: 1951–1956', *Journal of Chinese Cinemas*, vol. 5, no. 1, pp. 5–12.
Brand, D. (1991), *The Spectator and the City in Nineteenth-century American Literature*, Cambridge: Cambridge University Press.
Browne, N. (1994), 'Introduction', in N. Browne, P. G. Pickowicz, V. Sobchack and E. Yau (eds), *New Chinese Cinemas: Forms, Identities, Politics*, Cambridge: Cambridge University Press.
Buck, D. (1984), 'Changes in Chinese urban planning since 1976', *Third World Planning Review*, vol. 6, no. 1, pp. 5–26.
Burgess, J. S. (1930), 'The guilds and trade associations of China', *Annals of the American Academy of Political and Social Science*, vol. 152, no. 1, pp. 72–80.
Certeau, M. de (1984), *The Practice of Everyday Life*, Berkeley: University of California Press.
Chan, K. W. and L. Zhang (1999), 'The hukou system and rural-urban migration in China: processes and changes', *China Quarterly*, no. 160, pp. 818–48.
Chen, X. (2005), 'A spiritual sketch of Wang Xiaoshuai's films – from *The Days* to *Shanghai Dreams* [Wang Xiaoshuai dianying jingshen sumiao – cong *Dongchun de rizi* dao *Qing Hong*]', *Art Criticism [Yishu pinglun]*, no. 7, pp. 20–5.
Chen, J. (2011), '*Buddha Mountain*: fury and depression without a cause [Guanyin shan: wuyin de fennu yu juewang]', *Film Art [Dianying yishu]*, no. 3, pp. 41–3.
Chen, J., Z. Wang and L. Zhou (2015), 'Making films I love indeed [Zuo ziji zhenzheng reai de dianying]', *Contemporary Cinema [Dangdai dianying]*, no. 7, pp. 62–7.
Cheng, T. and M. Selden (1994), 'The origins and social consequences of China's hukou system', *China Quarterly*, vol. 139, pp. 644–68.
Cheng, Q. and W. Xu (1996), 'Right here waiting: an interview with Zhang Ming [Ciqing kedai: Zhang Ming fantan lu]', *Journal of Beijing Film Academy [Beijing dianying xueyuan xuebao]*, no. 1, pp. 285–93.
Cheng, J., S. Li and Z. Xing (1978), *A History of Chinese Film [Zhongguo dianying fazhan shi]*, Hong Kong: Wen hua zi liao gong ying she.
China approves new state-level SEZ in Gansu (2012), China.org.cn, <http://www.china.org.cn/business/2012-08/29/content_26371712.htm> (last accessed 1 December 2017).
China-Lanzhou/Climate Award (2015), CCTVPLUS, <http://www.cctvplus.com/news/latest.shtml?!keyword=Today%20Reform%20Progress%20Prize> (last accessed 27 January 2018).
Chow, R. (1995), *Primitive Passions: Visuality, Sexuality, Ethnography, and Contemporary Chinese Cinema*, New York: Columbia University Press.
Chow, R. (2007), *Sentimental Fabulations, Contemporary Chinese Films: Attachment in the Age of Global Visibility*, New York: Columbia University Press.
Chow, R. (2013), 'Fetish power unbound: a small history of "woman" in Chinese cinema', in C. Rojas and E. C. Chow (eds), *The Oxford Handbook of Chinese Cinema*, Oxford: Oxford University Press, pp. 490–506.

Chow, Y. F. and J. D. Kloet (2013), 'Flânerie and acrophilia in the postmetropolis: rooftops in Hong Kong cinema', *Journal of Chinese Cinemas*, vol. 7, no. 2, pp. 139–55.

Clark, P. (1987), *Chinese Cinema: Culture and Politics Since 1949*, Cambridge: Cambridge University Press.

Creekmur, C. K. (2011), 'The American Western film', in N. S. Witschi (ed.), *A Companion to the Literature and Culture of the American West*, Oxford: Blackwell Publishing, pp. 395–408.

Cui, S. (2003), *Women Through the Lens: Gender and Nation in a Century of Chinese Cinema*, Honolulu: University of Hawai'i Press.

Cui, S. (2006), 'Negotiating in-between: on new-generation filmmaking and Jia Zhangke's films', *Modern Chinese Literature and Culture*, vol. 18, no. 2, pp. 98–130.

Cui, S. (2011), 'Searching for female sexuality and negotiating with feminism', in L. Wang (ed.), *Chinese Women's Cinema: Transnational Contexts*, New York: Columbia University Press, pp. 213–32.

Dai, J. (2002), *Cinema and Desire: Feminist Marxism and Cultural Politics in the Work of Dai Jinhua*, London: Verso.

Dai, J. (2016), *Landscape in the Mist: Chinese Film Culture 1978–1998 [Wuzhong fengjing: Zhongguo dianying wenhua 1978–1998]*, Beijing: Peking University Press.

Data Report (2012), National Bureau of Statistic of the People's Republic of China, <http://www.stats.gov.cn/tjsj/tjgb/rkpcgb/dfrkpcgb/201202/t20120228_30383.html> (last accessed 22 November 2017).

Davis, D. S. (2014), 'Privatization of marriage in post-socialist China', *Modern China*, vol. 40, no. 6, pp. 551–77.

Debord, G. (1996a), 'Introduction to a critique of urban geography', in L. Andreotti and X. Costa (eds), *Theory of the Derive and Other Situationist Writings on the City*, Barcelona: Museu d'Art Contemporani de Barcelona.

Debord, G. (1996b), 'Theory of the dérive', in L. Andreotti and X. Costa (eds), *Theory of the Derive and Other Situationist Writings on the City*, Barcelona: Museu d'Art Contemporani de Barcelona.

Deng, X. (2000), *A Speech at the National Congress of the Communist Party of China (23 September 1985)*, People.com.cn, <http://www.people.com.cn/GB/channel1/10/20000529/80767.html> (last accessed 21 Feburary 2018).

Deppman, H.-C. (2014), 'Reading docufiction: Jia Zhangke's *24 City*', *Journal of Chinese Cinemas*, no. 1, pp. 1–21.

Dimendberg, E. (2004), *Film Noir and the Spaces of Modernity*, Cambridge, MA: Harvard University Press.

Du, M. (2011), *The Up and Down of Li Yu*, *Jinghua Weekly*, <http://paper.people.com.cn/jhzk/html/2011-06/01/content_959378.htm?div=-1> (last accessed 28 May 2017).

Esherick, J. W. (2000), 'Modernity and nation in the Chinese city', in J. W. Esherick (ed.), *Remaking the Chinese City: Modernity and National Identity, 1900–1950*, Honolulu: University of Hawaii Press, pp. 1–16.

Fried, D. (2007), 'Riding off into the sunrise: genre contingency and the origin of the Chinese Western', *Modern Language Association*, vol. 122, no. 5, pp. 1482–98.
Giannetti, L. D. (2008), *Understanding Movies*, 11th edn, Upper Saddle River, NJ: Pearson Education.
Hsueh, F.-h. (1995), *Beijing: The Nature and Planning of a Chinese Capital City*, Chichester: Wiley.
Huo, J. (2002), 'A summary of the artistic elements of *Life Show* [*Shenghuo Xiu* yishu zongjie]', *Film Art [Dianying yishu]*, no. 4, pp. 39–40.
Jameson, F. (1986), 'Third-World literature in the era of multinational capitalism', *Social Text*, vol. 15, no. 15, pp. 65–88.
Jameson, F. (1992), *The Geopolitical Aesthetic: Cinema and Space in the World System*, London: British Film Institute.
Jia, Z. (2009), *A Collective Memory of Chinese Working Class [Zhongguo gongren fangtan lu]*, Jinan: Shandong Huabao Chubanshe.
Jia, L. and S. Song (2011), 'A dialogue with Huang Jianxin [Yong yingxiang xieke minzu de xinling shi]', *Contemporary Cinema [Dangdai dianying]*, no. 7, pp. 23–9.
Jia, Z., S. Rao, Y. Zhou and X. Chen (2007), 'Discussion on new movies: *Still Life* [Xinzuo pingyi: *Sanxiao haoren*]', *Contemporary Cinema [Dangdai dianying]*, no. 2, pp. 19–27.
Jorn, A. (1996), 'Architecture for life', in L. C. Andreotti and X. Costa (eds), *Theory of the Derive and Other Situationist Writings on the City*, Barcelona: Museu d'Art Contemporani de Barcelona.
Kirby, L. (1997), *Parallel Tracks: The Railroad and Silent Cinema*, Durham, NC: Duke University Press.
Kuoshu, H. H. (2010), *Metro Movies: Cinematic Urbanism in post-Mao China*, Carbondale: Southern Illinois University Press.
Lai, H. H. (2002), 'China's Western Development Program: its rationale, implementation, and prospects', *Modern China*, vol. 28, no. 4, pp. 432–66.
Lai, L. C.-H. (2007), 'Whither the walker goes: spatial practices and negative poetics in 1990s Chinese urban cinema', in Z. Zhang (ed.), *The Urban Generation: Chinese Cinema and Society at the Turn of the Twenty-first Century*, Durham, NC: Duke University Press, pp. 205–40.
Lefebvre, H. (1991), *The Production of Space*, trans. D. N. Smith, Oxford: Blackwell.
Leyda, J. (1972), *Dianying: An Account of Films and the Film Audience in China*, Cambridge, MA: MIT Press.
Li, D. (2007), *History of Chinese Film Criticism*, Beijing: Peking University Press.
Li, D. (2009), *24 City: Jia Zhangke's Exploration of Meeting the Mainstream [Ershisi cheng ji: Jia Zhang yu zhuliu xiangyu de tansuo]*, Sina Film and Music, <http://ent.sina.com.cn/m/c/2009-03-04/15272401757.shtml> (last accessed 20 May 2017).
Li, D. (2012), 'Cultural variety and the establishment of an ecosystem for the Chinese Western [Wenhua duoyangxing yu zhongguo xibu dianying shengtai xitong goujian]', *Film Art [Dianying yishu]*, no. 2, pp. 88–92.

Li, H. (2013), 'Gender roles and their displacements in *Tuya's Marriage*', *Journal of Chinese Cinemas*, vol. 7, no. 2, pp. 123–37.

Li, T., W. Cui, Z. Jia, C. Xi, J. Ouyang and H. Wang (2007), '*Still Life*: hometown, transformation and Jia Zhangke's realism [*Sanxia haoren*: guli, bianqian yu Jia Zhangke de xianshi zhuyi]', *Reading [Dushu]*, no. 1, pp. 3–31

Liu, K. C. (1988), 'Chinese merchant guilds: an historical inquiry', *Pacific Historical Review*, vol. 57, no. 1, pp. 1–23.

Liu, M. (2008), '*24 City*, an interview with Jia Zhangke: a history of fifty-years behind the film', *Cinema World*, vol. 6, pp. 42–43.

Liu, X. (2009), 'In the face of developmental ruins: place attachment and its ethical claims', in S. H. Lu and J. Mi (eds), *Chinese Ecocinema: In the Age of Environmental Challenge*, Hong Kong: Hong Kong University Press.

Liu, X. (2010), 'Adhere to spiritual wandering – an interview with Wang Xiaoshuai [Jianshou jingshen de liulang – Wang Xiaoshuai fangtan]', *Film Art [Dianying yishu]*, no. 4, pp. 95–100.

Liu, H. (2018), 'Black comedy films in postsocialist China: case study of Ning Hao's *Crazy* series', *Journal of Chinese Cinemas*, pp. 1–16.

Lu, C. (2010a), *City Imagination and Cultural Expression in Chinese Cinema [Zhongguo dianying zhong de chengshi xiangxiang yu wenhua biaoda]*, Beijing: Beijing Normal University Publishing Group.

Lu, L. (2010b), *Disclosure and Representation: The Subaltern Space Constructed by the Chinese New Generation of Directors [Qubi yu xianxian: zhongguo xinshengdai daoyan de diceng kongjian goujian]*, Beijing: China Film Press.

Lu, S. H. (2001), *China, Transnational Visuality, Global Postmodernity*, Stanford, CA: Stanford University Press.

Lu, T. (2006), 'Trapped freedom and localized globalism', in P. G. Pickowicz and Y. Zhang (eds), *From Underground to Independent: An Alternative Film Culture in Contemporary China*, Lanham: Rowman and Littlefield, pp. 123–41.

Lu, S. H. (2007a), *Chinese Modernity and Global Biopolitics: Studies in Literature and Visual Culture*, Honolulu: University of Hawai'i Press.

Lu, S. H. (2007b), 'Tear down the city: reconstruction urban space in contemporary Chinese popular cinema and avant-garde art', in Z. Zhang (ed.), *The Urban Generation: Chinese Cinema and Society at the Turn of the Twenty-First Century*, Durham, NC: Duke University Press, pp. 137–60.

Lu, S. H. (2012), 'Alternative history, alternative memory: cinematic representation of the Three Gorges in the shadow of the dam', in C. Y. Henriot and W.-H. Yeh (eds), *History in Images: Pictures and Public Space in Modern China*, Berkeley: Institute of East Asian Studies, University of California, pp. 245–57.

Luo, Y. (2005), 'Zhong Dianfei and film aesthetics [Zhong Dianfei yu dianying meixue]', *Literature and Arts Studies [Wenyi yanjiu]*, no. 1, pp. 81–94.

Luo, T. (2015), 'Neither here nor there: the representation of post-socialist space in the world and *Still Life* and Jia Zhangke's transcendence of realism', *Sungkyun Journal of East Asian Studies*, vol. 15, no. 2, pp. 149–71.

Luo, T. (2019), 'Expression and prohibition of desire: cinematic representation of dreams as alternative aesthetics in modern Chinese film', *Sungkyun Journal of East Asian Studies*, vol. 19, no. 2, pp. 121–46.

McGee, T. G., G. C. S. Lin, A. A. Marton, M. Y. L. Wang and J. Wu (2007), *China's Urban Space: Development Under Market Socialism*, London: Routledge.

McGrath, J. (2008), *Postsocialist Modernity: Chinese Cinema, Literature, and Criticism in the Market Age*, Stanford, CA: Stanford University Press.

McGrath, J. (2016), 'Realism', *Journal of Chinese Cinemas*, pp. 1–3.

Marchetti, G. (2007), *Andrew Lau and Alan Mak's Infernal Affairs – The Trilogy*, Hong Kong: Hong Kong University Press.

Massey, D. (1994), *Space, Place and Gender*, Cambridge: Polity.

Mello, C. (2015), 'If these walls could speak: from slowness to stillness in the cinema of Jia Zhangke', in T. D. Luca and B. J. Nuno (eds), *Slow Cinema*, Edinburgh: Edinburgh University Press, pp. 137–49.

Mennel, B. (2008), *Cities and Cinema*, London: Routledge.

Mi, J. (2009), 'Framing ambient unheimlich: ecoggedon, ecological unconscious, and water pathology in New Chinese Cinema', in S. H. Lu and J. Mi (eds), *Chinese Ecocinema: In the Age of Environmental Challenge*, Hong Kong: Hong Kong University Press.

Moll Murata, C. (2008), 'Chinese guilds from the seventeenth to the twentieth centuries: an overview', *International Review of Social History*, vol. 53, no. S16, pp. 213–47.

Monument to the Three Gorges Migrants (Sanxia yimin jinianbei) (2010), Baidu. Baike, <http://baike.baidu.com/item/%E4%B8%89%E5%B3%A1%E7%A7%BB%E6%B0%91%E7%BA%AA%E5%BF%B5%E7%A2%91> (last accessed 26 March 2017).

Naughton, B. (1988), 'The Third Front: defence industrialisation in the Chinese interior', *China Quarterly*, vol. 115, pp. 351–86.

Ni, Z. (1995), 'Contrasts in ordinary life under a magnifier – my jotting on *Days of Winter and Spring* [Fangdajing xia de heibai rensheng – *Dongchun de rizi* suixiang]', *Journal of Beijing Film Academy [Beijing dianying xueyuan xuebao]*, no. 1, pp. 128–32.

Ni, Z. (2011), 'Interview with the director of *Buddha Mountain:* my film no longer denounces man [*Guanyin Shan* daoyan zhuanfang: Wo de dianying buzai kongsu nanren]', Mtime, <http://news.mtime.com/2011/03/04/1452614.html> (last accessed 28 May 2017).

Ni, Z. and Y. Xu (2012), 'Pursue a cinematic life: the film road of Wu Tianming [Zhizhuo zhuiqiu de dianying rensheng: Wu Tianming de dianying chuangzuo daolu]', *Contemporary Cinema [Dangdai dianying]*, no. 9, pp. 24–31.

Nie, J. (2009), 'A city of disappearance: trauma, displacement, and spectral cityscape in contemprary Chinese cinema', in S. H. Lu and J. Mi (eds), *Chinese Ecocinema: In the Age of Environmental Challenge*, Hong Kong: Hong Kong University Press.

Nochimson, M. P. (2009), 'Passion for documentation: an interview with Jia Zhangke', *New Review of Film and Television Studies*, vol. 7, no. 4, pp. 411–19.
Phillips, T. (2017), 'China goes west: a ghost city in the sand comes to life', *The Guardian*, <https://www.theguardian.com/cities/2017/mar/21/china-west-ghost-city-comes-to-life-lanzhou-new-area> (last accessed 27 March 2017).
Pickowicz, P. (2012), *China on Film: A Century of Exploration, Confrontation, and Controversy*, Lanham, MD: Rowman and Littlefield.
Pinder, D. (2005a), 'Arts of urban exploration', *Cultural Geographies*, vol. 12, no. 4, pp. 383–411.
Pinder, D. (2005b), *Visions of the City: Utopianism, Power and Politics in Twentieth-century Urbanism*, Edinburgh: Edinburgh University Press.
Pratt, G. and R. M. S. Juan (2014), *Film and Urban Space: Critical Possibilities*, Edinburgh: Edinburgh University Press.
Pugsley, P. (2013), *Tradition, Culture and Aesthetics in Contemporary Asian Cinema*, Farnham: Ashgate Publishing.
Ramos Monteiro, L., A. Gaudreault and M. Martin (2015), 'Remaking a European, post-catastrophic atmosphere in 2000s China: Jia Zhangke's *Still Life*, iconology and ruins', *Cinémas*, vol. 25, no. 2–3, pp. 97–117.
Rashkin, E. (1993), 'Rape as castration as spectacle: the price of Frenzy's politics of confusion', in T. Lu (ed.), *Gender and Sexuality in Twentieth-century Chinese Literature and Society*, Albany: State University of New York Press.
Schultz, C. K. N. (2015), 'Worker, peasant, soldier . . . middle class? Class figures in Jia Zhangke's *24 City*', *Asian Cinema*, vol. 26, no. 1, pp. 43–59.
Schultz, C. K. N. (2016), 'Ruin in the films of Jia Zhangke', *Visual Communication*, vol. 15, no. 4, pp. 439–60.
Seremetakis, C. N. (1996), *The Senses Still: Perception and Memory as Material Culture in Modernity*, Chicago: University of Chicago Press.
Shi, Y. (2007), 'Maintaining law and order in the city – new tales of the people's police', in Z. Zhang (ed.), *The Urban Generation: Chinese Cinema and Society at the Turn of the Twenty-first Century*, Durham, NC: Duke University Press.
Shiel, M. (2001), 'Cinema and the city in history and theory', in M. Shiel and T. Fitzmaurice (eds), *Cinema and the City: Film and Urban Societies in a Global Context*, Oxford: Blackwell, pp. 1–18.
Silbergeld, J. (1999), *China into Film: Frames of Reference in Contemporary Chinese Cinema*, London: Reaktion Books.
Soja, E. W. (1996), *Thirdspace: Journeys to Los Angeles and Other Real-and-imagined Places*, Cambridge, MA: Blackwell.
Song, H. (2010), 'Yongtai ancient town: an sample of the military stronghold of the Ming and Qing dynasties [Yongtai guzhen: yige Ming and Qing junshi yaosai de biaoben]', *Chinese National Geography [Zhongguo guojia dili]*, no. 3.
National Bureau of Statistics (2011), *The Report of the 2010 Population Census*, <http://www.stats.gov.cn/tjsj/tjgb/rkpcgb/qgrkpcgb/201104/t20110429_30328.html> (last accessed 11 December 2016).

Tang, X., S. Hu, J. Shen, G. Yao, N. Tang, Z. Bian, B. Zhou, X. Qian and S. Bian (1988), 'The "urban cinema" has a great prospect: a special forum on the "urban cinema" by the editorial department of the *New Films*', *New Films [Dianying xinzuo]*, no. 6, pp. 54–63.

Teo, S. (2013), *The Asian Cinema Experience: Style, Space, Theory*, London: Routledge.

Teo, S. (2016), *Eastern Westerns: Film and Genre Outside and Inside Hollywood*, London: Routledge.

Tester, K. (1994), *The Flâneur*, London: Routledge.

Thompson, K. and D. Bordwell (2003), *Film History: An Introduction*, 2nd edn, Boston: McGraw-Hill.

Tu, Y. (2011), '*Buddha Mountain*: nirvana from a mist [Guanyin shan: niepan zhizhong de miwu]', *Journal of Beijing Film Academy [Beijing dianying xueyuan xuebao]*, no. 2, pp. 104–7.

Walcott, S. M. (2003), 'Xi'an as an Inner China Development Model', Eurasian Geography and Economics, vol. 44, no. 8, pp. 623–40.

Wang, R. (1996), 'The locality of guild hall and regional difference of guild hall [Diyuxing huiguan yu huiguan de diyuxing chayi]', *Journal of Chinese Historical Geography [Zhongguo lishi dili luncong]*, no. 1, pp. 100–16.

Wang, D. (1998a), 'Street culture: public space and urban commoners in late-Qing Chengdu', *Modern China*, vol. 24, no. 1, pp. 34–72.

Wang, H. (1998b), 'The development of action film in mainland China since the 1980s [Bashi niandai yilai Zhongguo dalu dongzuo leixingpian de fazhan yanbian]', *Journal of Beijing Film Academy [Beijing dianying xueyuan xuebao]*, no. 3, pp. 56–65.

Wang, Y. (2009), 'The mode of the Chinese Western and its termination: the rise and fall of a film cultural paradigm [Zhongguo xibu dianying mokuai jiqi zhongjie: yizhong dianying wenhua fanshi de shuailuo]', *Film Art [Dianying yishu]*, no. 1, pp. 55–8.

Wang, Y. (2013), *Remaking Chinese Cinema: Through the Prism of Shanghai, Hong Kong, and Hollywood*, Hong Kong: Hong Kong University Press.

Williams, R. (1977), *Marxism and Literature*, Oxford: Oxford University Press.

Wing Chan, K. and W. Buckingham (2008), 'Is China abolishing the hukou system?', *China Quarterly*, vol. 195, pp. 582–606.

Wu, S. C. (2011), 'Time, history, and memory in Jia Zhangke's *24 City*', *Film Criticism*, vol. 36, no. 1, pp. 3–23.

Wu, J. W. and Z. Wang (2007), 'Remaining myself in the process of industrialization: Jia Zhangke's lecture at the Hong Kong Baptist University [Zai chanyehua chaoliu zhong jianchi ziwo: Jia Zhangke zai Xianggang Jinhui Daxue de yanjiang]', *Film Art [Dianying yishu]*, no. 1, pp. 27–34.

Xiao, Y. (2009), 'The significance of the Chinese Western for Chinese cinema [Xibu dianying dui zhongguo dianying de yiyi]', *Journal of Xi'an Jiaotong University: Social Science Edition [Xi'an jiaotong daxue xuebao, shehui kexue ban]*, vol. 29, no. 3, pp. 81–6.

Ying, Z. (2006), 'The transformation of traditional Chinese guilds in modern times', *Frontiers of History in China*, vol. 1, no. 2, pp. 292–306.
Zhang, Y. (1996), *The City in Modern Chinese Literature and Film: Configurations of Space, Time, and Gender*, Stanford, CA: Stanford University Press.
Zhang, Y. (2002), *Screening China: Critical Interventions, Cinematic Reconfigurations, and the Transnational Imaginary in Contemporary Chinese Cinema*, Ann Arbor: Center for Chinese Studies University of Michigan.
Zhang, A. (2003), 'Chinese Western film in the context of globalisation [Quan qiu hua yujing yu zhongguo xibu dianying de shengcun yu fazhan]', *Film Art [Dianying yishu]*, no. 4, pp. 74–7.
Zhang, H. (2004a), 'The stories of filming the *Mysterious Grand Buddha* [Wo pai Shenmi de dafo de qianqian houhou]', *Film Art [Dianying yishu]*, no. 1, pp. 81–7.
Zhang, Y. (2004b), *Chinese National Cinema*, London: Routledge.
Zhang, Z. (2007), 'Bearing witness: Chinese urban generation in the era of 'transformation' (zhuanxing)', in Z. Zhang (ed.), *The Urban Generation: Chinese Cinema and Society at the Turn of the Twenty-first Century*, Durham, NC: Duke University Press, pp. 1–45.
Zhang, X. (2008a), 'Ziyou (Freedom), occupational choice, and labor: bangbang in Chongqing, People's Republic of China', *International Labor And Working-Class History*, no. 73, pp. 65–84.
Zhang, Y. (2008b), 'An Exposition on *Curiosity Kills the Cat*', *Contemporary Cinema [Dangdai dianying]*, no. 9, p. 102.
Zhang, H. (2009), 'Ruins and grassroots: Jia Zhangke's cinematic discontents in the age of globalisation', in S. H. Lu and J. Mi (eds), *Chinese Ecocinema: In the Age of Environmental Challenge*, Hong Kong: Hong Kong University Press.
Zhang, Y. (2010a), *Cinema, Space, and Polylocality in a Globalising China*, Honolulu: University of Hawaii Press.
Zhang, Z. (2010b), 'Transfiguring the postsocialist city: experimental image-making in contemporary China', in Y. Braester and J. Tweedie (eds), *Cinema at the City's Edge: Film and Urban Networks in East Asia*, Hong Kong: Hong Kong University Press.
Zhong, D. (1994), *An Anthology of Zhong Dianfei*, Beijing: Huaxia Press, vol. II.
Zhou, X. (2001), 'From behind the wall' the representation of gender and sexuality in modern Chinese film', *Asian Journal of Communication*, vol. 11, no. 2, pp. 1–17.
Zhou, X. (2007), *Young Rebels in Contemporary Chinese Cinema*, Hong Kong: Hong Kong University Press.
Zhou, B. (2012), 'Diversified development of Chinese Western production [Zhongguo xibu dianying chuangzuo de duoyuanhua fazhan]', *Hundred Schools in Arts [Yishu Baijia]*, no. 1, pp. 49–55.
Zhu, D. and Y. Tu (2004), 'An interview with Wang Quan'an: the director of *The Story of Ermei* [Gengduo chengyi, gengda yuanwang, gengduo zhixian: fang Jingzhe daoyan Wang Quan'an]', *New Films [Dianying xinzuo]*, no. 4, pp. 19–22.

Index

Note: page numbers in **bold** refer to figures

After Separation, 75
Aftershock, 94
American Westerns, 8, 9–10, 20, 181
Andrew, D., 83
Anti-Japanese War 1937–45, 30, 37, 38, 136
anxiety, 54, 55, 81
The Arrival of a Train at La Ciotat Station, 164

Back to Back, Face to Face, 32, 133, 134, 209
    enclosed spaces and *flânerie*, 137–42
    guild hall and tradition and power, 140, **141**, 142–6, **143**
    from rural to urban space, 146–51, **147**, **150**
Backlight, 14
Bai Mang, 159
Balzac and the Little Chinese Seamstress, 40
bangbang, 48–9, **49**, 59–60
banned films, 61
Bao Shihong, 44, 45, 46–7, 48–9, 54–5, 101
Battleship Potemkin, 109
Baudelaire, Charles, 'The Painter of Modern Life', 137–8
Bazin, André, 8, 12, 82, 83
On the Beat, 74
A Beautiful New World, 75
Beidaihe, 174
Beijing, 14, 15–16, 23, 39, 43, 69, 75, 166, 168, 170
    compared with Xi'an, 174–8, **176**, **177**

Beijing Bastards, 69
bell hooks, 156, 209
Belt and Road International Film Festival Alliance, 210
Benjamin, W., 138
Berlin, 79
Berry, Chris, 106, 159
Bertolucci, Bernardo, 16
The Black Cannon Incident, 9, 134, 151
Black Snow, 69
borders and boundaries, 3, 15, 29, 53, 74, 77, 155, 157–8, 162, 165, 188, 198, 209
Boss Yu, 158, 160
Braester, Yomi, 13
The Bride, 70
Brother Dao, 55, 56
Buddha Mountain, 32, 94, 119, 120–1, 176, 208
    dysfunctional and broken families in the urban landscape, 124–8, **125**
    nature, a railway station and religious redemption, 122–4, **123**
    searching for home in an anonymous city, 128–9
Bumming in Beijing, 11–12
Buried, 94

cable cars, 44–5
The Call of Maiji Mountain, 183
Carina Lau, 50
Cellphone, 15, 52, 53
Central Film Studio, 38
Certeau, Michel de, 20, 26–8, 110, 191
chai, 78, 79–80, 134, 176, **177**

INDEX

Chambers, Iain, 115
Chang Yueqin, 121, 122, 123, 124, **125**, 126, 127
Chen Bolin, 121
Cheng Fen, 152
Chen Jianbin, 33, 100, 181, 184–5, 187, 194, 201
Chen, Joan, 108, 114
Chen Kaige, 16, 155, 188
Chen Qing, 62–3, 65, **67**, 68, 71–2, 73–4
Chen Zhenghua, 44
Chen Zhongshi, 135
Chengdu, 16–17, 23, 40
   24 City, 25, 31–2, 48, 91, 95, 96–118, **97**, **99**, **102**, **103**, **112**, **116**, **117**, 166, 170, 176, 208
   Buddha Mountain, 32, 94, 119–29, **123**, **125**, 176, 208
   character of, 92, 93
   cityscape, 91
   disconnection between past and present, 113–18, **116**, **117**
   dysfunctional and broken families in the urban landscape, 124–8, **125**
   in films, 91–6
   as a home city, 110–13, **112**
   loss and disillusion, experience of, 108–9
   modern space, making way for, 96–8, **97**
   searching for home in an anonymous city, 128–9
   settings in *Buddha Mountain*, 122–4, **123**
   socialist spatial design for working and living, 98–104, **99**, **102**, **103**
   vanishing socialist utopia, 104–9
   Wenchuan earthquake, 93–5, 96, 119, 122–3, **123**
Chengdu, I Love You, 94
chengshi, 10–11
children, 127–8, 199, 201, 202
   one child policy, 139–40
China Affair, 70
China Motion Picture Studio, 38
China Western Development, 211
China's Unnatural Disaster: The Tears of Sichuan Province, 94

Chinese Documentary Movement, 11–12
Chinese Western cinema, 3, 4–10, 133–4, 181
   American Westerns, influence of, 8, 9–10
   concept of, 4–5
   geographical base, 7, 9
   Han-centred depictions, 7
   representations, 8–9
   urban influences, 8, 9
Chongqing, 11, 16–17, 30–1, 37–60, 38
   cities and the human body, 54–60, **58**, **59**
   class stratification and infidelity, 50–4
   Crazy Stone, 43–50, **46**, **49**, 54–60, **58**, **59**, 208
   Curiosity Kills the Cat, 30–1, 37, 40–1, 43, 50–4, 208–9
   in films, 38–43, **39**, **42**
   high and low spaces, stratification of, 43–8, **46**, **58**
   spatial arrangements, 37
   unique urban space and vernacular culture, 41, 43
   urban village and its inhabitants, 48–50, **49**
Chongqing Blues, 40, 41, **42**
Chongqing Hot Pot, 40
Chow, Ray, 127, 167
Chyi Chin, 114
cities, 69
   as an absent presence in films, 181–4
   and cinema affinity, 13–14, 210
   concept of, 10–11
   and the human body, 54–60, **58**, **59**
commercialisation, 7, 8, 15, 28, 39, 60, 77, 101, 128, 187
   and desire, 62–9, **64**, **66**, **67**, **68**
Confucianism, 124, 127, 161
consumption, 7–8, 23, 24, 32, 91, 101, 104
   transition from a space of production, 105–8
A Corner in the City, 14, 23–4
Crazy Stone, 30, 37, 41, 101, 208
   cities and the human body, 54–60, **58**, **59**
   high and low spaces, stratification of, 43–8, **46**
   urban village and its inhabitants, 48–50, **49**

Crossroads, 12, 16
Cui, S., 113
Cultural Revolution, 13, 23, 30, 39, 92, 106, 154, 161
Curiosity Kills the Cat, 30–1, 37, 40–1, 43, 208–9
    class stratification and infidelity, 50–4

Datong, 78
Deadly Delicious, 40–1
death, 184, 202
Deep in the Heart, 211
Defend Our Land, 38
dérive, 119, 120, 121
Design of Death, 92, 93
desire, and commercialisation, 62–9, **64**, **65**, **66**, **67**, **68**
détournement, 120, 207
Ding Bo, 121, 126, 127
Ding Jiali, 152
disease and illness, 168, 171, 174, 184
Dislocation, 9, 134
Distant Thunder, 41
docufiction, 48, 91, 97–8, 114
documentaries, 11–12, 94, 95
drifting, 27–8, 32, 109, 119, 120, 121, 207
drunkenness, 160, 163

earthquakes, 32, 93–5, 96, 119, 122, 122–3, **123**
education, 18, 100, 137, 182, 183
Einstein and Einstein, 137
Eleven Flowers, 23
Ermo, 8, 15, 52, 53
Evening Rain, 39, **39**
extramarital affairs, 50–4

Factory 420, 96–7, 99, **99**, 100, **102**, **103**, 105, 108, 110, 113, 114, 118
Fallen City, 94
families
    dysfunctional and broken families, 123, 124–8, **125**
    one child policy, 139–40
Fan Bingbing, 121
Farewell My Concubine, 16
Fate of Graduates, 12
fathers, 127–8

Fei Long, 121
Feizao, 121, 126, 127
feminism, 162
Feng Hai, 46, 49, 57
Feng Jinlong, 158
Feng Qianyu, 50, 51–2
Fengjie, 11, 37, 76, 79
fetishism, 167
film studios, 9
flânerie, 27–8, 32, 44, 57, 133, 134–5, 207
    concept of, 137–9
    and enclosed spaces, 137–42
Fly with the Crane, 183, 184
A Fool, 33, 181, 183, 184–201, 208–9
    rear-view mirror scenes, **192**, **193**, 194–5
    urban and rural mental and social space, 195–201, **200**
    urban and rural physical space compared, 184–91, **186**, **189**, **190**
Forgetting to Know You, 41
Foucault, Michel, 20
Frightening Moment, 94
funerals, 184

Gansu, 203
Gao Qunshu, 183
Gao Xing, 136
Gaotai, 183–4
Ge Zhijun, 144
geographical mobility, 52–3
globalisation, 3, 9, 16, 17, 19, 20, 53, 109, 201, 209
Good Husband, 38
A Good Rain Knows, 94
Gou Yujia, 151, 153–4
'grassroots' people, 201
Great Iron Wall, 99, **99**, 100
Great Western Development project, 3, 18, 40
Gu Minhua, 108, 109, 114
Guangzhou, 39
Guan Ermei, 156–60, 161–5
Guan Fengjiu, 99, 109
guilds, 140
    and tradition and power, **141**, 142–6, **143**, 151
Guo Tao, 44

Han Sanming, 77, 78, **78**, 79, 81, 83, 85, 86–7, **86**
Hao Dali, 105, 106, 107, 108, 109, 114
He Ping, 9
He Xikun, 98–9
Hearing Implant, 182–3, 184
In the Heat of the Sun, 23
Heipi, 55, 56
Hero, 9–10
High Noon, 8
Hollywood, 9, 20, 56–7, 210
Hong Kong, 57
Hooper, Barbara, 54, 171
Horse Thief, 7
Hou Lijun, 101, 104, 108, 109
Hou Zhenfeng, 153–4
household registration system (*hukou* system), 104–5, 108, 152
Hu Jun, 50
Huang Bo, 55
Huang Jianxin, 32–3, 133–5, 134, 139, 142, 145, 151
human body, 54–60
    female body as the medium of social representation, 160–4
    female space and bodies, 155–78
    naked female bodies, 167–8
human trafficking, 195–6
Huo Jianqi, 41

individualism, 24, 53, 69, 111, 129
    individual subjectivity, 61, 83, 115
infidelity, 50–4

Jia Pingwa, 136
Jia Zhangke, 12, 23, 31–2, 37, 41, 48, 70–1, 76, 78, 79, 81, 82, 83, 91, 95, 97–8, 100, 104, 112, 114, 164, 166, 170
Jiang Qinqin, 185
Jin Shijia, 185
Jingzhe, 156, 157
Jinzhizi, 185, 196, 197
jishi zhuyi, 12
Jü Hao, 151

Kang Aishi, 153
The King of Masks, 91–2, 93

Kirby, L., 164
Kracauer, Siegfried, 12

Lai, L. C.-H., 65
landscape, 5, **6**, 9–10, 19–20, 40
Lanzhou, 16, 17, 40
    as an absent presence in films, 181–4, 194
    A Fool, 33, 181, 183, 184–201
    Lanzhou New Area, 182
    modernisation and environmental concerns, 201–3
    River Road, 33, 183, 184, 201–3, 208
    urban and rural mental and social space, 195–201, **200**
    urban and rural physical space compared, 184–91, **186**, **189**, **190**
Lao Ma, 146, **147**, 148, 149
Lao Mo, 62, 73
Lao Wang, 159–60, 162
Laochai, 151, 153
The Last Emperor, 16
Last Train Home, 95
Latiaozi, 185, 188, 190–1, 194, 195–7, 198, 199, **200**, 201
Lefebvre, Henri, 20, 22, 25, 70, 146
    Production of Space, 21
legends, 62
Lei Kesheng, 146
Leng Bingbing, 144, 145
Leng (father), 144, 146
Li Bing, 63
Li Datou, 185, 194, 195, 196, 198
Li (headmaster), 151, 153
Li Li, 165–7, 168, 171, 174, 176, 178
Li Qiang, 140
Li Ruijun, 183–4, 202
Li Yu, 32, 119
Lian Jin, 56
Liang Xiaoxia, 50, 51–2, 53
Liao Fan, 50
Life, 5
Life Show, 40–1
Lili (sex worker), 63, 65
Lin Chong's final fight (opera), 77
Little Flower, 114
Liu Fendou, 50, 51, 52, 53
Liu Gang, 48

Liu Hui, 60
Liu Xiaodong, 76
Liu Yanbing, 158
Liu Ye, 55
Living Forever in Burning Flames, 38–9
Lost, Indulgence, 41
Lou Ye, 12
A Love Story in Chengdu, 94
Lü Dou, 152
Lü Liping, 105
Lu, Sheldon, 83, 106–7, 176
Lumière brothers, 164

Ma Bing, 63
Ma Qianli, 50
Ma Zheng, 158
McGrath, Jason, 53, 106–7
magical realism, 37, 76, 82–7, **84**, 86
Mai Qiang, 62–3, **64**, 65, **66**, 68, 73–4
Man With a Movie Camera, 164
manipulation, 50–4
Mao Nü, 157, 158, 159–60, 161–2, 165
Mao Tse-tung, 23, 65, 106, 160
March of Victory, 38
Marchetti, G., 57
marriage, 53, 77
  arranged marriage, 156, 161, 162–4
  extramarital affairs and infidelity, 50–4
The Marriage Certificate, 137
martial arts, 9, 10, 13
masculinity, 162
'Master Hand' characterisations, 56–7
The Melody of Qiang Flute, 94
memory and nostalgia, 27, 40, 47, 79, 106–7, 112–13, 115
Meng Tianfang, 136
Mennel, B., 79
Mi Jiashan, 14, 75
migration, 72, 76, 85–6, 95, 104, 105, 108
Mike, 49, 54, 56–7
mise-en-scène, 28–9, 50
The Missing Sheep, 182, 183
Mission Impossible, 56
modernisation, 3, 12, 14, 15, 16, 19, 38, 53, 74, 79, 134, 135, 208, 209–10
  and environmental concerns, 201–3
  Four Modernity, 139
moral decadence, 190–1

Mr Zhao, 52, 53
My Homeland, 38
My Memories of Old Beijing, 14
Mysterious Grand Buddha, 91, 92–3

Nan Feng, 121, 126, 127
A Narrow Lane Celebrity, 92
national identity, 5, 8, 20, 69, 210
New Chinese Cinema, 5
New Film (journal), 10
New York City, 26–7, 110
news coverage, 114–15
The Next Life, 94
Ning Hao, 30, 37, 43
Niu Zhenhua, 139, 151
No Man's Land, 9–10
nomads, 33, 183, 184, 202, 203

Ocean's Eleven, 56
Old Beast, 211
The Old Donkey, 183, 184
Old Well, 5, 135
Once a Thief, 56
opera, 44, 76–7, 93, 109, 126, 160
Orphan Rescues Grandfather, 12

pain, 54, 55
Paoge (gangsters), 92
Paris, 119–20, 137–9
Peng Bo, 44
People First, 94
personal possessions, 79–81
Pickowicz, P.G., 8, 135
The Pickpocket, 70–1, 78
Platform, 71, 164
police, 74
politics of difference, 171, 174
post-socialism, 82–3
power, 148, 162, 207
  hegemonic power, 77, 81
  and tradition, 140, 142, 144–6, 149
Power Fighter in Vast Sky, 114
Pretty Big Feet, 183
private life, 154, 178
production, 17, 23, 25, 32, 47, 91, 97, 101, 104
  transition to a space of consumption, 105–8

psychogeography, 120, 121
public toilet/bathroom spaces, 55, 167–8

Qiao Liansheng, 158–9, 160, 164, 165

railway stations, 122
Rainclouds over Wushan, 31, 37–8, 40, 61, 61–75, 86, 208
  commercialisation and desire, 62–9, **64, 66, 67, 68**
  everyday life, depictions of, 70–1, 73, 74
  fish images, 65, **66, 67**, 68–9, **68**
  relations between people and police, 74
  subjective time, 71–5, **73**
  Three Gorges Dam Project and effects on life, 71–5
Raise the Red Lantern, 167
rape, 62, 73–4
rationalism, 120
realism, 82
  magical realism, 37, 76, 82–7, **84, 86**
  neorealism, 83
  on-the-site-realism, 14
  on-the-spot-realism, 12
The Red Awn, 181–2, 184
The Red Detachment of Women, 161
Red Sorghum, 4, 5, 135
Red Suspicion, 114
redemption, 79
religion, 123, 124, 127, 161, 201, 202
Rickshaw Boy, 14
Ripples Across Stagnant Water, 92
Ritchie, Guy, 60
River Road, 33, 183, 184, 201–3, 208
Road and Belt Initiative, 3, 18
Rock 'n' Roll Kids, 14
ruins, 76, 77, 78–81, **78, 80**, 170–1, **173**, 174, 176, **177**
rural traditions, **150**, 156–7, 161, 184
  modernisation and environmental concerns, 201–3
  rural space transformed to urban space, 146–51, **147, 150**
  urban and rural mental and social space, 195–201, **200**
  urban and rural physical space compared, 184–91, **186, 189, 190**

Samsara, 134
Sanbao, 48
Sanwa, 158, 159–60
Schultz, C. K. N., 84
Secondspace, 21, 25, 26
Sentinels Under the Neon Light, 13
Seremetakis, C.N., 109
Seven Swords, 9–10
Seventeen Years, 74
Shane, 8
Shanghai, 12–13, 14, 15–16, 23–4, 39, 43, 69, 191
Shanghai Fever, 75
Shaozi, 185, 188, 190, 195, 196–7
Shen Hong, 77, 83
Shi Dongshan, 38
Shi Xiaoping, 168
Shi Xiaoxia, 158
Signal Left, Turn Right, 25, 32–3, 133, 134, 139, 151–4, 209
Sister Jiang, 38
Situationist International (SI), 119, 120
social class, 22, 30, 33, 38, 51, 61
  class stratification and infidelity, 50–4
  economic gap between social classes, 51, 194, 195, 198, 199
  female social status in rural and urban spaces, 156–60
  low social status, 63, 76, 79, **80**, 81, 85, 86, 101, 106, 174
social mobility, 51, 81, 201
socialist utopia, 91, 95, 104–9, 165
Soja, Edward, 19, 20–1, 22, 25, 26, 75, 77, 91, 138, 140, 142, 160, 162, 171, 202, 207, 208
Song Jia, 50
Song Weidong, 100–1, 109, 114
songs, 113, 114, 168, 170, 178
space, 17, 18
  acting out concrete spaces, 110
  centrifugal space, 25
  centripetal space, 24–5
  and cinema, 20–8
  disappearing space, 61, 62
  enclosed space transition to urban space, 133–54

space (*cont.*)
   enclosed spaces and *flânerie*, 137–42
   female social status in rural and urban spaces, 156–60
   female space and bodies, 155–78
   high and low spaces, stratification of, 43–8, 57, **58**
   making way for modern space, 96–8, **97**
   and migration, 52–4
   moving from enclosed space to sprawling urban space, 151–4
   ruins as a lived space, 79, **80**, 81, 170–1, **173**, 174, 176, **177**
   and social relationships, 110–11
   socialist spatial design for working and living, 98–104, **99, 102, 103**
   space in film and film in space, 210–11
   spatial and social division, 178
   spatial imagination, 207–12
   train themes, 164–5
   transition from rural to urban space, 146–51, **147, 150**
   uneven relationship between rural and urban, 163–4
   urban and rural mental and social space, 195–201
   urban and rural physical space compared, 184–91, **186, 189, 190**
   urban space as a given condition, 134
   urban space as morally decadent, 190–1
   urban space, mental and psychological effects, 119–20
   urban space transition to production space, 91, 96–8, **97**, 105–8
   vanishing socialist utopia, 104–9
   as visual communication, 28–9
Spider Man, 56
Stagecoach, 8
Stand Straight, Don't Bend Over, 134
standardisation, 120
state-owned enterprise, 165–78, 182
state welfare, 104–5, 108
Still Life, 31, 37–8, 40, 61, 76–87, 112, 176, 208
   hegemonic power, 77, 81
   magical realism, 82–7, **84, 86**
   Monument to the Three Gorges Migrants, 84–5, **84**
   ruins, 76, 77, 78–81, **78, 80**
   UFOs, 83–4

Storm on the Border, 38
The Story of Ermei, 33, 135, 155, 208–9
   female body as the medium of social representation, 160–4
   female social status in rural and urban spaces, 156–64
   the train as representing an alternative life, 164–5
The Story of Qiu Ju, 135, 187–8, 197–8, 198–9
Street Angel, 12, 16
Su Na, 110, 111–12, 113
subaltern concept, 34, 56, 59–60, 76, 85, 86, 136, 185, 195, 207, 208, 209, 210, 212
The Summer is Gone, 211
The Swordsman in Double Flag Town, 9

Tarantino, Quentin, 60
Teng Wenji, 23–4
A Terracotta Warrior, 136
theft, 54–5, 56–7
Third Front Project, 3, 17, 99–100, 152, 211
Thirdspace concept, 19, 20–1, 22, 23, 25–6, 28, 31, 38, 61, 75, 181, 201, 211–12
   Thirdspace of resistance, 209
This Life of Mine, 74
Three Gorges Dam, 3, 17–18, 37, 38, 40, 61, 62, 208, 211
   in *Rainclouds over Wushan*, 71–5
   social consequences of, 76, 81, 85–6
   in *Still Life*, 78–87
ti cai, 5
Tian Zhuangzhuang, 14
Tibet, 7
time, subjective time, 71–5
Time until the Mountain Leaves, 39, 40
tourists, 17, 39, 47, 72, 86
towns, 11, 70
train themes, 122, 164–5
trauma, 79, 119, 121
The Trouble Shooters, 14, 75
Troubled Laughter, 13
Tuya's Marriage, 201–2
24 City, 23, 25, 31–2, 48, 91, 95, 166, 170, 176, 208
   Chengdu as a home city, 110–13, **112**
   disconnection between past and present, 113–18, **116, 117**

making way for modern space,
    96–8, **97**
photo poses of anonymous people,
    115, **116, 117**
socialist spatial design for working and
    living, 98–104, **99, 102, 103**
vanishing socialist utopia, 104–9

UFO, 83–4
Unknown Pleasures, 71, 78
*Up to the Mountain, Overlooking the
    Running River*, 182
urban cinema, 3, 10–28
    cities and cinema affinity, 13–14,
        210
    cities as an absent presence in films,
        181–4
    cities, concept of, 10–11
    development of, 12–13
    urban and rural mental and social
        space, 195–201, **200**
    urban and rural physical space
        compared, 184–91, **186, 189, 190**
    urban exploration: cinema and space,
        20–8
    Urban Generation, 12, 14, 69
    urban image, transformation of,
        16–20
    urban representation, domination of,
        15–16
    vernacular everyday life, 14–15
urban villages, 48–50
utilitarianism, 120

vernacularism, 14–15, 185
Vertov, Dziga, 164
violence, 55, 56

wages, 166, 167
Wan Xia, 110
Wang Gang, 151
Wang Jinsong, 152
Wang Quan'an, 23, 33, 135, 155,
    167, 170
Wang Shuangli, 139–40, 142, 144, 146,
    148, 148–9, **150**, 151
Wang Wenqiang, 62
Wang Xiaoshuai, 12, 41, 43, 69–70
Wang Xuebing, 185
Wang Yichuan, 7

Weaving Girl, 23, 33, 135, 155, 165–78,
    208
    portrayal of Xi'an as a time capsule of
        socialist China, 166–74, **169, 170,
        172, 173**
    Xi'an and Beijing compared, 174–8,
        176, 177
Weekend Lover, 69
White Deer Plain, 135
In the Wild Mountains, 5
Wind Blast, 9, 183
A Woman, a Gun and a Noodle Shop, 9
Woman Sesame Oil Maker, 8, 15, 52, 53
women, 155–78
    emancipation movement, 160–1
    female body as the medium of social
        representation, 160–4
    female workers and state-owned
        enterprise, 165–78
    inversion of gender roles, 202
    sexual harassment, 158–9
    social status in rural and urban spaces,
        156–65
The World, 83
'The World Outside', 114
Wu Gang, 62, 65, **68**, 72, 73–4
Wu Tianming, 133
Wu Wenguang, 11–12
Wujie, 168, 171
Wushan, 11, 37, 62, 70, 75; *see also
    Rainclouds over Wushan*; *Still Life*

Xi'an, 16, 17, 23, 32–3, 40, 146–51
    and adjacent area on screen, 133–7
    Back to Back, Face to Face, 32, 133,
        134, 137–51, **141, 147, 150**
    compared with Beijing, 174–8,
        176, 177
    enclosed space to sprawling urban
        space, 151–4
    enclosed spaces and *flânerie*, 137–42
    female body as the medium of social
        representation, 160–4
    female social status in rural and urban
        spaces, 156–60
    gates and walls, 149, **150**, 151, 152
    guild hall and tradition and power, 140,
        141, 142–6, **143**, 149
    Signal Left, Turn Right, 25, 32–3, 133,
        134, 139, 151–4

Xi'an (*cont.*)
  The Story of Ermei, 33, 135, 155, 156–60
  as a time capsule of socialist China, 166–74, **169, 170, 172, 173**
  Weaving Girl, 23, 33, 135, 155, 165–78, 208
Xi'an Film Studio, 9, 133–4
Xi'an Incident, 136
Xiao Yan, 140, 146, 148–9
Xiaobai (child character), 50
Xiaojun, 55
Xie Jin, 161
Xie (manager), 44, 45, 46, 47
Xie Xiaomeng, 44, 46, 55
Xining First International Film Festival (FIRST), 210–11
Xiu Zongdi, 62
xiyang yingxi, 12
Xu Zheng, 46

Yamaha Fish Stall, 13–14
Yan Li, 162
Yan Ruisheng, 12
Yang Liu, 63
Yellow Earth, 4, 5, **6**, 20, 135, 188
youth, 83
  and disillusionment, 69–70
Yu Nan, 156, 165
Yu Nannan, 144
Yuan Wenshu, 4
Yue Xiaojun, 55

Zhang Aijia, 121
Zhang Liang, 13–14
Zhang Ming, 31, 37–8, 61–2, 70, 72, 75
Zhang Suo, 162–3
Zhang Xianming, 62
Zhang Yibai, 30–1, 37, 40–1, 43, 45, 51
Zhang Yimou, 93–4, 136, 155, 167, 187, 197–8
Zhang Yingjin, 19, 69, 191
Zhang Yuan, 12, 69–70
Zhang Zhen, 134
Zhao Gang, 110–12, 113, 114
Zhao Luhan, 168, 174, 176, 178
Zhao Tao, 85, 110
zhen concept, 11, 82
Zheng Zhong, 50–2
Zhong Dianfei, 4, 5
Zhong Ping, 62

EU representative:
Easy Access System Europe
Mustamäe tee 50, 10621 Tallinn, Estonia
Gpsr.requests@easproject.com

www.ingramcontent.com/pod-product-compliance
Lightning Source LLC
Chambersburg PA
CBHW071838230426
43671CB00012B/1990